Selected Titles in This Series

Parallel Algorithms

DIMACS
Series in Discrete Mathematics and Theoretical Computer Science

Volume 30

Parallel Algorithms

Third DIMACS Implementation Challenge
October 17–19, 1994

Sandeep N. Bhatt
Editor

NSF Science and Technology Center
in Discrete Mathematics and Theoretical Computer Science
A consortium of Rutgers University, Princeton University,
AT&T Labs, Bell Labs, and Bellcore

American Mathematical Society

This volume resulted from the Third DIMACS Implementation Challenge which was conducted as part of the 1993–1994 Special Year on Parallel Algorithms. This Implementation Challenge was held at DIMACS on October 17–19, 1994.

1991 *Mathematics Subject Classification.* Primary 68-06; Secondary 68Q22, 68-04.

Library of Congress Cataloging-in-Publication Data
Parallel algorithms : third DIMACS implementation challenge / Sandeep N. Bhatt, editor.
    p. cm. — (DIMACS series in discrete mathematics and theoretical computer science, ISSN 1052-1798 ; v. 30.)
    "NSF Science and Technology Center in Discrete Mathematics and Theoretical Computer Science, a consortium of Rutgers University, Princeton University, AT&T Labs, Bell Labs, and Bellcore."
    ISBN 0-8218-0447-2
    1. Parallel programming (Computer science)—Congresses. 2. Computer algorithms—Congresses. I. Bhatt, Sandeep Nautam. II. DIMACS (Group) III. Challenge Workshop (1991 : DIMACS) IV. Series.
QA76.642.P36   1997
004′.35—dc21
                                     96-52111
                                          CIP

Contents

Foreword

This volume resulted from the Third DIMACS Implementation Challenge which was conducted as part of the 1993–1994 Special Year on Parallel Algorithms. The implementation challenges have become a regular part of DIMACS programs and the center is proud to sponsor and host them.

We are very grateful to Sandeep Bhatt and Pangfeng Liu, his assistant in this work, for their work to plan the challenge and coordinate the work of many individual projects. Sandeep Bhatt also earns our appreciation for the additional work of editing this volume and bringing it to fruition. We are also thankful to David Culler, David S. Johnson, Lennart Johnnson, and Charles Leiserson for their assistance as a steering committee for the year's activities.

DIMACS gratefully acknowledges the generous support that makes these programs possible. The National Science Foundation through its Science and Technology Center program, the New Jersey Commission on Science and Technology, and DIMACS partners at Rutgers, Princeton, AT&T Labs, Bell Labs, and Bellcore all generously supported the Special Year and the Implementation Challenge.

Fred S. Roberts
Director

Bernard Chazelle
Co-Director for Princeton

Stephen R. Mahaney
Associate Director

Preface

The past decade witnessed the development of parallel computers which were successfully used to solve large-scale numerical problems, typically arising from scientific and engineering applications. The use of massive parallelism in non-numerical applications received considerably less attention. However, this period also witnessed a flurry of research in the design of algorithms for discrete combinatorial applications. Despite the large body of theoretical work on parallel algorithms for combinatorial problems, it was unclear what kinds of parallel algorithms would be effective in practice, and how well these would compete with standard sequential algorithms.

The Third Annual DIMACS Implementation Challenge was formulated with the view to provide a forum for a concerted effort to study effective algorithms for combinatorial problems, and to investigate opportunities for massive speedups on parallel computers. The challenge included two problem areas for research study: (a) tree searching algorithms, used in game search and combinatorial optimization for example; and (b) algorithms for sparse graphs.

Participants at sites in the U.S. and Europe undertook projects during the period from November 1993 to October 1994. The Challenge workshop was held at DIMACS on October 17 and 18, 1994. Following the workshop, participants were encouraged to share test instances where possible, to rework their implementations in light of the feedback at the workshop, and to submit a final report for the proceedings. Nine papers were selected for this volume.

Approximately 50 researchers attended the workshop; there were 17 project presentations, 7 invited talks, and a panel discussion. The specific application problems presented at the workshop included connected components and shortest paths in graphs, geometric clustering and dominance, graph partitioning, N-body algorithms for astrophyiscs, branch-and-bound techniques, and massively parallel chess. The invited presentations focused on topics ranging from good experimental methodology (Guy Blelloch, David Johnson); the interplay between modeling, algorithm design, and implementation (David Culler); and specific applications such as factoring (Arjen Lenstra), traveling salesman (David Applegate), and mesh partitioning (Shanghua Teng, Zdenek Johann).

The expert assistance of the DIMACS staff in hosting and arranging the workshop is gratefully acknowledged. The NSF STC grant supported Pangfeng Liu as a DIMACS post-doctoral fellow to help coordinate the Challenge. Thanks to Pangfeng for his efforts, and also to the rest of the Challenge Steering Committee, which included David Culler (UC Berkeley), David Johnson (AT&T Labs), Lennart Johnsson (Univ. of Houston) and Charles Leiserson (MIT).

Sandeep Bhatt
November 1996

xi

DIMACS Series in Discrete Mathematics
and Theoretical Computer Science
Volume **30**, 1997

Connected Components on Distributed Memory Machines

Arvind Krishnamurthy, Steven S. Lumetta, David E. Culler,
and Katherine Yelick

ABSTRACT. The efforts of the theory community to develop efficient PRAM
algorithms often receive little attention from application programmers. Although there are PRAM algorithm implementations that perform reasonably
on shared memory machines, they often perform poorly on distributed memory machines, where the cost of remote memory accesses is relatively high.
We present a hybrid approach to solving the connected components problem, whereby a PRAM algorithm is merged with a sequential algorithm and
then optimized to create an efficient distributed memory implementation. The
sequential algorithm handles local work on each processor, and the PRAM algorithm handles interactions between processors.

Our hybrid algorithm uses the Shiloach-Vishkin CRCW PRAM algorithm
on a partition of the graph distributed over the processors and sequential
breadth-first search within each local subgraph. The implementation uses the
Split-C language developed at Berkeley, which provides a global address space
and allows us to easily manipulate the distributed graph data structure. We
present our first version, then provide a detailed account of the optimizations
used to create the final version. For graphs from real-world problems, we
obtain speedups on the order of 20 on a 32-processor CM-5 and 238 on a
512-processor CM-5.

1. Introduction

Although the theory community has studied the asymptotic running times of
numerous PRAM algorithms, comparatively few of these algorithms are used in
practice. The implementations that do exist generally appear on small shared
memory platforms such as the Cray C90 or on SIMD machines such as the CM-2
or Maspar, where messages between processors require only a single, very long cycle. Large parallel machines, however, typically have a distributed memory model:

1991 *Mathematics Subject Classification.* Primary 68Q22, 68R10; Secondary 68P05.

This material is based in part upon work supported by a National Science Foundation
Graduate Research Fellowship, by the National Science Foundation Infrastructure Grant numbers
CDA-8722788 and CDA-9401156, by the Lawrence Livermore National Laboratory Grant LLL-
B28 3537, by the National Science Foundation award number CCR-9210260, by the Advanced
Research Projects Agency of the Department of Defense monitored by the Office of Naval Research
under contract DABT63-92-C-0026, by the Department of Energy under grant number DE-FG03-
94ER25206. The content of the information does not necessarily reflect the position or the policy
of these organizations.

off-the-shelf processors loosely coupled via a fast network (e.g., TMC CM-5, Meiko CS-2, Cray T3D, Intel Paragon, IBM SP-1). In this paper, we demonstrate the process of adapting a PRAM algorithm to execute efficiently on a distributed memory machine. We start with the PRAM algorithm for finding the connected components of a graph, and, through a gradual process of refinement, we develop an efficient hybrid parallel algorithm.

Labeling the connected components of a graph has a wide range of uses, including applications in computer vision and condensed matter physics. Grouping adjacent pixels of similar intensity to identify edges and planes, for example, helps to analyze images for object recognition. By creating a graph in which adjacent pixels of equal intensity are connected and then finding the connected components of the graph, we find the homogeneous regions of the image. Connected component labeling is used in Physics to implement clustering in Monte Carlo algorithms such as that of Swendsen and Wang [13], which simulates physical systems near critical temperatures by repeatedly grouping particles into clusters (connected components) and choosing a new state for each cluster.

The graphs used for these applications have underlying grid topologies in either two or three dimensions. Because of the underlying topology, the graphs decompose easily into smaller fragments with only a small fraction of edges crossing between fragments, allowing much of the work in finding connected components to be performed locally. For our results, we use the graphs typical of Physics problems. These graphs are generated randomly, using a fixed probability for the presence of each edge from an underlying lattice graph. For problems in vision and image recognition, the presence of an edge from the underlying grid is not independent of the presence of other edges.

Although we are primarily interested in graphs from actual problems, we also consider an artificial graph type. The graph, denoted AD3 for "average degree three," is generated by having each node pick zero to three other random nodes as neighbors. AD3 is a variant of the Tertiary graph used by Greiner [7] for benchmarking connected components algorithms.[1] Graphs corresponding to physical systems usually exhibit locality in their structure. However, the AD3 graph exhibits almost no locality, and could therefore be viewed as an extreme input to our algorithm.

Previous parallel implementations of connected components algorithms have focused primarily on shared-memory machines [7]. For distributed memory machines, a straightforward implementation of a PRAM algorithm is generally of little use because of the high cost of remote accesses and the frequency of such accesses in most PRAM algorithms. A more sophisticated approach employs a PRAM algorithm in conjunction with a standard sequential algorithm, using the latter to manage operations local to each processor and the former to manage the interaction between processors. This hybrid approach is illustrated in Figure 1 for the connected components problem. The two algorithms are merged, then the result is optimized.

In this paper, we present a hybrid algorithm for finding the connected components of a graph on a distributed memory machine. We implemented and optimized the algorithm on a CM-5 using the Split-C language developed at Berkeley [4].

---

[1] Each node in an instance of Greiner's Tertiary graph randomly selects three other nodes as neighbors, resulting in an average degree of six and a graph that has only one connected component with high probability.

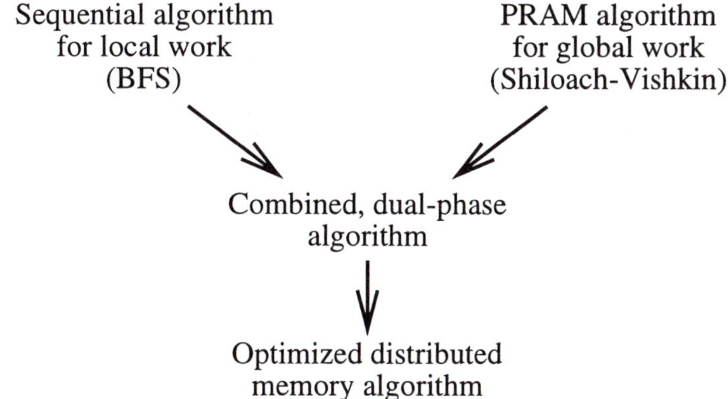

FIGURE 1. Hybrid algorithm strategy. We combine a PRAM algorithm with a sequential algorithm and optimize the result to create an efficient algorithm for distributed memory machines.

We discuss the PRAM algorithm in Section 2 and give details of the first hybrid implementation in Section 3. In Section 4, we describe the sequence of optimizations through which we developed the final version of our algorithm. Section 5 discusses the graphs used and our methodology for measuring performance. In Section 6, we present our results.[2] Section 7 compares the results with other implementations of the algorithm, and Section 8 concludes.

2. The PRAM Algorithm

Sequential solutions for identifying the connected components of a graph are generally based on variants of depth-first search, breadth-first search, or union-find. The solutions have running times linear in the number of edges and vertices in the graph and are easy to implement. Many efficient parallel solutions [2, 6, 12] have been devised, but these solutions are often complex and difficult to implement. Our implementation is a hybrid of a sequential search on the subgraph local to each processor and a variant of the Shiloach-Vishkin PRAM algorithm [12] on the global collection of subgraphs. In this section, we briefly describe the key components of the PRAM algorithm.

In the following discussion, we denote the vertex set of the input graph by V and the edge set by E. Each vertex has an associated *Value* attribute that is a unique number at the beginning of the algorithm. When the computation terminates, all vertices within the same connected component share the same value. We use the notation (u, v) to denote an edge between the vertices u and v.

Given a graph with n vertices and m edges, the Shiloach-Vishkin algorithm requires $O(\log n)$ parallel steps and a total of $O(m \log n)$ work. The algorithm repeatedly groups vertices that have edges between them using two basic operations: *pointer doubling* and *hooking*. The algorithm maintains a *forest* of trees, and makes progress either by decreasing the number of trees in the forest or by decreasing the height of the trees. The algorithm terminates when no two trees in the forest share an edge and all trees in the forest are of height one.

---

[2] A separate paper [9] presents more detailed results for the algorithm on several different platforms and demonstrates the best connected components performance seen to date.

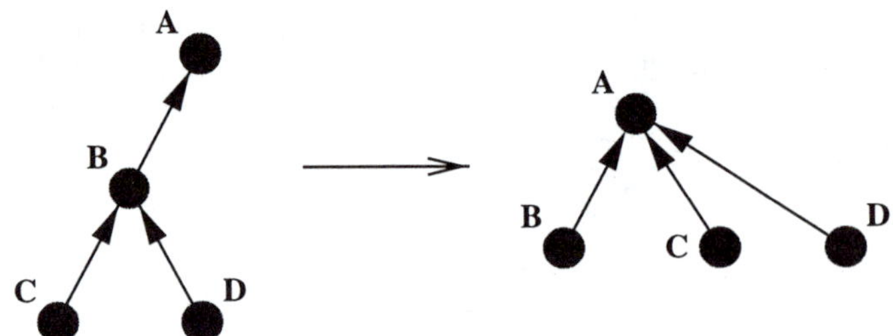

FIGURE 2. Pointer doubling operation. The parent of each vertex is replaced with the vertex' grandparent. The root of a tree is assumed to be its own parent.

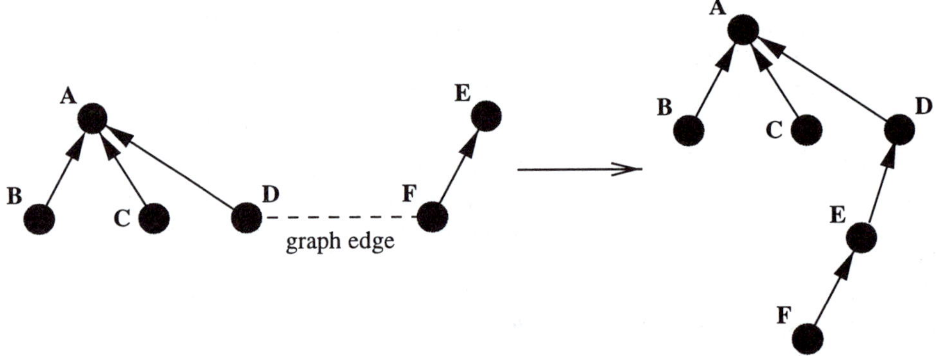

FIGURE 3. Hooking operation. A graph edge between two trees in the forest is replaced with a parent link, merging the two trees into a single tree.

The *pointer doubling* operation replaces the parent of each vertex with the vertex' grandparent, as shown in Figure 2. This operation decreases the distance from the root of the tree to the leaves, and terminates when the tree becomes a *star*, which is a tree of height 1. During the pointer doubling operation, the algorithm also propagates the value of the new parent to the child. By making the parent of the root of a tree the root itself, we simplify the operation to the form:

$$Parent(v) \leftarrow Parent(Parent(v))$$
$$Value(v) \leftarrow Value(Parent(v))$$

The *hooking operation* hooks a star in the forest to another tree in the forest if the star contains a vertex adjacent to a vertex in the target tree, as shown in Figure 3. The operation comes in two flavors: conditional and unconditional. A conditional hooking operation is permitted only when the *Value* attribute of the first vertex[3] is less than that of the adjacent vertex. An unconditional hooking operation links the two trees irrespective of their values.

In order to guarantee termination, the algorithm must ensure that the parent relationship remains acyclic. The conditional hooking operation prevents the

---

[3]Note that the *Value* of every vertex in a star is the same, as the *Value* propagates from parent to child during pointer doubling.

formation of cycles by requiring that the *Value* attribute monotonically increases from the leaves to the root of a tree. The same is not true of the unconditional hooking operation, however. The algorithm prevents the creation of cycles by first applying the conditional hooking operation, and then applying the unconditional hooking operation only to those stars that were not hooked in the conditional hooking phase. This scheme prevents two stars from linking to one another since at least one of the stars has had an opportunity to link to the other star during the conditional hooking phase. Unconditional hooking is necessary to obtain $log(n)$ bound on the running time, but is not necessary for correctness [**12**].

The algorithm follows:

1. For each vertex u, set
   Parent(u) $\leftarrow$ u
2. Repeat until no change occurs in an iteration:
   - a. For each vertex u such that u is part of a star, pick v such that $(u, v) \in E$ and $Value(u) < Value(v)$ and set
      $Parent(Parent(u)) \leftarrow v$.
   - b. For each vertex u such that u is part of a star that neither hooked to another vertex nor had another vertex hooked to it, pick v such that $(u, v) \in E$ and set
      $Parent(Parent(u)) \leftarrow v$.
   - c. For each vertex u, set
      $Parent(u) \leftarrow Parent(Parent(u))$ and
      $Value(u) \leftarrow Value(Parent(u))$

Given one processor for each vertex and each edge in the graph, the loop requires $O(log\ n)$ iterations to terminate. The vertex processors perform during steps 1 and 2c, while the edge processors perform during steps 2a and 2b. The processors execute in a lock-step manner and must be able to read and write a single memory location concurrently for each step to execute in unit time. Steps 2a and 2b, for example, require the concurrent write ability, since multiple children of a vertex may attempt to change the parent. Note, however, that the algorithm makes no assumptions about the policy for disambiguating writes to the same location.

3. Implementation

In this section, we describe our initial implementation of the connected components algorithm. We start with a hybrid algorithm, which composes the local sequential breadth-first search with a global PRAM-based algorithm. Although this implementation proved to be inefficient, the description introduces the general style of the program and facilitates understanding of the optimizations discussed later.

The natural implementation of many algorithms on distributed memory machines involves a combination of local and global phases. During the local phases, the algorithm deals only with data that reside in the processor's local memory. In the global phases, the algorithm must address the issues of efficient remote data access and synchronization between processors. The global phases are hence more difficult to program.

Fortunately, we can make use of the Split-C language [**4**] to simplify the task. Split-C provides the abstraction of a global address space on a distributed memory

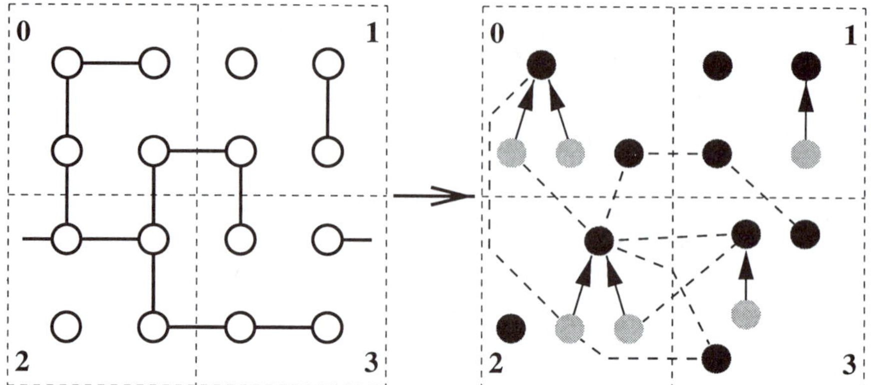

FIGURE 4. Local phase. In this phase, the algorithm processes all local edges to find local connected components, then passes the reduced graph into the global phase.

machine.[4] Any processor can access any location in the global address space using *global pointers*, and each processor owns a specific region of the global space, its local region. A global pointer is used just like a local pointer, but can reference the entire global address space, while standard pointers reference only the portion local to the accessing processor. The notion of a global pointer allows us to represent a graph whose vertices are spread across processors and whose edges are represented using global pointers. Another useful aspect of global pointers is the ability to determine the processor that owns the object pointed to by a global pointer without actually dereferencing the pointer. In our implementation, we use this ability in the local phase to explore only those edges that point to local vertices. The distinction between local and global objects provides a clear cost model for introducing optimizations that we examine later.

Having briefly discussed the language used to code our implementation, we now introduce the algorithm:

1. **Local Phase.** Perform purely local computations to decrease the size of the graph processed during the global phase. Figure 4 illustrates the effect of the local phase.
    a. *Search Step.* On each processor, find local connected components among local nodes and edges using Breadth First Search (BFS). Ignore remote edges.
    b. *Star Formation Step.* Assign a unique value to each node. Choose a representative node for each local connected component. Move all remote edges from nodes in the component to the representative and collapse the component into a star. The representative node becomes the root of the star, and the value of the representative node becomes the value of the star.
2. **Global Phase.** Beginning with a list of components on each processor, all of which are stars and are marked with unique values, apply a modified Shiloach-Vishkin algorithm. Iterate over the following steps until done:

---

[4]Implementations of the language exist on a variety of machines including the IBM SP-2, the Intel Paragon, the Cray T3D, and the Meiko CS-2 [1, 8, 10, 11].

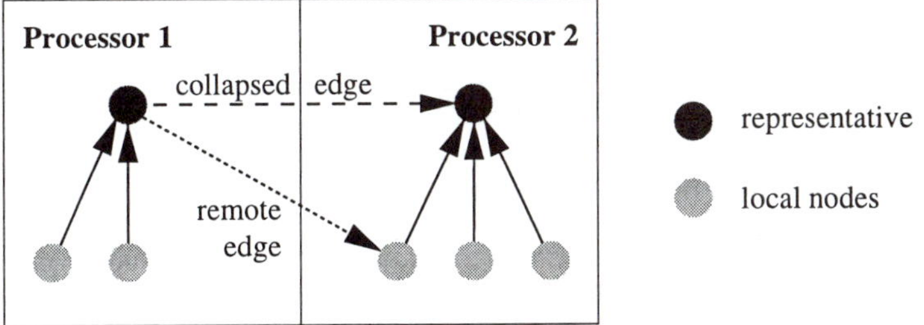

FIGURE 5. Collapsing remote edges. By collapsing remote edges before entering the global phase, we reduce the amount of work required for each iteration of that phase.

  a. *Termination Check.* Move star components with no remaining remote edges to a finished component list. If all components on all processors are finished, quit.
  b. *Conditional Hooking Step.* Attach star components to other components if the value of the other component is larger. Remove newly attached components from the component list.
  c. *Pointer Doubling Step.* Double parent pointers one or more times for each node and update the node's value from the new parent.
  d. *Star Marking Step.* Determine whether each component is a star: first mark all components as stars, then mark the grandparent of each node as a non-star if it is distinct from the parent of the node.
  e. *Edge-List Concatenation Step.* For each node, pass remote edges to the parent of the node.
  f. *Self-Loop Removal Step.* For each star, remove edges that point to nodes with the same value (nodes within the star).

The initial implementation does not include an unconditional hooking phase. We introduce this phase and study its effect in the next section.

4. Optimization

In this section, we describe the sequence of optimizations that we used to improve the performance of our implementation on distributed memory machines. On a CM-5, the optimized code runs roughly twenty times faster than does the basic version described in the last section. The optimizations make use of three simple concepts in parallel optimization: reducing the amount of computation, reducing the number of remote references, and balancing the workload between processors.

4.1. Collapsing remote edges. The local phase leaves all local components in star form. We first consider the role of the leaf nodes of these stars, which we call the *local nodes.* As the local nodes make up the bulk of the graph in most cases, we want to eliminate any reference to them within the global phase. Although we have chosen representative nodes (which are the roots of the stars) during the local phase of the algorithm and have moved one end of each edge to the representative nodes, the other end of each edge remains unchanged, and often refers to a local node. To avoid creating a cycle in the graph, we must keep the unique component values for the local nodes consistent in each iteration of the global phase. By extending the

| | | Avg. Nodes |
Graph	Nodes	in Star
2D40	10,000	4.2
2D60	10,000	27
3D20	8,000	2.3
3D40	8,000	14
AD3	10,000	1.05

TABLE 1. Average star size after the local phase. Graphs used in real-world problems form large stars; artificial graphs might not. All measurements used a 32-processor CM-5, and the "Nodes" column shows the number of graph nodes per processor.

algorithm slightly, we remove edge references to the local nodes and greatly reduce the amount of work done in the global phase.

The first extension involves collapsing the remote edges just before beginning the first iteration of the global phase. For each remote edge, we replace the remote node with the parent of the remote node, as shown in Figure 5. Since each local component has the form of a star after the local phase, the parent of any node is that node's representative. The extension adds the following step just after the local phase:[5]

1.c. *Remote Edge Collapse Step.* Replace each remote edge (u, v) with the collapsed edge $(u, Parent(v))$.

The local nodes can then be safely ignored during the global phase, and their component values can become inconsistent without affecting the correctness of the algorithm.

The second extension involves updating the unique component values of the local nodes after the global phase completes, bringing them back into consistency with the reduced graph. Since all representative nodes are updated in the global phase, we need merely copy the component value of each local node from its parent, an operation requiring no remote references as the parent of a local node is always local. We add an update phase after the global phase:

3. **Update Phase.** For each local node, update the value of the node from the value of its parent.

How these two extensions affect the execution time of the algorithm depends upon the balance between the computation and communication architectures and upon the structure of the graph. The first extension potentially adds an additional remote reference for each remote edge, but allows us to forgo updating the values of local nodes during the global phase. We must eventually update these values at least once, and do so in the second extension after the global phase completes. In a graph where the number of local nodes is small compared to the number of remote edges, or on a machine on which the cost of a remote reference is large compared to the cost of a cache miss, the changes described in this section can increase the

---

[5]The new step accesses remote data and should technically not be a part of the local phase, but the numbering used indicates both the appropriate insertion point for the step and fact that the step is not part of the global phase iteration.

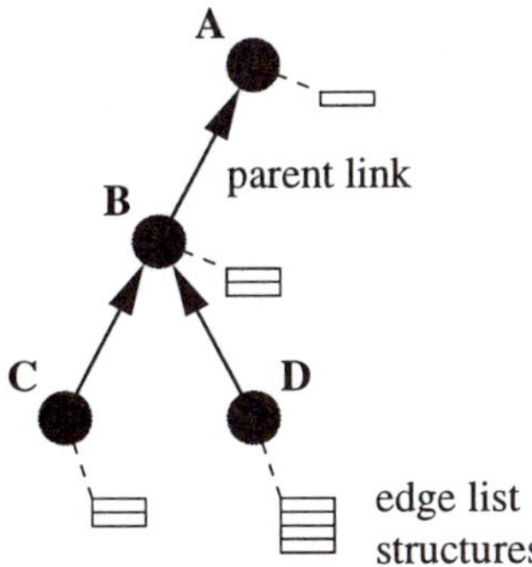

FIGURE 6. Postponing edge list concatenation. Race conditions in edge motion make efficient design difficult; waiting until the tree has collapsed into a star eliminates races and allows further optimization.

execution time. In our case, however, they greatly reduced that time. Table 1 shows the average star size for our graphs.

4.2. Postponing edge list concatenation. The initial implementation moved remote edges from leaf nodes to their parents after every pointer doubling, concatenating each leaf's list to that of its parent. Unless we are careful in designing the interactions for this step, races between the parent and children of a node make the code very unstable. To understand the problem, consider the tree shown in Figure 6. The edge list structures exist in the global address space, so that accessing or modifying an edge might involve a remote access. In one correct solution, each node maintains pointers to the first and last edge list structures in its list of edges. Before sending edges to its parent, a node saves copies of these two pointers and zeroes the originals in an atomic fashion, protecting the edge list from corruption by incoming edges. The node then sends both the start and end pointers to its parent. When the parent node receives these pointers from a child, it replaces its own first edge with the child's first edge and, if the parent already had edges, modifies the child's last edge to point to the parent's previous first edge. The latter operation requires a message to the processor on which the child's last edge list structure resides, but since the parent is the only node that has a pointer to this edge list structure, no races exist.

Unfortunately, the method outlined above requires too much information to take advantage of the short messages available on the CM-5, and using a slightly longer message adds a significant amount of overhead and complexity. The solution we chose is to delay the motion of edge lists. By postponing the edge list concatenation on a tree until pointer doubling has collapsed the tree into a star, we sidestep the difficulties of designing a correct and efficient method for this step. The cost is moderate—the root of each tree must handle all of the link messages instead of handling one or more rounds from each immediate child (a very small cost when the height of the trees is small)—and the change allows us to take advantage of a more significant optimization, as we discuss in the next section. We modify step 2e to affect only stars:

    2.e. *Edge-List Concatenation Step.* For all leaf nodes of star components, pass remote edges to the star root.

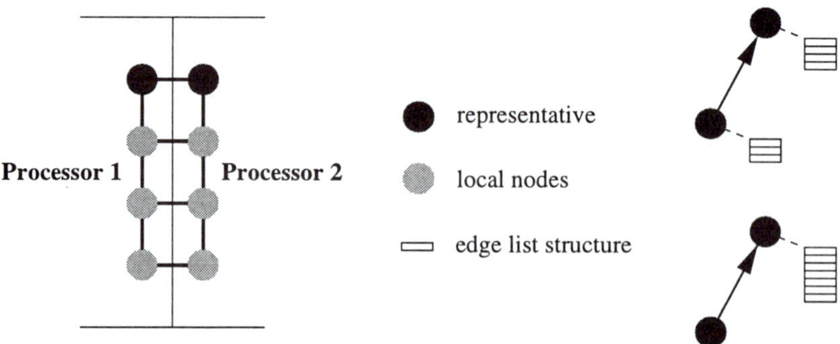

FIGURE 7. Removing duplicate edges before concatenation. Pushing duplicate edges to the root of a star forces the root to handle the destruction of all duplicates. Eliminating the duplicates first improves load balance.

4.3. Removing duplicate edges before concatenation. After the local phase completes, many components are left with *duplicate edges* in their edge lists. The graph segment depicted in Figure 7, for example, gives rise to a set of four duplicate edges in both local components. Detecting duplicate edges at this point requires sorting the edge lists and fails to catch duplicate edges created in the global phase (when two local components are collapsed into a single component). For this reason, the original algorithm checked for duplicate edges at the end of each global phase iteration, when they appear as edges in a star that point to other nodes within the star.

The problem with such an approach is that the root of the star must perform all of the remote references needed to detect duplicate edges. The upper righthand section of the figure shows the two representative nodes and their edge list structures after one node has been hooked to the other (eliminating one edge). In this figure, all of the edge list structures reside on the same processor as the associated node, and all of the edges point to remote nodes. The lower righthand section shows the nodes after edge list concatenation; in this case, three of the edge list structures are remote, and the complementary structures (the other four) point to remote nodes. In both cases, each edge list structure requires one remote access to determine its duplicate nature, but in the upper figure, the cost of these accesses is shared between two processors, while a single processor must perform all remote accesses in the lower figure. By checking for duplicate edges before concatenating the edge lists, we create a better load balance between the processors. We swap the two steps:

2.e. *Self-Loop Removal Step.* For each star, remove edges that point to nodes with the same value (nodes within the star).

2.f. *Edge-List Concatenation Step.* For all leaf nodes of star components, pass remote edges to the star root.

Since the root of a star must perform a remote reference for each edge when scanning the list for duplicates, the benefits of this optimization outweigh the small costs incurred by delaying concatenation in the earlier section, where the root of a star need make only one remote reference per edge list.

Graph	Nodes	Iteration	Components	Stagnant	Percentage
2D40	2,000,000	1	472,538	425	0.090%
2D60	2,000,000	1	70,141	157	0.22%
3D20	4,000,000	1	1,673,284	1,915	0.11%
3D20	4,000,000	2	1,627,463	15	0.00092%
3D40	4,000,000	1	251,734	823	0.33%
3D40	4,000,000	2	228,101	2	0.00088%
AD3	1,600,000	1	1,525,032	47,560	3.1%
AD3	1,600,000	2	252,240	6,624	2.6%
AD3	1,600,000	3	100,671	25	0.025%

TABLE 2. Usefulness of unconditional hooking. The stagnant components make up a small fraction of the total, but lead to additional iterations of the global phase. All measurements in the table were made on a 32-processor CM-5.

4.4. Unconditional hooking. Certain pathological graphs require unconditional hooking to prevent the possibility of requiring one iteration per node to find connected components. But the stagnation information needed for unconditional hooking requires extra work and extra remote references, and the unconditional hooking phase itself adds still more overhead. As we are not concerned with these pathological cases, we chose not to implement unconditional hooking in our initial implementation.

We found, however, that unconditional hooking serves a practical purpose, as demonstrated by the data in Table 2. For each graph type, the table shows the number of components left stagnant during each iteration of the global phase. Although the stagnant fraction is generally small, the number is large enough to increase the number of iterations required in the global phase. Adding unconditional hooking results in fewer iterations, and the time gained by eliminating iterations outweighs the overhead costs.

We modify the conditional hooking step and add the new step as follows:

2.b.1) *Conditional Hooking Step.* Mark all stars as stagnant. Attach star components to other components if the value of the other component is larger. Remove each newly attached component from the component list and remove the stagnant marker from the component to which it attached.

2.b.2) *Unconditional Hooking Step.* Attach stagnant star components to other components. Remove each newly attached component from the component list.

4.5. Asynchronous pointer doubling. The standard approach to pointer doubling, as shown in Figure 8, requires that each processor iterate over its local set of nodes and double the parent link for each vertex (replace the parent with the grandparent). The processors then synchronize and repeat the doubling procedure some number of times. The synchronization guarantees that each doubling decreases the height of all trees by a factor of two.

An alternative approach reverses the loop structure and eliminates the synchronization; each processor iterates over vertices and replaces the parent of each

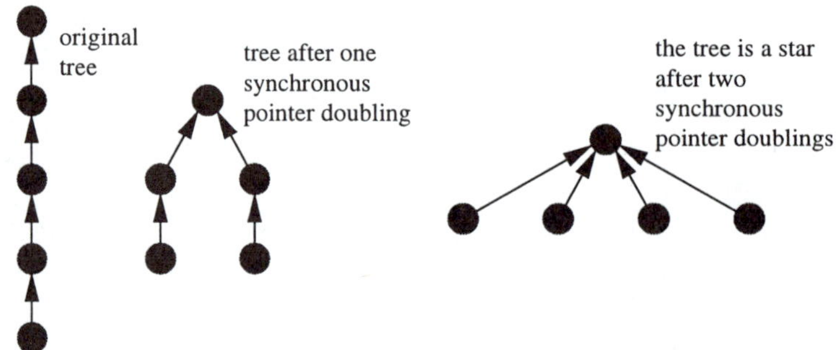

FIGURE 8. Asynchronous pointer doubling. Synchronized pointer doubling guarantees fully collapsed trees in time logarithmic in the height of the trees. Asynchronous doubling offers no such guarantee, but requires much less overhead.

vertex with the node found by following the parent link some number of times. This second approach has much less overhead than the first: not only does it lack multiple synchronizations between processors, but it requires only one loop through a processor's vertices. However, the approach does not guarantee that the depth of the tree decreases exponentially.

We implemented both schemes and compared the results. Surprisingly, execution times were very close. The extra overhead of synchronization and multiple list traversals compensated for the benefits of guaranteed exponential decrease. Keep in mind, however, that barrier synchronization is relatively inexpensive on the CM-5. On machines with more heavyweight barriers, asynchronous pointer doubling is more beneficial.

4.6. Maximal pointer doubling. The last optimization we discuss involves tuning the number of doublings performed in each pointer doubling phase. We studied the effect of the number on execution time and found the the optimal number varied from three to seven, depending on the structure of the graph. We next tried maximal pointer doubling, in which pointer doubling continues until every tree is reduced to a star. Although execution times were slightly worse, maximal pointer doubling enabled numerous other optimizations. Since every tree entering an iteration of the global phase was a star, we removed the star-marking phase entirely and eliminated all conditionals that checked a tree's star property. The resulting program ran faster than the one that performs an optimal number of pointer doublings. The algorithm outlined below reflects the numerous minor changes made with maximal pointer doubling.

4.7. Final Algorithm. The optimized algorithm follows:

1. **Local Phase.** Perform purely local computations to decrease the size of the graph processed during the global phase.
    a. *Search Step.* Each processor finds local connected components among its nodes using Breadth First Search (BFS). The search ignores remote edges.
    b. *Star Formation Step.* Assign a unique value to each node. Choose a representative node for each local connected component. Move all remote edges from nodes in the component to the representative and

    collapse the component into a star. The representative node becomes the root of the star, and the value of the representative node becomes the value of the star. Make a list of star roots for each processor.

    c. *Remote Edge Collapse Step.* Replace each remote edge (u, v) with the collapsed edge $(u, Parent(v))$.

2. **Global Phase.** Beginning with a list of components on each processor, all of which are stars and are marked with unique values, apply a modified Shiloach-Vishkin algorithm. During this phase, ignore any nodes not on the local star root list. Iterate over the following steps until done:

    a. *Termination Check.* Move components with no remaining remote edges to a finished component list. If no components need still be processed on any processor, quit.

    b. *Hooking Steps.* Merge components into larger components.

        1) *Conditional Hooking Step.* Mark all components as stagnant. Attach components to other components if the value of the other component is larger. Remove each newly attached component from the component list and remove the stagnant marker from the component to which it attached.

        2) *Unconditional Hooking Step.* Attach stagnant components to other components. Remove each newly attached component from the component list.

    c. *Pointer Doubling Step.* Double parent pointers for each node until the parent and the grandparent are the same; that is, collapse all components into stars. Update the node's value from the new parent.

    d. *Self-Loop Removal Step.* For each component, remove edges that point to nodes with the same value (nodes within the component).

    e. *Edge-List Concatenation Step.* For all leaf nodes of components, pass remote edges to the component root.

3. **Update Phase.** For each node with a local parent, update the value of the node from the value of its parent.

5. Graphs and Methodology

We begin this section with a description of the graphs used to measure the performance of our optimized implementation. We then discuss our measurement methodology.

5.1. Graph construction. As our results depend fairly heavily upon the types of graphs studied, we first describe those graphs. We used five separate types of graphs; four are drawn directly from the work of Greiner [7], and the fifth is a modified form of another graph used in that work.

The first two graphs are built on a two-dimensional toroidal mesh. Each edge in the mesh is present with some fixed probability, either 40% or 60% in our measurements. Since one expects a graph with average degree below two to be fairly disconnected and a graph with average degree above two to be fairly connected, these two percentages outline the boundary region for the two dimensional grid. We call these graphs 2D40 and 2D60, following the notation given by Greiner. We divide the underlying rectangular mesh into P square chunks, where P is the number of processors.

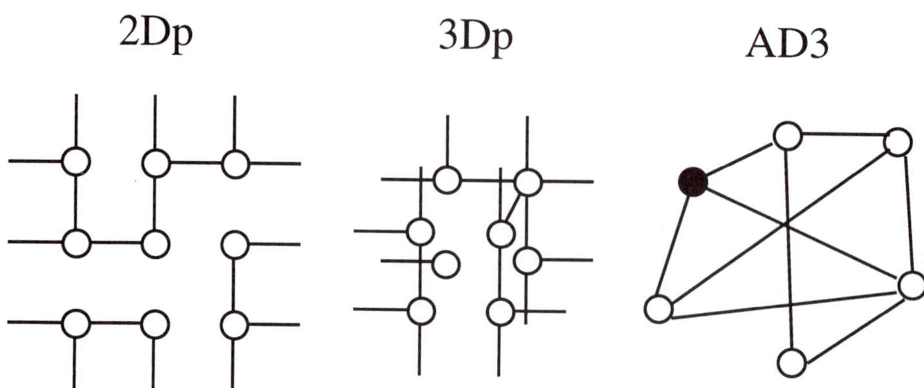

FIGURE 9. Graph types. The left and middle graphs correspond to real problems; p is the probability of presence for each edge on the underlying grid. The right graph is artificial; each node selects zero to three other nodes as neighbors.

The second two graphs are built in the same fashion on a three dimensional toroidal mesh. The boundary between fairly connected and fairly disconnected graphs falls near 33% in the three dimensional case, so our measurements use edge presence probabilities of 20% and 40%. We call these graphs 3D20 and 3D40. The underlying mesh again provides the best method of partitioning the graph among processors.

The last type of graph, AD3, is a randomly generated graph of average degree three. Each node randomly selects zero to three other nodes as neighbors, resulting in a graph with average degree three (although the degree of a particular node may vary from zero to $3n + 3$). The lack of an underlying coordinate space and the nature of the generation method for AD3 lead to extremely poor locality.

5.2. Methodology. Except where noted, all measurements were averaged over several runs of the algorithm using distinct random seeds. Variation in execution time between multiple runs arises from three sources. In decreasing order of significance, these sources are the random nature of the graph, the non-deterministic behavior of the algorithm, and irreproducible timing fluctuations on the CM-5.

An unforeseen side effect of our random number generation led to a graph independent of the random seed on one processor, introducing some amount of systematic error into our measurements. Although the error is practically irrelevant for large numbers of processors, the advantage of averaging is nullified in the single processor data. We blame this problem in several cases for bumps in our data, where the runs with many processors found graphs from both the high and low end of the execution time distribution, but the single processor runs found only a single graph.

Table 3 shows variation in execution time for large samples of all graph types running on 32 processors. Twenty seeds were chosen at random and fed into the algorithm for each graph type. The table shows the size of the graphs, the average time, and the standard deviation in seconds and as a percentage of the average. The variations are larger for more strongly connected graphs and tend to rise around the boundary regions between mostly connected and mostly disconnected graphs.

Graph	Nodes	Edges	Avg. Time (sec)	Std. Dev. (sec)	SD/Avg.
2D40	2,000,000	1,600,000	1.13	0.064	5.69%
2D60	2,000,000	2,400,000	1.63	0.12	7.59%
3D20	4,000,000	2,400,000	2.59	0.14	5.52%
3D40	4,000,000	4,800,000	4.83	0.97	20.1%
AD3	1,600,000	2,400,000	9.29	2.8	30.3%

TABLE 3. Variation in execution time. The random nature of the graph proved to be the most significant factor in execution time variance.

Size	Nodes	Time (sec)	Per Node (usec)
18x18x18	5,832	0.1451	24.88
19x19x19	6,859	0.1711	24.95
20x20x20	8,000	0.1960	24.50
21x21x21	9,261	0.2319	25.04
22x22x22	10,648	0.2559	24.03
23x23x23	12,167	0.2900	23.83
24x24x24	13,824	0.3308	23.93

TABLE 4. Variation in execution time per node as a function of graph size. Measurements of a 3D20 graph on a 32-processor CM-5 show only minor variations in cost per node, validating our scaling of measurements.

The largest variation occurs in the AD3 graphs, where the variation in number of references is amplified by the higher average cost of each reference.

In addition to averaging, some of the results are scaled linearly from graphs close to the same size. As the graph creation section of the program allowed only for square (cubic) sections on each processor for the 2D (3D) graphs, we were unable to obtain graphs with exactly the same number of nodes when doubling the number of processors. To justify our choice of linear scaling, we investigated the effect of graph size on execution time for various graphs. Since the number of nodes in the actual graphs measured are quite close to the desired number of nodes, we require only that the effect be reasonably approximated by a line. The data in Table 4 show the results for 3D20 graphs. The cost does not vary by more than 5% over the range shown, and demonstrates no clear trend.

6. Performance Measurements

In this section, we discuss our measurements of the optimized algorithm running on a 32-processor CM-5 and on a 512-processor CM-5 (we were able to obtain only one set of data on the latter). We first explore the efficiency of the parallel algorithm by comparing execution times for graphs of fixed size running on a variable number of processors. Next, we scale the graph size with the number of processors to demonstrate scalability for large graphs. Finally, we look at two performance factors in detail: convergence and load balance.

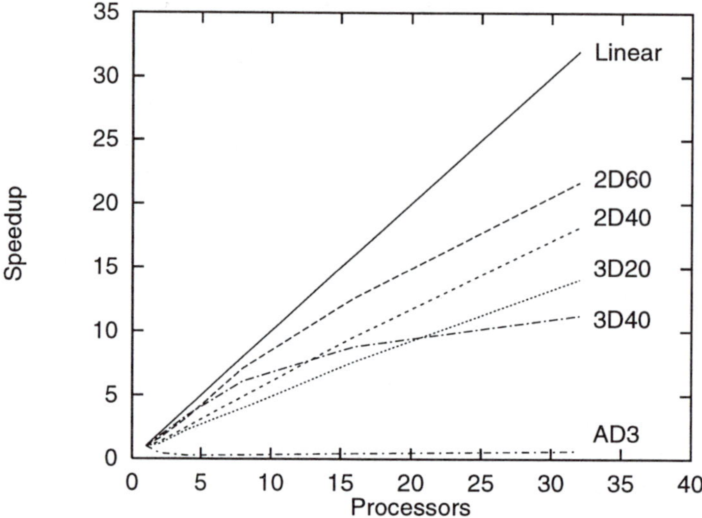

FIGURE 10. Speedup a problem size of 256K nodes.

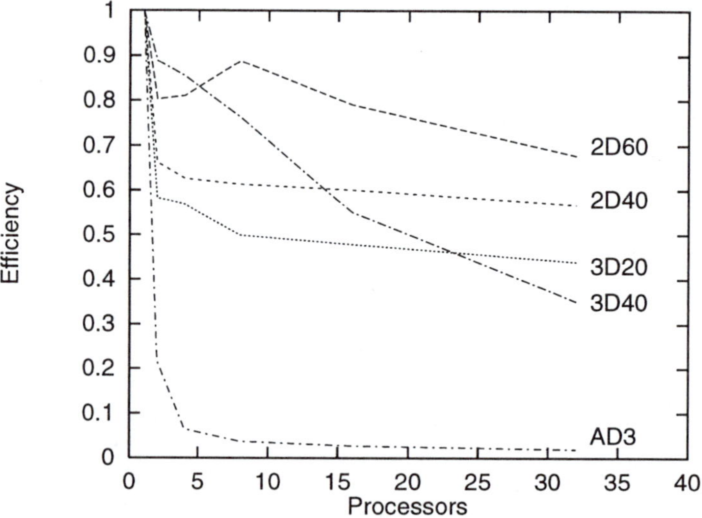

FIGURE 11. Efficiency for a problem size of 256K nodes.

6.1. Speedup. Speedup of the parallel version is measured by comparing to a sequential implementation that contains only step 1a of the algorithm. Although the algorithm requires no communication on a single processor, it takes a significant amount of time that is not relevant to the sequential execution time of the program.

Figure 10 shows the speedup for a fixed problem size (262,144 nodes) on between 1 and 32 processors of a CM-5. Ignoring AD3 for the moment, the speedups are roughly linear after discounting the overhead in moving from one processor to two. The exception is 3D40, for which the chunk owned by each processor has become small enough that the fraction of remote edges rises significantly and limits the speedup. AD3 never regains a speedup of 1, because the nonlocal structure of the

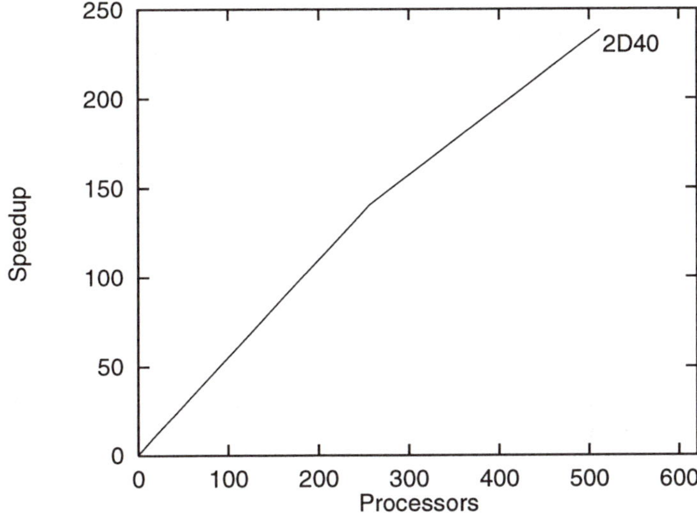

FIGURE 12. Speedup for a 2D40 graph up to 512 processors. The problem size is 256K nodes between 1 and 32 and 8M nodes between 32 and 512.

graph leads to unavoidable communication. Figure 11 shows the efficiency for the same data set. Again, we see that 2D40, 2D60, and 3D20 fall rapidly to a fairly level plateau, indicating good scalability on these problems.

Figure 12 extends the speedup for 2D40 graphs on machine sizes up to 512 processors using an 8 million node graph. Because this graph does not fit on a small number of processors, the speedups from 1 to 32 are computed using the smaller, 256 thousand node, graph and setting the speedup for 8 million nodes on 32 processors equal to the speedup for 256 thousand nodes on 32 processors.[6]

A second definition of speedup, *scaled speedup*, uses a problem size proportional to the number of processors. In Figure 13, we see the results for the graphs using this definition and varying numbers of nodes per processor (dependent upon graph type). They follow the same pattern as did the previous set, with slightly better values. Finally, in Figure 14, we see the scaled efficiency for the algorithm on all graph types. The plateaus in this case are flatter because the fraction of remote edges remains roughly constant across the graph, except between 1 and 2 processors.

6.2. Convergence and load imbalance. Most runs of the algorithm converged in about 2 or 3 iterations for the 2D and 3D graphs. AD3 graphs took a few more iterations, averaging about 3 or 4. In Figure 15, we see the number of remote edges remaining after each iteration normalized by the number of remote edges existing immediately after the local phase (iteration 0). The rate at which edges are removed depends on the degree of graph connectivity: the mostly unconnected graphs, 2D40 and 3D20, lose over 95% of their edges in the first iteration; the mostly connected graphs, 2D60 and 3D40, lose between 75% and 90% of their edges in the first iteration; and the most strongly connected graph, AD3, loses just

---

[6]Note that this method underestimates the speedup on large graphs—the larger chunks have relatively fewer remote edges and should therefore have better speedup than the smaller chunks.

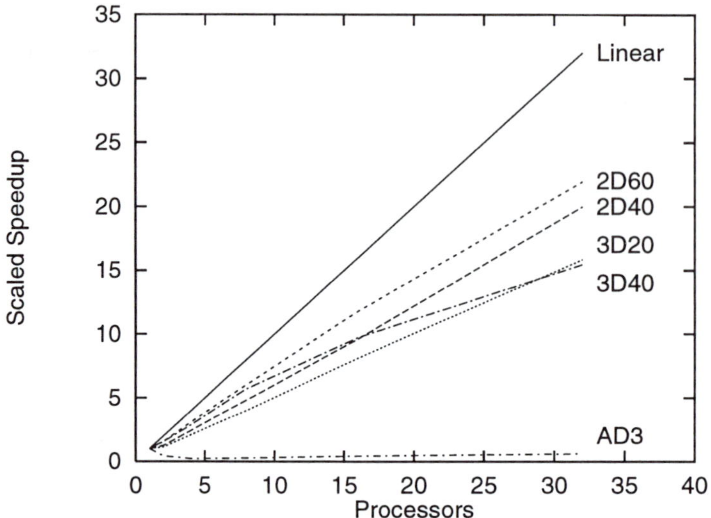

FIGURE 13. Scaled speedup. The problem size per processor is fixed: 62,500 nodes for 2D40 and 2D60, 125,000 for 3D20 and 3D40, and 50,000 for AD3.

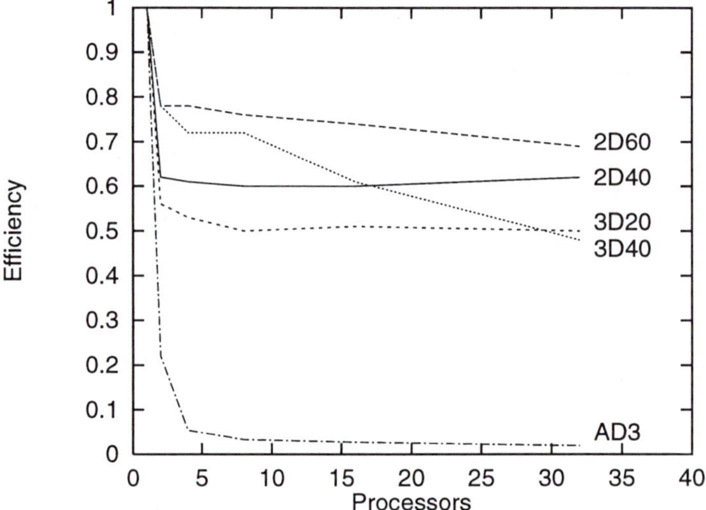

FIGURE 14. Scaled efficiency. The problem size per processor is fixed: 62,500 nodes for 2D40 and 2D60, 125,000 for 3D20 and 3D40, and 50,000 for AD3.

over half of its edges in the first iteration, retaining nearly 40% after the second as well.

For all but AD3, the number of components after completion of the local phase is within 10% of the final number, and decreases rapidly in the first two iterations. For AD3 (with 1,600,000 nodes), the data appears in Table 5.

One of the biggest problems with most graph algorithms on distributed memory machines lies in managing to partition the graph across processors in such a way

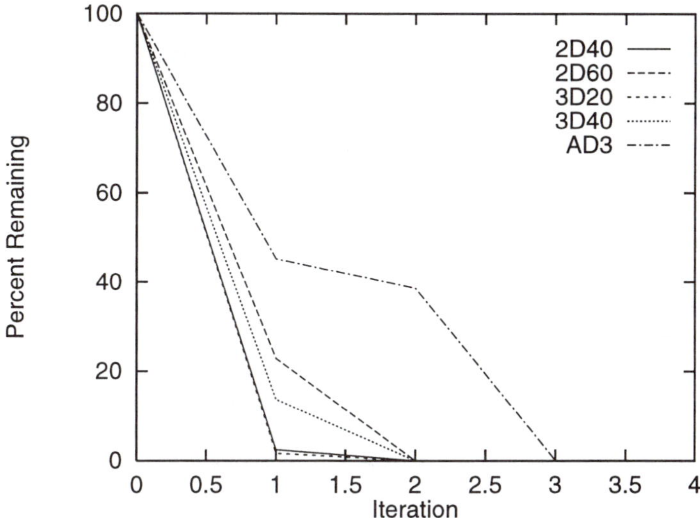

FIGURE 15. Percentage of remote edges remaining after each iteration. 100% corresponds to the state at the completion of the local phase.

Iteration	Components	Percent of Final Value
0	1,525,032	1602%
1	252,240	265%
2	100,671	106%
3	95,191	100%
4	95,190	100%

TABLE 5. Number of components remaining. For an AD3 graph with 1.6 million nodes, the table lists the number of components remaining after each iteration of the global phase.

that each processor has an approximately equal amount of work at each stage. For the 2D and 3D graphs, the natural partitioning provided by the underlying mesh performs quite well, keeping the variance across processors small except during the very last iteration (for which the time spent is much smaller anyway).

For AD3 graphs, however, there is no underlying topology, but the random nature of the graph helps to create a fair load balance. Unfortunately, the methods used for hooking in this algorithm tend to cause load imbalance fairly early in the AD3 processing, with a factors as high as 2.25 between some processors and the average arising while a significant fraction of edges and components remain. We plan to further optimize the solution of this type of graph as time permits.

7. Comparison with Earlier Work

Though a lot of research has been done in proposing theoretically optimal algorithms for finding connected components of a graph, not much work has been done in implementing these algorithms efficiently on parallel machines. Greiner [7] implemented the connected components algorithm on the Cray C-90 and on the

Connection Machine 2. However, the C-90 is a shared bus multiprocessor system, and the CM-2 is a SIMD machine. These machines are easier to program than distributed memory machines, which are however more scalable. Therefore, our work on implementing the connected components algorithm on the CM-5 exposes a new set of concerns and optimizations that were non-issues on the C-90 and the CM-2. By introducing the optimizations described in Section 4, we have created a highly efficient implementation of the connected components algorithm. For some of the graphs that we studied (*e.g.*, the 2D40 graphs), the execution time of our implementation is comparable to the results obtained by Greiner on the C-90. This is highly encouraging considering that our results were obtained on a 32-processor CM-5 without vector units, which is a much cheaper machine.

Another piece of related work is the implementation of the parallel clustering algorithm by Flanigan and Tamayo [5] on a CM-5 using CMMD, which is a message passing library provided by Thinking Machines Corporation. As mentioned earlier, the clustering algorithm requires a connected components labeling on a 2D mesh. Their implementation achieves a peak performance of finding connected components for about 12M nodes in a second on a 256-processor CM-5, a result comparable to our own. However, their implementation is optimized to labeling a 2D graph, which allows a compact representation of the edge list. As a result, they are able to greatly reduce the storage requirements for their algorithm. Bader and Jájá [3] adopt a similar strategy for identifying components of 2D images such that each component is a maximal collection of adjacent pixels with the same intensity. Our algorithm is more general-purpose since the input graph can have arbitrary connectivity, and we still obtain similar performance results. Also, our implementation is more portable than Flanigan and Tamayo's implementation since Split-C runs on a variety of parallel machines including the Paragon, the IBM SP-1 and SP-2, the Cray T3D, the Meiko CS-2, and a network of workstations. In fact, we were able to run our connected components program on a network of workstations without any change.

8. Conclusions

We have implemented the connected components algorithms on a distributed memory machine. We used a hybrid algorithm that combines the important aspects of the sequential and the PRAM algorithms. By using the Split-C language, which exposes the underlying machine to the programmer, we were able to enhance the performance of our implementation by treating local and global subgraphs separately, by paying attention to locality, and by tolerating remote memory access latencies. The resulting implementation is very efficient and obtains speedups on the order of 20 on a 32-processor CM-5 and 238 on a 256-processor CM-5. In related work [9], we demonstrate that our algorithm is the fastest in the world.

References

[1] R. H. Arpaci, D. E. Culler, A. Krishnamurthy, S. Steinberg, K. Yelick, "Empirical Evaluation of the Cray T3D: A Compiler Perspective," *Proceedings of the International Symposium on Computer Architecture*, 1995.

[2] B. Awerbuch, Y. Shiloach, "New connectivity and MSF algorithms for Ultracomputer and PRAM," International Conference on Parallel Processing, 1983, pp. 175-179.

[3] D. Bader and J. Jájá, "Parallel Algorithms for Image Histogramming and Connected Components with an Experimental Study," Journal of Parallel and Distributed Computing, June 1996.

[4] D. E. Culler, A. Dusseau, S. C. Goldstein, A. Krishnamurthy, S. Lumetta, T. von Eicken, K. Yelick, "Parallel Programming in Split-C," Proceedings of Supercomputing '93, Portland, Oregon, November 1993, pp. 262-273.

[5] M. Flanigan, P. Tamayo, "A Parallel Cluster Labelling Method for Monte Carlo Dynamics," International Journal of Modern Physics C, Vol. 3, No. 6, 1992, 1235-1249.

[6] H. Gazit, "An Optimal Randomized Parallel Algorithm for Finding Connected Components in a Graph," *SIAM Journal of Computing* **20(6)**, December 1991.

[7] J. Greiner, "A Comparison of Parallel Algorithms for Connected Components," to appear in the Symposium on Parallel Algorithms and Architectures 1994.

[8] L. T. Liu, D. E. Culler, "Evaluation of the Intel Paragon on Active Message Communication," Proceedings of the Intel Supercomputer Users Group Conference, 1995.

[9] S. S. Lumetta, A. Krishnamurthy, D. E. Culler, "Towards Modeling the Performance of a Fast Connected Components Algorithm on Parallel Machines," Proceedings of Supercomputing '95, San Diego, California, December 1995, available at *http://www.supercomp.org.sc95/proceedings/465_SLUM/SC95.HTM.*

[10] S. Luna, "Implementing an Efficient Portable Global Memory Layer on Distributed Memory Multiprocessors," U. C. Berkeley Technical Report #CSD-94-810, May 1994.

[11] K. E. Schauser, C. J. Scheiman, "Experience with Active Messages on the Meiko CS-2," *Proceedings of the International Parallel Processing Symposium*, 1995.

[12] Y. Shiloach, U. Vishkin, "An *O(log n)* Parallel Connectivity Algorithm," Journal of Algorithms, No. 3, 1982, pp. 57-67.

[13] J. S. Wang, R. H. Swendsen, "Cluster Monte Carlo Algorithms," Physica A, No. 167, 1990, pp. 565-579.

COMPUTER SCIENCE DIVISION, UNIVERSITY OF CALIFORNIA AT BERKELEY, BERKELEY, CALIFORNIA 94720

E-mail address: {arvindk,stevel,culler,yelick}@CS.Berkeley.EDU

DIMACS Series in Discrete Mathematics
and Theoretical Computer Science
Volume **30**, 1997

Parallel Implementation of Algorithms for Finding Connected Components in Graphs

TSAN-SHENG HSU,

VIJAYA RAMACHANDRAN,

AND NATHANIEL DEAN

June 10, 1996

ABSTRACT. In this paper, we describe our implementation of several parallel graph algorithms for finding connected components. Our implementation, with virtual processing, is on a 16,384-processor MasPar MP-1 using the language MPL. We present extensive test data on our code.

In our previous projects [**21**, **22**, **23**], we reported the implementation of an extensible parallel graph algorithms library. We developed general implementation and fine-tuning techniques without expending too much effort on optimizing each individual routine. We also handled the issue of implementing virtual processing.

In this paper, we describe several algorithms and fine-tuning techniques that we developed for the problem of finding connected components in parallel; many of the fine-tuning techniques are of general interest, and should be applicable to code for other problems. We present data on the execution time and memory usage of our various implementations.

1991 *Mathematics Subject Classification.* Primary 68-04; Secondary 05-04, 05C85, 68Q22.

Key words and phrases. parallel algorithms, graph algorithms, connected components, implementation, MasPar.

The first author was supported in part by NSC of Taiwan, ROC, Grants 84-2213-E-001-005 and 85-2213-E-001-003. The second author was supported in part by NSF Grant CCR-90-23059 and Texas Advanced Research Projects Grant 003658386.

This paper is in final form and no version of it will be submitted for publication elsewhere.

1. Introduction

Over the past decade there has been a large amount of work in the theory of efficient, highly parallel graph algorithm design [25, 27, 31, 46]. Parallel algorithms that run in polylog time with linear or sub-linear number of processors have been developed for several fundamental problems on undirected graphs including connected components and spanning forest[§] [2, 5, 7, 13, 16, 17, 24, 26, 42], minimum spanning forest (MSF) [2, 5, 6], ear decomposition and 2-edge connectivity [32, 37, 43], open ear decomposition and biconnectivity [32, 37, 43, 52], triconnectivity [12, 36] and planarity [44]. All of these algorithms (with the exception of some algorithms for MSF) have the additional feature that they serialize into linear-time sequential algorithms. However, these algorithms are quite different from earlier linear time algorithms based on depth-first search [51] in that they are very modular in structure. For instance, the algorithm for ear decomposition calls subroutines for several basic problems such as connected components, spanning forest, the Euler tour technique on trees [52], least common ancestors in trees [47, 52] and range minima [47, 52]. More complex algorithms, such as those for triconnectivity and planarity call subroutines for open ear decomposition, in addition to subroutines for more basic problems. Thus an implementation of parallel algorithms for undirected graphs would have to proceed in a bottom-up fashion, starting with an implementation of basic primitives, and successively building up to more complex algorithms. Using this strategy, we have implemented efficient parallel algorithms for several combinatorial and graph problems [21, 22, 23].

Our implementations have been on the MasPar MP-1 in the parallel language MPL [34, 35], which is an extension of the C language [28]. In our previous papers [21, 22, 23], we reported on the implementation of an extensible parallel graph algorithms library using the approach outlined in the previous paragraph: We first built a *kernel* of basic parallel primitives and then implemented parallel graph algorithms in order of increasing complexity. In [22] we described general implementation and fine-tuning techniques used in the implementation of our parallel graph algorithms library; in this implementation we did not expend too much effort on optimizing each individual routine. Since the MasPar MP-1 does not support virtual processing in MPL, in [23] we handled the issue of implementing virtual processing. We then went into the basic routines we implemented in the kernel, and performed extensive fine-tuning; this is reported in [21]. In this paper, we present our work on fine-tuning the first parallel graph algorithm we implemented, that for finding connected components in an undirected graph. All of the non-trivial parallel graph algorithms that we have implemented, except the one for finding minimum spanning tree, call the routine for finding connected components before performing any further computation.

[§]In this paper, a spanning forest of a graph G is a maximal subgraph of G (w.r.t. the edges in G) that is a forest.

In this project we implemented several different parallel algorithms for the connected components problem, including one randomized algorithm, and tested our code with respect to various fine-tuning techniques.

Related work on implementing combinatorial algorithms on massively parallel machines can be found in [**1, 3, 4, 8, 9, 10, 11, 15, 16, 18, 19, 30, 38, 39, 41, 48**]. Also there has been work reported on implementing combinatorial algorithms on a vector super computer [**16, 45, 49**] and on a distributed memory machine [**29**].

The rest of the paper is organized as follows. Section 2 describes the algorithms implemented which includes an algorithm that we devised for this project. Section 3 gives general fine-tuning techniques for our code. Section 4 describes the testing scheme. Section 5 gives performance data. Finally Section 6 gives concluding remarks.

2. Algorithms

Given a list of vertices and edges in a graph, an algorithm for finding connected components assigns a unique component number $c(u)$ to each vertex u. Two vertices u and v are in the same component if and only if $c(u) = c(v)$. In addition to computing $c(u)$ for each vertex u, our implementation for finding connected components also returns the total number of connected components in the input graph. In this section, we describe four parallel algorithms that we have implemented.

All of the parallel algorithms we implemented use the well-known 'hooking-and-pointer-jumping' technique for finding connected components. Since our code takes care of isolated vertices at the start of the computation, we will assume here for convenience that there is no isolated vertex in the input graph. The execution of this type of computation proceeds in iterations. In each iteration, the following hooking and pointer jumping operations are performed. Initially, each vertex is assigned to a different set by itself. During execution, if two sets of vertices are found to belong to the same connected component, then these two sets are merged. We repeat the merging process until all vertices in each connected component are in the same set. The data structure for a set of vertices during the execution is a *tree loop*, where each vertex in the set has an outgoing pointer that points to another vertex in the set with the constraint that exactly one vertex has a pointer that points to itself. (Note that this is sometimes called a 'zero-tree-loop' in the literature [**20**].) Let the height of a tree loop T be the number of vertices in a longest simple directed path in T. A tree loop whose height is 2 is a *rooted star*. The vertex with self loop in a tree loop is the *root*. Two tree loops are merged by changing the pointer of the root of a tree loop to a vertex in the other tree loop. During the execution, it is desirable to reduce the height of a tree loop by performing a pointer jumping on vertices in the tree loop. When the algorithm terminates, all tree loops become rooted stars. The

```
each vertex is in a tree loop by itself;
assign a unique number α(u) to each vertex u;
let p(u) be the current pointer of the vertex u;
repeat
1.   /* Conditional star hooking.  */
      for all edges (u,v) execute in parallel
           if u is in a rooted star and α(p(u)) > α(p(v)) then
1.1             p(p(u)) ← p(v);
2.   /* Unconditional star hooking.  */
      for all edges (u,v) execute in parallel
           if u is in a rooted star and p(u) ≠ p(v) then
2.1             p(p(u)) ← p(v);
3.   /* Pointer jumping.  */
      perform a pointer jumping operation on all vertices
until there is no change in the current set of tree loops;
```

ALGORITHM 1. An algorithm for finding connected components
by Awerbuch and Shiloach [2].

component number can thus be assigned on the roots and the component number
of each vertex is the component number of its root. The number of connected
component is equal to the number of tree loops.

Based on the method used to determine the set of tree loops to be merged,
we can have many different algorithms. We implemented the following four
algorithms, all of which run in $O(\log n)$ time (with high probability for the randomized algorithm) using a linear number of processors on a CRCW PRAM.
Although techniques are known to reduce to the number of processors used in
the algorithms [7], we chose not to implement them because the associated algorithms are quite complicated and the overhead is likely to be too large. The use
of CRCW PRAM algorithms involved dealing with concurrent memory accesses;
we discuss our implementation of concurrent memory accesses in Sections 3.4
and 3.7.

2.1. Awerbuch and Shiloach. The algorithm by Awerbuch and Shiloach
[2] is shown in Algorithm 1. In each hooking-and-pointer-jumping iteration
of this algorithm, two hooks are performed. The first hook, which is called
conditional star hooking, makes the root of a rooted star point to a tree loop.
In order to prevent two rooted stars from hooking to each other, the algorithm
requires the root of the hooking star to have a smaller vertex number than the
vertex number of the vertex to which it points. The second hook, which is called
unconditional star hooking, makes the root of a rooted star point to a tree loop
that is not itself.

Note that steps 1.1 and 2.1 are concurrent write operations. Note also that
this algorithm needs to check which vertices are in rooted stars. This can be
implemented using 2 concurrent read operations and one current write operation
as follows. Using one concurrent read, each vertex finds its grandparent (i.e., the

```
each vertex is in a tree loop by itself;
assign a unique number α(u) to each vertex u;
let p(u) be the current pointer of the vertex u;
repeat
1.   /* Conditional hooking. */
       for all edges (u, v) execute in parallel
           if (u is the root or a child of a root) and α(p(u)) > α(p(v)) then
1.1           p(p(u)) ← p(v);
2.   /* Unconditional star hooking. */
       for all edges (u, v) execute in parallel
           if u is in a rooted star and p(u) ≠ p(v) then
2.1           p(p(u)) ← p(v);
3.   /* Pointer jumping. */
       perform a pointer jumping operation on all vertices
until there is no change in the current set of tree loops;
```

ALGORITHM 2. An algorithm for finding connected components
by Shiloach and Vishkin [**50**] as described in Chapter 5.1.3 of
JáJá [**25**].

parent of its parent). For each vertex whose grandparent is different from its
parent, we mark (concurrent write) a flag f for its grandparent. Any vertex that
is marked is not in a rooted star. Every unmarked vertex reads the flag f from
its grandparent. Unmarked vertices whose grandparents are marked are also not
in rooted stars.

2.2. Shiloach and Vishkin. The next algorithm we implemented (Algorithm 2) is by Shiloach and Vishkin [**50**] and also appears in Chapter 5.1.3 of
JáJá [**25**]. In each of the hooking-and-pointer-jumping iteration of this algorithm, two hooks are performed as in Algorithm 1. The first hook, which is
called *conditional hooking*, is similar to conditional star hooking as described
in Algorithm 1, except that the root of a tree loop (rather than a rooted star)
is made to point to another tree loop. The second hook is the same with the
unconditional star hooking as described in Algorithm 1. This algorithm needs to
check which vertices are in rooted stars only once during each iteration, instead
of twice as in Algorithm 1.

2.3. A Revised Deterministic Algorithm. Algorithm 3 is a revised deterministic algorithm that we developed for this implementation project. In each
hooking-and-pointer-jumping iteration of this algorithm, only one hook is performed. This is a conditional star hooking similar to the one in Algorithm 1
except that the tie-breaking rule when two rooted stars try to hook to each
other alternates between the following two rules: In even-numbered iterations,
the algorithm favors the rooted star with a larger vertex number while in odd-
numbered iterations, the algorithm favors the rooted star with a smaller vertex
number. This guarantees termination in a logarithmic number of iterations.
Note that this algorithm tries to balance the amount of work performed and

```
each vertex is in a tree loop by itself;
assign a unique number α(u) to each vertex u;
let p(u) be the current pointer of the vertex u;
repeat
1.   /* Conditional star hooking.  */
        for all edges (u,v) execute in parallel
            if the number of iterations executed so far is even then
                if u is in a rooted star and α(p(u)) > α(p(v)) then
1.1                 p(p(u)) ← p(v);
            else
                if u is in a rooted star and α(p(u)) < α(p(v)) then
1.2                 p(p(u)) ← p(v);
2.   /* Pointer jumping.  */
        perform a pointer jumping operation on all vertices
until there is no change in the current set of tree loops;
```

ALGORITHM 3. A revised deterministic algorithm for finding
connected components.

the number of tree loops reduced in each iteration. There is only one hook per
iteration.

2.4. A Simple Randomized Algorithm. Algorithm 4 is a simple randomized algorithm (see, e.g., Chapter 4.3 in [**46**]) that avoids the checking of rooted
stars by making sure that each tree loop is a rooted star at the beginning of each
hooking-and-pointer-jumping iteration. In each iteration, two hooks between
rooted stars are performed. By using a random bit in each vertex, the root of a
rooted star with the random bit 1 is made to point to the root of a rooted star
with the random bit 0. By enforcing the tie-braking rule using random bits, the
height of each resulting tree loop is less than four. After a pointer jumping, all
height-three tree loops become rooted stars. This simple randomized algorithm
differs from the previous three algorithms by saving the efforts of checking for
rooted stars in each iteration. Note that in this algorithm, the height of each
tree loop is at most 2 after step 2. Thus all vertices are in rooted stars (or isolated vertices) after step 3. By using random bits to break ties in hooking, this
algorithm avoids the construction of a tree loop with height larger than 2. Thus
it is possible that it would take a larger number of iterations for the algorithm
to terminate.

During the implementation of this algorithm, we found that when the number of vertices is small relative to the number of physical processors, the system
pseudo random bits that we generated do not have good random behavior. Thus
it usually took a very large number of iterations and a very long time for the algorithm to terminate. (The same problem is also reported in our implementation
of a randomized list ranking algorithm [**21**].)

To avoid the above problem, we revised our algorithm as follows. We execute
our randomized algorithm until the number of live edges left is less than half
of the number of physical processors. Then we switch to the deterministic code

```
each vertex is in a tree loop by itself;
initially all edges are live;
let p(u) be the current pointer of the vertex u;
while there is a live edge do
1.   /* Coin tossing on vertices.  */
       assign a random bit β(u) to each vertex u;
2.   /* Hooking */
       for all live edges (u,v) execute in parallel
           if p(u) = p(v) then (u,v) is dead;
           else if β(p(u)) = 1 and β(p(v)) = 0 then
2.1            p(p(u)) ← p(v);
           else if β(p(u)) = 0 and β(p(v)) = 1 then
2.2            p(p(v)) ← p(u);
3.   /* Pointer jumping.  */
       perform a pointer jumping operation on all vertices
end ;
```

ALGORITHM 4. A simple randomized algorithm for finding connected components (see, e.g., Chapter 4.3 in [46]).

(without virtual processing) as described in [22]. Since it is possible for a very dense graph to have a small number of vertices, but a very large number of edges, the problem with the system pseudo random bits remained for dense graphs even after this modification. To handle this problem, we also revised the way our randomized algorithm picks (pseudo) random bits. Let n be the number of vertices. The randomized algorithm first picks a random bit for each vertex. Then we count the number of random bits that are 1. If the number of 1 bits is less than $\frac{n}{8}$ or is greater than $\frac{7n}{8}$, then we use the following algorithm to re-pick pseudo random bits. We generate a positive 32-bit pseudo random number for each physical processor that contains some vertices. We assign the number 0 to each physical processor that does not contain vertices. Then we compute the ranks of the random numbers generated. Let b_i be the parity of the rank associated with the ith physical processor. We assign the bit $(b_i + j)$ mod 2 to the jth vertex in the ith physical processor. Since we need to compute ranks, the second method takes more time than the first method. Thus we use the first method to generate pseudo random bits and switch to the second method only if the first method fails.

We found that when the number of vertices is more than a quarter of the number of physical processors, we never use the second method in our testing. When the second method is used, the number of vertices in each physical processor is at most 1. As a result, the number of 1 bits and the number of 0 bits differ by at most 1.

3. General Fine-Tuning Techniques

In this section, we describe several fine-tuning techniques.

3.1. Compressed Data Structure for Edges. Three of our algorithms (Algorithms 1–3) require that two copies of an undirected edge to be stored for processing. To save memory usage, we store only one copy. Whenever we need to perform operations based on the set of edges, our code performs the same operations twice, assuming that we have two copies of the same edge available. As indicated in [23], the amount of extra computation time used is negligible. By doing this, we are able to handle input sizes up to twice as large as we could without the compressed data structure.

3.2. Special Routine for the First Iteration of Hooking. During the first iteration of the first three algorithms, isolated vertices instead of the roots of rooted stars hook into other tree loops. Checking for isolated vertices requires only one concurrent write operation and is much faster than checking for rooted stars. Thus we can use special routines to compute the first iteration of Algorithms 1–3.

3.3. Check for Live Edges. Algorithm 4 introduces a techniques to get rid of edges connecting two vertices that are inside the same tree loop (i.e., that are already known to be in the same connected component). The check works as follows: An edge (u, v) is known to be in the same connected component if u and v have the same parent pointer. Let edge (u, v) be *dead* if the current parent pointers of u and v are the same. An edge is *live* if it is not dead. At the start of the each iteration, the algorithm checks the parent pointers for the endpoints of edges that are currently live. Dead edges do not participate in further computation.

Algorithm 4 uses this check of live edges not only to remove dead edges, but also to detect the termination of computation. In addition, by getting rid of dead edges, the total number of operations performed during each iteration is reduced. This technique can be applied to the other three algorithms as well.

3.4. Implementation of Concurrent Write Operations. In our algorithms, we need to implement arbitrary concurrent write operations. The system-provided routine `rsend` in MPL language can be used to directly implement arbitrary write operations. The execution time of an arbitrary concurrent write operation increases when the maximum number of concurrent write requests per physical processor increases. This is the 'Queue-Write' model that is addressed in [14].

Another way of implementing concurrent write in MPL is to use the routine `sendwith`. This routine executes the standard simulation of a concurrent write step on an exclusive write PRAM [27], and requires the use of sorting and additional working memory space. The execution time of a concurrent write operation when `sendwith` is used depends only on the total number of write requests, and not on the maximum number of concurrent write requests per physical processor. Further, with this routine, one can implement priority write with the same delay as an arbitrary write. This delay is considerably less than the delay caused by the routine **rsend** when the maximum concurrency at a memory location is large, but the reverse is true when the concurrency at every memory location is small.

Our experimental data indicates that if we modify our connected components algorithms and use priority write operations in places where arbitrary concurrent write operations are needed, we tend to have fewer number of iterations. For example, if there are several candidates which the root r of a tree loop can hook to, using an arbitrary write operation causes r to hook to an arbitrary tree loop. Instead, if we use a priority write operation and cause r to hook to a vertex with the largest vertex number, the maximum height of the resulting tree loops tends to be smaller than the maximum height of the tree loops formed using an arbitrary write operation. In our implementation we used both arbitrary concurrent writes using the **rsend** routine and priority concurrent writes using the **sendwith** routine and compared the performance of the resulting codes. (The performance data will be shown and discussed in Section 5.1.)

In addition to using just **rsend** or just **sendwith** to implement concurrent write operations, we can also use the following hybrid implementation. We note that our algorithms usually have a large number of hooks (and thus a high probability of having large number of concurrent write requests per physical processor) during the first iteration. The number of hooks performed tends to be smaller after the first iteration. Thus we can use priority concurrent write (with the **sendwith** routine) in the first iteration and arbitrary concurrent write (with the **rsend** routine) (i.e., queue-write [**14**]) in the remaining iterations. We will show in Section 5 that this hybrid implementation improves the performance of some of our algorithms.

3.5. Edge Condensation. During the execution of the algorithm, vertices in a tree loop can be viewed as a super vertex and can be collapsed. When collapsing vertices, multiple edges can be removed using sorting. We implement the collapsing of vertices by the following method. During each iteration, whenever we need to retrieve the pointer of an end point of an edge, we replace the end point with its pointer. We refer to this operation as *edge condensation*. If a tree loop is a rooted star, and an edge incident on it is examined, then all of the vertices in the tree loop are collapsed into a super vertex. After each iteration, we sort (lexicographically) the set of edges and remove multiple copies of the same edge.

3.6. Deferred Pointer Jumping. Given a tree loop, the depth of a vertex u is the number of vertices on the path from u to the root of its tree loop. The pointer of a vertex with depth less than or equal to 2 does not change when pointer jumping is performed. To reduce the number of pointer chasing operations performed during pointer jumping, we can use the following *deferred pointer jumping* scheme.

Note that it takes one concurrent write operation to check whether a non-root vertex is a leaf in a tree loop by marking a flag for the parent of each vertex. After the marking, i.e., concurrent write, the vertices remain unmarked are leaves. Initially, all vertices are active. During the beginning of each iteration, we mark the leaves in tree loops as 'inactive.' Inactive vertices keep their pointers, but do not participate further computation, and edge condensation is performed on edges incident on them to move these edges further up the tree loop. Given a set of tree loops, let the set of *active tree loops* be the induced subgraph on active vertices. Note that a rooted star that marks its leaves inactive becomes an isolated vertex. Thus in our new scheme, we hook active tree loops that are isolated vertices instead of rooted stars. We find the set of isolated vertices using one concurrent write operation as follows. We mark a flag for the parent of each vertex using concurrent write. After the marking, the vertices that remain unmarked and whose parent pointers are null or point to themselves are isolated vertices. Finally, after the original algorithm terminates, we mark all vertices active and perform pointer jumping until all tree loops are rooted stars.

Recall that the original star-checking algorithm as described in Section 2.1 uses two concurrent read operations and one concurrent write operation. Under the new scheme, it takes 1 concurrent write to find inactive vertices. After marking inactive vertices, rooted stars becomes isolated vertices. It takes only one concurrent write to find isolated vertices. Our experimental data indicates that this new method runs faster.

Note also that after removing inactive vertices, the height of each tree loop decreases (unless all tree loops are isolated vertices). Without using the new scheme, all depth-1 vertices (i.e., children of the root) in a tree loop perform a pointer jump operation even though their pointers do not change after the jump. This is a waste of communication bandwidth. Using our new scheme, leaves that are originally depth-1 do not participate in pointer jumping. Thus our new scheme not only reduces the time needed to check which tree loop to hook to, but also reduces the heights of the tree loops we work with, and the number of pointer chasing operations we perform during each iteration.

3.7. Implementation of Concurrent Read. In implementing pointer jumping, we need to use concurrent read operations. The MPL language provides system routine `rfetch` to directly implement it. The execution time of an concurrent read operation increases when the maximum number of concurrent read requests per physical processor increases [**21, 40**]. This is the 'Queue-Read' model that is addressed in [**14**]. As indicated in the experiments performed in [**21**], an exclusive read implementation of concurrent read operations using sorting outperforms the `rfetch` concurrent read implementation when the maximum number of concurrent read requests on one processor is larger than 256. We found that when performing pointer jumping on dense graphs with less vertices than the number of physical processors in the system, the maximum number of concurrent read requests on one physical processor becomes quite large at the very last few iterations. Thus it is desirable to switch to an exclusive read implementation during this stage. Hence in our implementations we use `rfetch` for deferred pointer jumping in the initial iterations, but when the number of vertices becomes less than or equal to the number of physical processors we use an exclusive read implementation to perform deferred pointer jumping operations. We will show in Section 5 this hybrid implementation of concurrent read operations improves the performance of some of our algorithms.

4. Testing Scheme

4.1. Computing Platform. All of our parallel implementations are on a MasPar MP-1 with 16,384 processors. The MasPar computer [33] is a fine-grained massively parallel single-instruction-multiple-data (SIMD) computer. All of its parallel processors synchronously execute the same instruction at the same time. A description of the hardware architecture and the software environment of MasPar MP-1 can be found in [22].

We used 4 kilo-bytes of memory per physical processor to test our various implementations for connected components. We show the performance of our code running on the largest data that we could fit into the system.

4.2. Test Inputs. In our code, an undirected graph is represented by a list of edges in it. We tested our programs using random graphs of three different edge densities[*]:
  - dense graphs where $m = \frac{n^2}{4}$;
  - intermediate-density graphs where $m = n^{1.5}$;
  - sparse graphs where $m = \frac{3n}{2}$.

To generate a random graph with n vertices and m edges, we first generated an empty graph with n vertices. Then we added one edge at a time with each edge being chosen with uniform probability until exactly m edges were generated. For each size and sparsity, we generated four different test graphs. We ran each program on each test graph for 10 iterations and recorded the average of the 40 trials.

We also used the following special classes of graphs that are reported in the experiments conducted in [16].
  - Two-dimensional wrap-around grids that are squares with 30% and 60% of their edges (chosen randomly). Thus given a graph in this class, $m = 0.6 \cdot n$ when the edge density is 30% and $m = 1.2 \cdot n$ when the edge density is 60%.
  - Three-dimensional wrap-around grids that have the same size in each dimension with 20% and 40% of their edges (chosen randomly). Thus

---

[*]In this paper, n and m always represent the number of vertices and edges in the input graph, respectively.

given a graph in this class, $m = 0.6 \cdot n$ when the edge density is 30% and $m = 1.2 \cdot n$ when the edge density is 60%.
- Tertiary graphs in which each vertex randomly selects three neighbors. Note that tertiary graphs are multi-graphs and $m = 3 \cdot n$.
- Random graphs with $m = 0.02 \cdot \frac{n \cdot (n-1)}{2}$.

5. Performance Data

We implemented the Algorithms 1 through 4 described in Section 2. All of our code used the compressed data structure that represents each undirected edge only once, a special routine for the first iteration, and performed the check for live edges. We also did not use deferred pointer jumping in Algorithms 1 and 2, since we found that there is no performance improvement by adding this feature.

5.1. Deterministic Algorithms. We first tested the following 5 different deterministic code using 16,384 PE's with 4 kilo-bytes of memory per PE.
- Code A: Algorithm 2.
- Code B: Code A with edge condensation, but does not remove duplicated edges.
- Code C: Algorithm 1.
- Code D: Code C with edge condensation, but does not remove duplicated edges.
- Code E: Algorithm 3 with edge condensation and deferred pointer jumping, but does not remove duplicated edges.

For each code, we tested two different methods to implement concurrent write. In the first version, we used arbitrary concurrent write operations (using the **rsend** routine), and in the second version we used priority concurrent write operations (using the **sendwith** routine). The performance data is shown in Table 1. We observe that for dense graphs, most of the runs terminate in a few iterations, and Algorithm 2 (i.e., Code A and Code B) outperforms the rest. Algorithm 1 (i.e., Code C) outperforms others on priority write implementation. Algorithm 3 (i.e., Code E) performs better when the graph is very sparse. We also observe that the priority write version decreases the number of iterations needed for code to terminate. However, the total execution time does not necessary decrease because of the overhead involved in implementing priority concurrent write operations using the **sendwith** routine.

Removing Duplicated Edges and Implementing Hybrid Concurrent Read/Write. We re-ran the above code with the modification of removing duplicated edges in each iteration. We found that the performance for Code A through D does not improve. We also used hybrid concurrent read and write in our code. We found that the performance of Code A through D did not improve too much. However, the performance of Code E greatly improves and

		$m = n^2/4$		$m = n^{3/2}$		$m = 3n/2$	
		seconds	iterations	seconds	iterations	seconds	iterations
Code A	Arbitrary CW	3.6	5.0	2.9	6.0	50.3	8.5
	Priority CW	5.2	3.5	4.2	4.2	52.8	7.0
Code B	Arbitrary CW	3.6	5.0	2.9	6.0	46.1	7.2
	Priority CW	5.2	3.5	4.2	4.2	47.3	6.2
Code C	Arbitrary CW	5.0	6.0	6.7	8.0	103.3	11.5
	Priority CW	2.2	3.0	4.0	5.0	72.5	7.0
Code D	Arbitrary CW	13.7	6.0	21.5	7.8	105.3	10.8
	Priority CW	12.0	3.0	17.8	5.0	84.0	7.0
Code E	Arbitrary CW	33.4	14.5	33.7	17.0	17.4	19.5
	Priority CW	8.9	5.0	18.8	9.0	22.0	19.5

TABLE 1. Performance for 5 different deterministic code when $m = 262,142$. We show both the execution time (in seconds) and the number of iterations the algorithm needs to terminate.

outperforms all other code in all classes of graphs. The performance data is shown in Table 2.

5.2. Randomized Algorithm. We incorporated the features of removing duplicated edges and deferred pointer jumping in our randomized algorithm. The performance of our code is shown in Table 3. We observe that the performance of our randomized code is slower than our best deterministic version on the set of graphs that we have tested.

5.3. Further Testing. We tested our code on several other classes of graphs which are shown in Section 4.2. The performance data for Code E with the features of removing duplicated edges and using hybrid concurrent write operations is shown in Table 4. The performance data for our randomized code is shown in Tables 5 and 6. We note that our randomized code outperforms our best deterministic code on grids. However, our deterministic code still outperforms our randomized code on random graphs and tertiary graphs.

5.4. Memory Usage. Using 16,384 physical processors and 4 kilo-bytes of memory per physical processor (which is $\frac{1}{16}$ of the total available memory), we were able to run our randomized algorithm for any graph with upto 0.52 million vertices and 0.52 million edges. That is, we are able to store 32 vertices and 32 edges in a physical processor. Our deterministic algorithm runs faster, though it requires more memory. We show the performance of our deterministic code for graphs with upto 0.26 million vertices and 0.26 million edges. For graph of this size, we store 16 vertices and 16 edges in a physical processor.

We observe that we do not occupy all 4 kilo-bytes of space by storing 16 vertices and 16 edges in a physical processor, and we should have enough space to pack 24 vertices and 24 edges. However, the sorting program that we used [41] requires that the number of data allocated in each physical processor to be power of 2. We use sorting to implement priority concurrent write operations (using the **sendwith** routine) and to remove duplicated edges. Thus we are unable to run our algorithms on larger graphs even though we have space left. For

			$m = 32,766$		$m = 65,534$		$m = 131,070$		$m = 262,142$	
			secs	itrs	secs	itrs	secs	itrs	secs	itrs
	code from [23]		0.6	NA	1.6	NA	2.4	NA	5.3	NA
	Code C	orig.	0.3	3.0	0.7	3.0	1.1	3.0	2.2	3.0
$m = n^2/4$	Pri. write	rev.	0.4	3.0	0.8	3.0	1.3	3.0	2.6	3.0
	Code E, Pri. write	orig.	1.1	5.0	2.0	5.0	4.3	5.0	8.9	5.0
	Code E	rev.	0.2	3.5	0.5	4.0	0.8	4.0	1.6	4.0
	code from [23]		0.9	NA	1.9	NA	3.4	NA	7.2	NA
	Code A	orig.	0.6	6.0	0.9	5.8	1.7	6.0	2.9	6.0
$m = n^{3/2}$	Arb. write	rev.	0.8	5.8	1.2	5.5	2.5	6.0	4.5	6.0
	Code E, Pri. write	orig.	2.3	9.0	4.6	9.0	9.1	9.0	18.8	9.0
	Code E	rev.	0.3	6.0	0.6	7.0	1.1	7.0	2.2	7.0
	code from [23]		7.4	NA	15.6	NA	33.4	NA	49.1	NA
	Code B	orig.	5.7	6.0	11.2	6.0	21.7	6.0	47.3	6.2
$m = 3n/2$	Pri. write	rev.	5.0	6.0	11.7	6.5	25.2	6.8	54.6	7.0
	Code E, Arb. write	orig.	1.4	15.5	3.4	18.0	8.2	20.0	17.4	19.5
	Code E	rev.	0.8	14.0	1.5	14.5	3.2	16.0	6.3	15.0

TABLE 2. The performance of our deterministic code after adding the feature of removing duplicated edges and also the features of hybrid concurrent read and write. For each class of graphs, we show the performance of the program which has the best performance among Code A through D and the fastest version of Code E. We apply the feature of removing duplicated edges in all of our tested code and apply the feature of hybrid concurrent write on Code E only. For comparison, we also list the performance of the code in [23] (based on Algorithm 1) which is not fine-tuned.

	$m = 32,766$		$m = 65,534$		$m = 131,070$		$m = 262,142$		$m = 524,286$	
	secs	itrs	secs	itrs	secs	itrs	secs	itrs	secs	itrs
$m = n^2/4$	1.2	3.0	2.0	3.1	3.5	4.1	6.6	4.0	13.4	4.5
$m = n^{3/2}$	1.2	3.3	1.9	4.0	3.7	4.9	6.4	4.7	13.0	5.2
$m = 3n/2$	1.9	6.0	3.2	7.6	5.6	7.7	11.6	8.5	25.4	9.8

TABLE 3. The performance of our randomized algorithm (with removing duplicated edges) is shown. We show both the total execution time (in seconds) and the number of iterations needed for the algorithm to reduce its number of edge to 8,192, in which case we switch to a deterministic algorithm.

	2-D grids		3-D grids		Tertiary graphs	Random graphs
	30%	60%	20%	40%		
n	261,121	218,089	250,047	216,000	87,380	5,119
m	157,285	262,142	157,285	262,142	262,140	262,142
seconds	4.5	6.7	5.5	5.9	5.8	2.3
iterations	12.5	20.0	16.5	17.0	11.5	7.0

TABLE 4. The performance of our best deterministic code on several special classes of graphs.

	2-D grids				3-D grids			
	30%		60%		20%		40%	
n	261,121	524,176	218,089	435,600	250,047	512,000	216,000	421,875
m	157,285	314,571	262,142	524,286	157,285	314,571	262,142	524,286
secs	4.0	8.8	5.7	12.6	4.1	9.3	7.6	16.4
itrs	7.0	8.0	9.0	11.0	7.1	8.1	9.6	11.0

TABLE 5. The performance of our randomized code on grid graphs.

	Tertiary graphs		Random graphs	
n	87,380	174,762	5,119	7,240
m	262,140	524,286	262,142	524,286
secs	9.6	21.3	7.0	15.2
itrs	6.7	7.9	4.8	5.5

TABLE 6. The performance of our randomized code on two special classes of graphs.

comparison, the code that we had for our previous implementation [23] (which is not fine-tuned) used 16 kilo-bytes of space to process upto 64 vertices and 64 edges per physical processor. Our randomized code used only half of the amount of memory because of the simplicity of the underlying algorithm. As a result of our fine-tuning, our current deterministic code uses 25% less memory than our earlier version in [23].

5.5. Comparison to Related Work. In [16], Greiner reported the implementation of several parallel algorithms for finding connected components on a massively parallel computer CM-2 using a quarter of the processors (8,192 processors) and all 32 kilo-bytes of memory in each processor. He also reported an implementation on a vector super computer Cray C-90 using one processor. Greiner implemented the algorithms of Shiloach and Vishkin [50] and Awerbuch and Shiloach [2], and the simple randomized algorithm that we implemented. Greiner did not use the system pseudo number generator for generating random bits in his randomized code. Instead, the ith "random" bit for a vertex is the $(i \bmod \log_2 n)$th bit of the vertex number. He implemented fine-tuning techniques which include routines similar to our first iteration of hooking, check of live edges, and edge condensation. He also implemented hybrid algorithms that combine features in the above three algorithms and an algorithm in Hirchberg, Chandra, and Sarwate [20]. His hybrid algorithm has the best performance for the classes of graphs tested. Greiner did not implement the compressed data structure for edges, various implementation of concurrent write operations, or deferred pointer jumping, all of which have been implemented in our work. Our revised deterministic algorithm is also different from any of the algorithms that he used.

Our code on the MasPar MP-1 is about half as fast as Greiner's code on the CM-2 for random graphs and tertiary graphs. On grids, his code is more than twice as fast. We observe that for grid graphs, his randomized code, though not the fastest overall, has about the same performance as his best code. His code on the Cray C-90 is about 15 times faster than his code on the CM-2. It should be noted that the CM-2 is a more expensive machine than the MasPar MP-1, and the Cray C-90 is a much more expensive machine than the MP-1.

The issue of memory usage is not addressed in [16]. Using four times the amount of total memory that we used, Greiner shows CM-2 performance data on random graphs with about 0.52 millions edges. He shows CM-2 performance data on grids and tertiary graphs with twice as many edges. As indicated in Section 5.4, our randomized code can run graphs with 0.52 millions edges. We also show performance data for our deterministic code on graphs with 0.26 millions edges. Since we use only quarter the amount of memory as Greiner's implementation on the CM-2, it appears that our code uses less space than his.

In [29], a distributed memory implementation of the algorithm by Shiloach and Vishkin [50] is reported. After fine-tuning, they obtain a speedup of 20 using a 32 processor CM-5 on grid graphs and obtain virtually no speedup on sparse random graphs. The performance of our massively parallel implementation seems to be more adaptable to different classes of graphs.

In [30], a mesh implementation of hooking-and-pointer-jumping type algorithms is reported on a MasPar MP-1 using 8,192 processors. By using the underlying mesh architecture and the fact that the mesh communication is more than 100 times faster than the global router communication, their implementation is generally faster than ours on dense graphs. Our implementation runs in about the same speed than theirs on very sparse graphs. In [30], the input graph is represented by an adjacency linked list on sparse graphs and is represented by an adjacency matrix on dense graphs while we use an arbitrary edge list to represent any input graph. It appears that our input data format is more flexible. Note that it takes non-trivial time to prepare an adjacency linked list or an adjacency matrix data structure for a graph. Because of the different data structures used for the input graph, our implementation also has a more efficient usage of the memory if the difference between the minimum vertex degree and the maximum vertex degree is large. We also have a more balanced usage of memory in each processor if the graph is very dense.

6. Concluding Remarks

In this paper, we have described our project on the implementation and fine-tuning of parallel code for the important problem of finding connected components in an undirected graph. Our fine-tuned code is more than 7 times faster than our original code on very sparse graph and also uses less memory. A randomized version of our code requires less memory, although it runs slower. This version can be used when memory is at a premium. We also note that our Code E with various revisions outperforms all other programs on all classes of graphs except grids. On grids, our randomized code has the best performance.

REFERENCES

1. R. Anderson and J. Setubal, *On the parallel implementation of Goldberg's maximum flow algorithm*, Proc. 4th ACM Symp. on Parallel Algorithms and Architectures, 1992, pp. 168–177.

2. B. Awerbuch and Y. Shiloach, *New connectivity and MSF algorithms for shuffle-exchange network and PRAM*, IEEE Tran. on Computers (1987), 1258–1263.

3. G. E. Blelloch, *Scan primitives and parallel vector models*, Ph.D. thesis, M.I.T., October 1989.

4. G. E. Blelloch, C. E. Leiserson, B. M. Maggs, C. G. Plaxton, S. J. Smith, and M. Zagha, *A comparison of sorting algorithms for the Connection Machine CM-2*, Proc. 3th ACM Symp. on Parallel Algorithms and Architectures, 1991, pp. 3–16.

5. K. W. Chong and T. W. Lam, *Finding connected components in $O(\log n \log \log n)$ time on the EREW PRAM*, Proc. 4th Annual ACM-SIAM Symp. on Discrete Algorithms, 1993, pp. 11–20.

6. R. Cole, P. N. Klein, and R. E. Tarjan, *A linear-work parallel algorithm for finding minimum spanning trees*, Proc. 6th ACM Symp. on Parallel Algorithms and Architectures, 1994, pp. 11–15.

7. R. Cole and U. Vishkin, *Approximate parallel scheduling. Part II: Applications to logarithmic-time optimal graph algorithms*, Information and Computation **92** (1991), 1–47.

8. E. Dekel, D. Nassimi, and S. Sahni, *Parallel matrix and graph algorithms*, SIAM J. Comput. **10** (1981), 657–675.

9. B. Dixon and A. K. Lenstra, *Factoring integers using SIMD sieves*, Manuscript, 1992.

10. ______ , *Massively parallel elliptic curve factoring*, Manuscript, 1992.

11. T. Feder, A. G. Greenberg, V. Ramachandran, M. Rauch, and L.-C. Wang, *Circuit switched link simulation: Algorithms, complexity and implementation*, Draft manuscript, 1992.

12. D. Fussel, V. Ramachandran, and R. Thurimella, *Finding triconnected components by local replacements*, SIAM J. Comput. **22** (1993), no. 3, 587–616.

13. H. Gazit, *An optimal randomized parallel algorithm for finding connected components in a graph*, SIAM J. Comput. **20** (1991), no. 6, 1046–1067.

14. P. B. Gibbons, Y. Matias, and V. Ramachandran, *The QRQW PRAM: Accounting for contention in parallel algorithms*, Proc. 5th ACM-SIAM Symp. on Discrete Algorithms, 1994, pp. 638–648, SIAM J. Comput., to appear.

15. A. G. Greenberg, B. D. Lubachevsky, and L.-C. Wang, *Experience in massively parallel discrete event simulation*, Proc. 5th ACM Symp. on Parallel Algorithms and Architectures, 1993, pp. 193–202.

16. J. Greiner, *A comparison of data-parallel algorithms for connected components*, Proc. 6th ACM Symp. on Parallel Algorithms and Architectures, 1994, pp. 16–25.

17. S. Halperin and U. Zwick, *An optimal randomized logarithmic time connectivity algorithm for the EREW PRAM*, Proc. 6th ACM Symp. on Parallel Algorithms and Architectures, 1994, pp. 1–10.

18. W. Hightower, J. Prins, and J. Reif, *Implementations of randomized sorting on large parallel machines*, Proc. 4th ACM Symp. on Parallel Algorithms and Architectures, 1992, pp. 158–167.

19. W. D. Hillis and G. L. Steele Jr., *Data parallel algorithms*, Communications of the ACM **29** (1986), 1170–1183.

20. D. S. Hirschberg, A. K. Chandra, and D. V. Sarwate, *Computing connected components on parallel computers*, Communications of the ACM **22** (1979), no. 8, 461–464.

21. T.-s. Hsu and V. Ramachandran, *Efficient massively parallel implementation of some combinatorial algorithms*, Theoretical Computer Science (1996, to appear).

22. T.-s. Hsu, V. Ramachandran, and N. Dean, *Implementation of parallel graph algorithms on the MasPar*, DIMACS Series in Discrete Mathematics and Theoretical Computer Science, vol. 15, American Mathematical Society, 1994, pp. 165–198.

23. ______ , *Implementation of parallel graph algorithms on a massively parallel SIMD computer with virtual processing*, Proc. 9th International Parallel Processing Symp., 1995, pp. 106–112.

24. K. Iwama and Y. Kambayashi, *A simpler parallel algorithm for graph connectivity*, Journal of Algorithms **16** (1994), 190–217.

25. J. JáJá, *An introduction to parallel algorithms*, Addison-Wesley, 1992.

26. D. R. Karger, N. Nisan, and M. Parnas, *Fast connected components algorithms for the EREW PRAM*, Proc. 4th ACM Symp. on Parallel Algorithms and Architectures, 1992, pp. 373–381.

27. R. M. Karp and V. Ramachandran, *Parallel algorithms for shared-memory machines*, Handbook of Theoretical Computer Science (J. van Leeuwen, ed.), North Holland, 1990, pp. 869–941.

28. B. W. Kernighan and D. M. Ritchie, *The C programming language*, Prentice Hall, Englewood Cliffs, NJ, 1988, Second Edition.

29. A. Krishnamurthy, S. Lumetta, D. E. Culler, and K. Yelick, *Connected components on distributed memory machines*, Presented at the 3rd DIMACS Implementation Challenge Workshop, October, 1994.

30. S. Kumar, S. M. Goddard, and J. F. Prins, *Connected-components algorithms for mesh-connected parallel computers*, Presented at the 3rd DIMACS Implementation Challenge Workshop, October, 1994.

31. F. T. Leighton, *Introduction to parallel algorithms and architectures: Arrays, trees, hypercubes*, Morgan Kaufmann, 1992.

32. Y. Maon, B. Schieber, and U. Vishkin, *Parallel ear decomposition search (EDS) and st-numbering in graphs*, Theoret. Comput. Sci. (1986), 277–298.

33. MasPar Computer Co., *MasPar system overview*, version 2.0 ed., March 1991.

34. MasPar Computer Co., *MasPar parallel application language (MPL) reference manual*, version 3.0, rev. a3 ed., July 1992.

35. MasPar Computer Co., *MasPar parallel application language (MPL) user guide*, version 3.1, rev. a3 ed., November 1992.

36. G. L. Miller and V. Ramachandran, *A new triconnectivity algorithm and its applications*, Combinatorica **12** (1992), 53–76.

37. ______, *Efficient parallel ear decomposition with applications*, Manuscript, MSRI, Berkeley, CA, January 1986.

38. B. Narendran and P. Tiwari, *Polynomial root-finding: Analysis and computational investigation of a parallel algorithm*, Proc. 4th ACM Symp. on Parallel Algorithms and Architectures, 1992, pp. 178–187.

39. P. M. Pardalos, M. G.C. Resende, and K.G. Ramakrishnan (eds.), *Parallel processing of discrete optimization problems*, DIMACS series in discrete mathematics and theoretical computer science, vol. 22, American Mathematical Society, 1995.

40. L. Prechelt, *Measurements of MasPar MP-1216A communication operations*, Tech. Report 01/93, Institute für Programmstrukturen und Datenorganisation, Fakultät für Informatik, Universität Karlsruhe, Germany, January 1993.

41. J. F. Prins and J. A. Smith, *Parallel sorting of large arrays on the MasPar MP-1*, Proc. 3rd Symp. on the Frontiers of Massively Parallel Computation, 1990, pp. 59–64.

42. T. Radzik, *Computing connected components on EREW PRAM*, Tech. report, King's College, London, 1994, Tech. Rep. 94/02.

43. V. Ramachandran, *Parallel open ear decomposition with applications to graph biconnectivity and triconnectivity*, Synthesis of Parallel Algorithms (J. H. Reif, ed.), Morgan-Kaufmann, 1993, pp. 275–340.

44. V. Ramachandran and J. Reif, *Planarity testing in parallel*, Jour. Comput. and Sys. Sci. **49** (1994), no. 3, 517–561, Special Issue for *FOCS '89*.

45. M. Reid-Miller, *List ranking and list scan on the CRAY C-90*, Proc. 6th ACM Symp. on Parallel Algorithms and Architectures, 1994, pp. 104–113.

46. J. H. Reif (ed.), *Synthesis of parallel algorithms*, Morgan-Kaufmann, 1993.

47. B. Schieber and U. Vishkin, *On finding lowest common ancestors: Simplification and parallelization*, SIAM J. Comput. **17** (1988), no. 6, 1253–1262.

48. J. T. Schwartz, *Ultracomputers*, ACM Trans. on Programming Languages and Systems **2** (1980), 484–521.

49. T. J. Sheffler, *Implementing the multiprefix operation on parallel and vector computers*, Proc. 5th ACM Symp. on Parallel Algorithms and Architectures, 1993, pp. 377–386.
50. Y. Shiloach and U. Vishkin, *An o(log n) parallel connectivity algorithm*, Journal of Algorithms (1982), 57–67.
51. R. E. Tarjan, *Depth-first search and linear graph algorithms*, SIAM J. Comput. **1** (1972), 146–160.
52. R. E. Tarjan and U. Vishkin, *An efficient parallel biconnectivity algorithm*, SIAM J. Comput. **14** (1985), 862–874.

INST. OF INFORMATION SCIENCE, ACADEMIA SINICA, NANKANG 115, TAIPEI, TAIWAN, ROC
E-mail address: tshsu@iis.sinica.edu.tw

DEPT. OF COMPUTER SCIENCES, UNIV. OF TEXAS AT AUSTIN, AUSTIN, TX 78712, USA
E-mail address: vlr@cs.utexas.edu

S/W PRODUCTION RESEARCH, AT&T BELL LABS., MURRAY HILL, NJ 07960, USA
E-mail address: nate@research.att.com

DIMACS Series in Discrete Mathematics
and Theoretical Computer Science
Volume **30**, 1997

CONNECTED COMPONENTS ALGORITHMS
FOR MESH-CONNECTED PARALLEL COMPUTERS

STEVE GODDARD, SUBODH KUMAR, AND JAN F. PRINS

ABSTRACT. We present a new CREW PRAM algorithm for finding connected
components. For a graph G with n vertices and m edges, algorithm $\mathcal{A}_0$ requires
at most $O(\log n)$ parallel steps and performs $O((n+m)\log n)$ work in the worst
case. The advantage our algorithm has over others in the literature is that it
can be adapted to a 2-D mesh-connected communication model in which all
CREW operations are replaced by $O(\log n)$ parallel row and column operations
without increasing the time complexity.

We present the mapping of $\mathcal{A}_0$ to a mesh-connected computer and describe
two implementations, $\mathcal{A}_1$ and $\mathcal{A}_2$. Algorithm $\mathcal{A}_1$, which uses an adjacency
matrix to represent the graph, performs $O(n^2 \log n)$ work. Hence, it only
achieves work efficiency on dense graphs. The second implementation, $\mathcal{A}_2$, uses
a sparse representation of the adjacency matrix and again performs $O(\log n)$
row and column operations but reduces the work to $O((m + n)\log n)$ on all
graphs.

We report MasPar MP-1 performance figures for implementations of the
algorithms described. The implementations are exercised on a variety of para-
metrically generated graphs, differing in structure and connectivity. These
graphs are generated externally and read in as input for the algorithms, per-
mitting comparison of different implementations on identical graphs.

1. INTRODUCTION

The problem of rapidly finding the connected components of an undirected graph
presents some substantial challenges for parallel computers.

First, parallel algorithms for this problem developed for the PRAM model make
extensive use of concurrent reads and writes (CRCW) to the shared memory, and
this abstraction is poorly supported by current parallel computers. Hence great
care has to be taken to minimize the impact of these operations.

Second, the standard sequential algorithm for this problem (based on depth-first
search) has optimal time complexity and small multiplicative constants, using only
a few operations per vertex and edge in the graph. Parallel algorithms for this problem rely on completely different techniques, and in many cases do not have optimal
work complexity or else perform a much larger number of operations per vertex and
edge. Thus achieving high absolute performance from parallel implementations can
be difficult.

In this paper we develop a new parallel algorithm for connected components that
is designed for the 2-D mesh communications model instead of the shared memory

Date: June 1996.

1991 *Mathematics Subject Classification*. Primary 68Q22; Secondary 68R10.

Key words and phrases. Connected Components Algorithms, Mesh-Connected Computers,
MasPar.

CRCW model and has variants with reasonable work efficiency for sparse and dense graphs.

The initial presentation of the algorithm, $\mathcal{A}_0$, is for the CREW-PRAM model of computation and is based on ideas found in the CRCW-PRAM algorithms for sparse graphs developed by Shiloach *et al.* in [SV82, AS87]. For a graph G with n vertices and m edges, $\mathcal{A}_0$ requires at most $O(\log n)$ parallel steps and performs $O((n + m) \log n)$ work (hence, like [SV82, AS87], is not quite work efficient).

$\mathcal{A}_0$ differs from [SV82, AS87] in that it can be adapted to a 2-D mesh-connected communication model in which all CREW operations are replaced by parallel row and column operations. In the case of the MasPar MP-1 and MP-2 machines that are the implementation targets for this work, row and column operations can use the high-bandwidth mesh network and offer better performance than concurrent read operations on global memory, which use the lower-bandwidth general-routing network. Even in machines like the Intel Paragon and the Cray T3D/T3E, where the general-routing network is based on the mesh connections, the regularity of the communication pattern and the elimination of read contention can still favor the use of row and column operations.

Algorithm $\mathcal{A}_1$ is the adaptation of $\mathcal{A}_0$ to the mesh, and is based on an adjacency matrix representation of G. This algorithm performs $O(\log n)$ parallel row and column reduction and broadcast operations, but performs $O(n^2 \log n)$ work, hence achieves very poor work efficiency on sparse graphs. Since sparse graphs are typical in applications requiring high-speed determination of connected components (see [Gre93]), this is unsatisfactory.

Algorithm $\mathcal{A}_2$ uses a sparse representation of the adjacency matrix and again performs $O(\log n)$ row and column operations but reduces the work to $O((m + n) \log n)$ on all graphs. A cyclic decomposition of the underlying adjacency matrix over processors, tends to distribute the sparse edge set uniformly over processors while insuring that the communication structure of the row and column operations is preserved.

On a 4096 node graph, our implementation of $\mathcal{A}_1$ on an 8,192 processor Mas-Par MP-1 (at approximately 0.2 Mops/sec per processor) achieves a performance varying from 10^5 to 10^8 edges per second with increasing density of the graph. Our implementation of $\mathcal{A}_2$ improves on $\mathcal{A}_1$ by about a factor of three for sparse graphs.

The rest of the paper is organized as follows. We introduce the basic PRAM algorithm $\mathcal{A}_0$ in section 2. Section 3 describes the implementation of $\mathcal{A}_1$ and $\mathcal{A}_2$ under a mesh-connected communication model. Section 4 reports on the implementation of $\mathcal{A}_1$ and $\mathcal{A}_2$ on the MasPar MP-1 and gives performance statistics. We discuss other connected components algorithms and compare their results with $\mathcal{A}_2$ in section 5. Section 6 shares our plans for further improvements to the algorithms. Finally we present our conclusions and ideas for continuing research in section 7.

2. Main Algorithm

Let $G = (V, E)$ be an undirected graph, with vertices $V = \{1, \ldots, n\}$ and $|E| = m$. For $u, v \in V$, there is a *path* between u and v, written as $u \leftrightsquigarrow v$, iff there exists a sequence of vertices $[w_1 \ldots w_k]$ such that $w_1 = u, w_k = v$, and $\forall\, i : 1 \leq i < k :: (w_i, w_{i+1}) \in E$.

The connected component problem is to compute for each $v \in V$ a label $P(v)$ such that $\forall\, u, v \in V : u \leftrightsquigarrow v$ iff $P(u) = P(v)$. We require that any labeling function satisfy $P : V \to V$ and $\forall\, u, v \in V : P(u) \leq u$. Under these conditions P is a *parent function* and induces a forest of *rooted trees* on V, with each tree rooted by some vertex r for which $r = P(r)$. A *rooted star* is a tree T of height one with a root r such that $P(v) = r$ for each vertex $v \in T$. Our solution to the connected components problem sets $P(v)$ to be the smallest vertex reachable from v, which defines a rooted star for each component.

Our PRAM algorithm, $\mathcal{A}_0$, starts with $P(v) = \min(v, \min\{u \mid (u, v) \in E\})$ for all $v \in V$ (i.e. for each v, the smallest vertex within distance one of v), and iteratively improves P until it converges on the solution. Note that the initial parent function may contain a tree of height as much as $n - 1$. Each iteration of the algorithm changes P as follows.

- *opportunistic pointer jumping:* Define the *chain* from a vertex $u \in V$ to be the sequence of vertices from u to the root of the tree containing u. The opportunistic pointer jumping step attempts to decrease the height of chains through a pointer doubling operation for each vertex u of the form $P'(u) := P(P(u))$, shrinking the height h of the chain to $\lceil \frac{h}{2} \rceil$. However, u can perform pointer jumping either through its own chain or through that of one of its neighbors in G. The neighbor v of u with the least value for $P(v)$ determines the chain into which u performs a pointer jumping step (see Figure 1). Therefore a vertex may switch trees or leave one rooted star for another as part of this step.

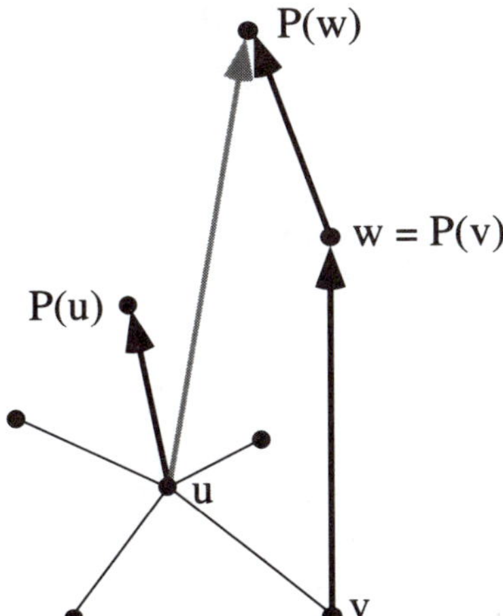

FIGURE 1. Opportunistic Pointer Jumping: Vertex u finds that of all of its neighboring vertices, v has the smallest numbered parent. Therefore, vertex u changes its parent to $P(w) = P(P(v))$ rather than $P(P(u))$.

- *tree hanging:* If a vertex v with parent $u = P(v)$ switches chains so that $P'(v)$ ends up a smaller value than $P'(u)$, then $P'(u)$ is switched to $P'(v)$. There may be multiple children of u that can improve $P'(u)$, in which case $P'(u)$ is set to the minimum of the new parents of all its children (see Figure 2). Subsequently a single normal pointer jumping step is used to ensure that rooted stars can be hung onto a tree without changing the tree's height. This step is not necessary for correct execution of $\mathcal{A}_0$, but simplifies the time

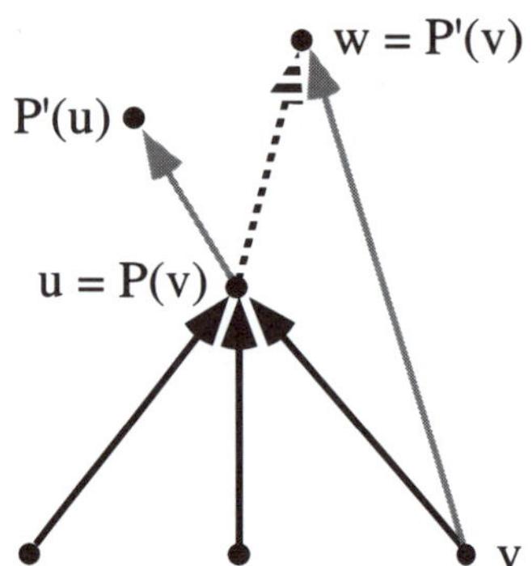

FIGURE 2. Tree Hanging: Vertex u finds that its former child, vertex v, has found a smaller numbered parent during the opportunistic pointer jumping step (i.e., $w = P'(v) < P'(u)$). The tree hanging step changes the parent of u from $P'(u)$ to $w = P'(v)$ if w is the minimum of the new parents of the old children of u.

complexity proof. The tree hanging operation is critical for rapid convergence and plays the same role as the grafting operation of [SV82].

The pseudo code of $\mathcal{A}_0$ follows.

FOREACH vertex u **IN G**
    $P(u) := \min\{u,\min\{v \mid$ vertex v is adjacent to u in G$\}\}$
REPEAT
    FOREACH vertex u **IN G**   */* Opportunistic Pointer Jumping */*
        $OldP(u) := P(u)$
        $P'(u):=P(\min\{P(u), \min\{P(v) \mid$ vertex v is adjacent to vertex u in G$\}\})$
    FOREACH vertex u **IN G**   */* Tree hanging */*
        $P(u) := \min\{P'(u), \min\{P'(v) \mid P(v) = u\}\}$
    FOREACH vertex u **IN G**   */* Normal Pointer Jumping */*
        $P(u) := P(P(u))$
UNTIL $P = OldP$

Algorithm $\mathcal{A}_0$ uses the combination of opportunistic pointer jumping and tree hanging to pull stagnant stars into other trees that comprise the same connected component. Since vertices are always trying to decrease their parent function, eventually all trees of a connected component are combined and contracted to a single rooted star. While the Shiloach-Vishkin algorithms of [SV82, AS87] must be very particular about how trees are grafted, $\mathcal{A}_0$ hangs a tree on any lower numbered vertex without concern for its height in the tree.

2.1. **Correctness.** Algorithm $\mathcal{A}_0$ terminates when all vertices of a connected component have the same parent.

Theorem 2.1. *On termination of* $\mathcal{A}_0$, $\forall u, v \in V$, $P(u) = P(v) \iff u \leftrightsquigarrow v$

Proof ($\Rightarrow$): $\forall u \in V$, $u \leftrightsquigarrow P(u)$ is an invariant of the loop: each change to P(u) preserves $u \leftrightsquigarrow$ P(u). Hence if P(u) = P(v), then $u \leftrightsquigarrow$ P(u) = P(v) $\leftrightsquigarrow v$ and therefore $u \leftrightsquigarrow v$.
($\Leftarrow$): By contradiction. Assume $\mathcal{A}_0$ has terminated with P(u) $\neq$ P(v) and $u \leftrightsquigarrow v$. Then $\exists\, (w_i, w_{i+1})$ on $u \leftrightsquigarrow v$ such that P(w_i) $\neq$ P(w_{i+1}). This means that P(w_i) <

$P(w_{i+1})$ or $P(w_i) > P(w_{i+1})$. In either case, the opportunistic pointer jumping step would change $P(w_i)$ or $P(w_{i+1})$ so that the termination condition (OldP = P) could not hold. This contradicts the assumption that $\mathcal{A}_0$ has terminated. $\blacksquare$

2.2. **Complexity.** Termination of $\mathcal{A}_0$ is guaranteed because each iteration of $\mathcal{A}_0$ satisfies $\forall u \in V : P(u) \leq OldP(u)$, which can be established by observing that (1) $P(u) \leq u$ is an invariant of $\mathcal{A}_0$ and (2) each change to $P(u)$ can only decrease its value or leave it the same. Since P is strictly decreasing on each iteration on which $\mathcal{A}_0$ does not terminate, and is bounded below by the connected components labeling, $\mathcal{A}_0$ must terminate.

In practice, we have observed that the number of iterations of the outer loop is very small, but the complexity is $O(\log n)$. To see this, observe that $\log n$ steps will reduce any tree formed by P, that does not have another tree hook onto it, to a rooted star. Any chain that did have trees hook onto it, may take another $\log n$ steps to shrink to height one. Note that the number of trees never increases. In most iterations both the number of trees and the height of each tree decreases. In the worst case, if all trees shrink to rooted stars without forming complete components, it takes one more step to get the final connected components of P and another $\log n$ iterations to shorten these new chains to rooted stars.

3. IMPLEMENTATION ON A MESH

The connected components algorithm of section 2 has the nice property that it can be mapped to a mesh-connected computer without needing costly concurrent read operations in a shared memory. The pseudo code presented below represents the mapping to the mesh utilizing only the row and column communication primitives shown below, which are quite efficient on computers like the MasPar. The graph edges are stored in the adjacency matrix A. Matrices Q and M are used to store intermediate results. The functions P, P' and $OldP$ from $\mathcal{A}_0$ are each represented as matrices in which the function values are replicated either on each row (P and $OldP$) or each column (P').

During the opportunistic pointer jumping and tree hanging steps, the parent values are stored in the columns of P', such that the parent of vertex j is stored in column j. The normal pointer jumping step then returns the parent values to the rows of P for the next iteration. All values needed at any step in the algorithm are in the row or column of one of the matrices. Hence, only row or column communications is required.

Functions:

$MinCol(M^{n \times n}) : Q^{n \times n}$
$MinRow(M^{n \times n}) : Q^{n \times n}$
$MinNeighbor(A^{n \times n}, u) : v$

$MinCol()$ finds the minimum value in each column of the matrix M and copies these values to every entry of the respective columns of the return matrix Q. $MinRow()$ performs the respective operations on the rows of the matrix. The third function, $MinNeighbor()$, returns the minimum of u and the minimum vertex adjacent to u in the adjacency matrix A (all necessary information for this function can be found in column u). Note that all three of these functions can be implemented quite efficiently on most mesh computers.

Variables:
 $A^{n\times n}$ adjancency matrix representation of the graph
 $P', P^{n\times n}$ values of parent function $P()$
 $M, Q^{n\times n}$ storage matrices

Initializations:

$$A(i,j) := \begin{cases} \text{True if } (i,j) \in E \text{ or } i = i \\ \text{False otherwise} \end{cases}$$

$$P_{i,j} := MinNeighbor(A, i)$$

Pseudo-Code for Connected Components Algorithm on a Mesh:
REPEAT
 $OldP := P$

            /* begin opportunistic pointer jumping */
 FORALL i, j **IN** $[1..n], [1..n]$

$$M(i,j) := \begin{cases} P_{ij} \text{ if } A_{ij} \\ \infty \text{ otherwise} \end{cases}$$

 $Q := MinCol(M)$
 FORALL i, j **IN** $[1..n], [1..n]$

$$M(i,j) := \begin{cases} P_{ij} \text{ if } Q_{ij} = i \\ \infty \text{ otherwise} \end{cases}$$

 $P' := MinCol(M)$

              /* begin tree hanging */
 FORALL i, j **IN** $[1..n], [1..n]$

$$M(i,j) := \begin{cases} P'_{ij} \text{ if } P_{ij} = j \\ \infty \text{ otherwise} \end{cases}$$

 $Q := MinCol(M)$
 FORALL i, j **IN** $[1..n], [1..n]$
  $P'(i,j) := min(P'_{ij}, Q_{ij})$

           /* begin normal pointer jumping */
 FORALL i, j **IN** $[1..n], [1..n]$

$$M(i,j) := \begin{cases} P'_{ij} \text{ if } i = j \\ \infty \text{ otherwise} \end{cases}$$

 $Q := MinRow(M)$
 FORALL i, j **IN** $[1..n], [1..n]$

$$M(i,j) := \begin{cases} P'_{ij} \text{ if } Q_{ij} = j \\ \infty \text{ otherwise} \end{cases}$$

 $P := MinRow(M)$
UNTIL $P = OldP$

The opportunistic pointer jumping and tree hanging steps both serve to move vertices closer to the correct root for the connected component to which they belong. A vertex may switch from following one parent to another if it finds that one of its neighbors has found a smaller vertex (or root). These two steps serve to group trees into connected components while reducing each connected component to a rooted star. In contrast the normal pointer jumping step of the algorithm can only shrink a tree to a rooted star, something the opportunistic pointer jumping step also does. Hence, in practice we find that replacing the normal pointer jumping step with another opportunistic pointer jumping step improves the performance of the algorithm. Since the next iteration will do another opportunistic pointer jumping step, we can further simplify the implementation of the algorithm by dropping the last pointer jumping step so the loop only consists of one opportunistic pointer jumping step followed by tree hanging.

A graph can be represented as a matrix or an adjacency list. The variation in representation gives rise to different behavior. While the first representation is well suited to dense graphs it is quite wasteful for sparse graphs. Algorithm $\mathcal{A}_1$, described in section 3.1, stores the graph as an adjacency matrix. Algorithm $\mathcal{A}_2$, described in section 3.2, stores the graph as an adjacency list. $\mathcal{A}_1$ is better suited for dense graphs while $\mathcal{A}_2$ is better suited for sparse graphs as shown in section 4.

3.1. Algorithm $\mathcal{A}_1$: Matrix Representation.

Consider a mesh of $p \times p$ processors (or PEs, for processing elements). In the following discussion we assume that wrap-around connections exist on the mesh, though it is not essential to the algorithm.

We combine matrices P and A by storing P_{ij} in A_{ij} if $(i, j) \in E$ and ∞ otherwise. Call this matrix M. We then use the diagonals of M to store OldP(), P'_{ij}. The matrix M is distributed by mapping $M(i, j)$ to PE($i \bmod p, j \bmod p$). Combining this mapping with our algorithm, PE(a, b) only accesses $M(i, j)$ if either $i \bmod p = a$ or $j \bmod p = b$. In both cases the required data is found within the row or column.

The work complexity of algorithm $\mathcal{A}_1$ is $O(n^2 \log n)$, each PE does $O((\frac{n}{p})^2)$ work per iteration. The total number of iterations is $O(\log n)$ and the total number of PEs is p^2.

3.2. Algorithm $\mathcal{A}_2$: Adjacency List Representation.

If most of the elements in M are ∞, we waste space and time performing operations on the adjacency matrix. So instead of distributing the entire matrix we can distribute only the non ∞ entries in the matrix — just the edges. Our approach is to store a *sparse* adjacency matrix. We use the cyclic decomposition from $\mathcal{A}_1$: an edge (u, v) is stored at the processor PE($u \bmod p, v \bmod p$), but we only store edges present in the graph and elide the ∞ values. Thus we have a list of (u, v) values at each processor. We can implement the row and column minimum operations by merging lists between processors, retaining the minimum u value for elements with equal v values or vice versa (for this to yield a constant cost per edge, we must keep the lists in sorted order). This implementation doesn't spoil the communication characteristics of the algorithm since the required information can still be found in the row or the column, but we may end up with load balancing problems if the edges are not uniformly distributed in the graph (see Section 6.1).

The adjacency list is constructed and pre-processed in parallel at each processor. The list is sorted using $min(u, v)$ as the key, and the *RowMin* and *ColMin* operations work locally on the list before communicating with other processors. The list pre-processing and the higher operation count per row or column operation increases the per edge cost compared to $\mathcal{A}_1$, but this is offset by the reduced work (relative to the n^2 adjacency matrix when the graph is sufficiently sparse).

The work complexity of this implementation is $O((n + m) \log n)$, since we represent only the m edges and the n values for P, P', etc. The number of iterations stays the same. In our current implementation of $\mathcal{A}_2$, each processor still does some work for vertices that do not have adjacent edges mapping onto that processor; eliminating this work will further improve the timings.

4. Performance Results

We tested the performance of algorithms $\mathcal{A}_1$ and $\mathcal{A}_2$ on star, chain, tertiary, 2D-mesh, 3D-mesh and random shaped graphs. We found that star graphs provided the best results while long chains yielded the worst. Since the star and chain graphs were created to exploit strengths and weakness specific to our algorithm, we do not present those timing results. We have chosen instead (for brevity) to report results measured on the canonical graph benchmarks of random and tertiary graphs and variations thereof.

Many algorithms are quite sensitive to the structure of the graph. For example, a class of graphs that are recursively defined as graphs of vertices which are themselves graphs (with different density and structure) pose difficulties for some connected component algorithms. Such graphs are sometimes called *hard graphs*. Due to the dependence of our algorithm on a chain's length, and not the actual structure of the graph, such graphs do not negatively impact the performance of our algorithms. In some cases our algorithms execute faster on hard graphs than the 'simple' graphs reported in this paper because hard graphs have more dense connections that shorten the chains in the graph.

Section 4.1 defines the graph terms we use to describe our suite of benchmark graphs. Section 4.2 describes how we built our test graphs. Section 4.3 addresses how graphs are read into the MasPar and distributed. Sections 4.4, 4.5, and 4.6 address the performance of algorithms $\mathcal{A}_1$ and $\mathcal{A}_2$ on random, tertiary, and grid graphs respectively. The timing tests reported in this paper (except the sequential algorithm) were performed on a 8192 processor MasPar MP-1.

4.1. Definitions. A graph in which each pair of distinct vertices is joined by an edge is called a *complete graph*. The number of edges in a graph as a percentage of complete cover is called its *density*: e.g., a $p\%$ dense graph has $\frac{p}{100} \cdot \frac{n(n-1)}{2}$ edges, n being the number of vertices in the graph. The number of edges incident on a vertex is called its *vertex degree* and the degree of the graph is its maximum vertex degree. A *2D* graph is a subset of a two-dimensional toroidal grid. The neighbors of a vertex in a 2D graph form a subset of the four neighbors on such a grid [Gre93]. Similarly, a *3D graph* is a subset of a three-dimensional toroidal grid [Gre93]. The vertices of a *random graph* are joined at random, and unless otherwise noted, the number of components is not constrained; it is a function of the random edge generation. Each vertex of a *tertiary* graph has degree 3. When no duplicate edges are allowed, a tertiary graph has $1.5n$ edges.

4.2. Generating Benchmark Graphs. Initially, we created graphs 'on the fly' as other research projects had done [KLCY94, HRD94]. However, we found that this method presented two problems. First, duplicate edges were created which inflated the 'actual' number of edges, resulting in better performance for our algorithms. The second problem was that creating graphs on the fly precluded the possibility of accurately comparing algorithms implemented on different machines (or by other groups).

We have created a tool, *mkgraph*, that was used to generate a suite of benchmark graphs for finding connected components. This program creates a binary graph file consisting of a list of unique, undirected edges that conform to the options provided on the command line.

The program can create graphs with a specific number of components that conform to one of four component structures: star, chain, mesh or random. The structure defines the minimal connections between the nodes when forming the component. After the initial component is created, the rest of the edges for that component are added at random.

The total number of edges in an n node graph is defined by the vertex degree or graph density. If a vertex degree is specified, all vertices of the resulting graph have the requested degree. Otherwise, the density parameter is used to define the total number of edges in the graph.

4.3. Reading and Distributing Graphs. All of our performance results were measured with graphs created by the *mkgraph* tool. The graphs were read into the MasPar and then distributed to the proper PEs in parallel. Although we measured the time taken to read and distribute the graphs, this time is *not* included in our performance results. Only the actual time to find the connected component is presented in this paper. It is interesting to note that the time to read and distribute the graphs ranged from 200 milliseconds to 2 seconds depending on the number of edges. While reading the file in parallel rather than sequentially significantly reduced the time it took to load the graph (by a few orders of magnitude), it still dominated the time it took to actually find the components for most graphs. We have determined that the limiting factor in loading the graph is the disk network itself and not the use of the router, which indicates that using the MasPar to find connected components must be part of a larger problem as opposed to a stand-alone program.

Each PE reads $\frac{m}{p}$ edges from the file where we have m edges and p processors. The edges are then distributed to the proper PE via parallel sends using the router. We studied several different decompositions and found a cyclic decomposition based on the vertex values provides the best performance on average.

Nodes, Edges	$\mathcal{A}_1$ time (ms)	$\mathcal{A}_2$ time (ms)	Comments
1000,9990	43.7	22.6	2% complete
2000,39980	125.4	47.2	2% complete
3000,89970	237.8	71.6	2% complete
4000,159960	387.7	103.8	2% complete
5000,249950	571.4	133.1	2% complete
6000,359940	766.1	164.1	2% complete
7000,489930	1014.2	197.6	2% complete
8000,639920	1294.4	335.1	2% complete

TABLE 1. **Random Graphs**: Other than density no other property is prescribed for this experiment. The times increase linearly with the size of the graph.

4.4. Random Graphs. Algorithms $\mathcal{A}_1$ and $\mathcal{A}_2$ perform well on random graphs, which are more dense than tertiary or grid graphs. We tested a variety of random graphs and compare results from both algorithms. Algorithm $\mathcal{A}_1$ has clear performance advantages in dense graphs, but when the density is under 20% $\mathcal{A}_2$ is the faster.

Table 1 shows our results when we varied the number of nodes from 1000 to 8000 while maintaining a constant density of 2%. The times for both algorithms increase almost linearly as the number of nodes is increased.

Our next suite of graphs all have 4096 nodes, but their density varies from 1% to 10%. Table 2 shows the timing results for both $\mathcal{A}_1$ and $\mathcal{A}_2$ in finding the connected components of these graphs.

Nodes, Edges	$\mathcal{A}_1$ time (ms)	$\mathcal{A}_2$ time (ms)	Density
4096,83865	407.2	133.3	1% complete
4096,167731	408.1	145.7	2% complete
4096,251596	408.9	158.5	3% complete
4096,335462	407.7	173.1	4% complete
4096,419328	300.2	136.4	5% complete
4096,503193	299.4	145.2	6% complete
4096,587059	298.7	154.9	7% complete
4096,670924	298.1	165.9	8% complete
4096,754790	297.3	176.1	9% complete
4096,838656	296.4	186.7	10% complete

TABLE 2. **Varying Density of 4096 Node Random Graphs**: On sparse graphs, $\mathcal{A}_2$ always outperforms $\mathcal{A}_1$. The times increase nearly linearly with the density of the graph.

Table 3 amplifies the efficiency of $\mathcal{A}_1$ for very dense graphs. When the number of nodes is held constant, as in Table 2, and the density approaches 100%, $\mathcal{A}_1$ gets faster. The inverse is true for $\mathcal{A}_2$ whose time to find the connected components increases almost linearly with the increased number of edges. Table 3 also shows what happens when the density is kept constant at 50%, but the number of nodes is increased (as in Table 1 with 2% dense graphs).

Increasing Density				Increasing size,50% dense		
Nodes, Edges	Density	$\mathcal{A}_1$ ms	$\mathcal{A}_2$ ms	Nodes, Edges	$\mathcal{A}_1$ ms	$\mathcal{A}_2$ ms
4096,4193280	50%	268.4	547.8	1024,261888	35.5	55.7
4096,5031936	60%	264.6	631.7	2048,1048064	92.4	169.7
4096,5870592	70%	261.8	720.4	4096,4193280	268.4	547.8
4096,6709248	80%	260.2	799.7	8192,16775168	432.7	799.7

TABLE 3. **Dense Graphs**: The time for $\mathcal{A}_1$ goes down as we start approaching the completeness of the graph since the distance of any vertex to the lowest numbered vertex in its component decreases, which is what drives the complexity of algorithm $\mathcal{A}_1$.

4.5. Tertiary Graphs. Regular tertiary graphs are included in our benchmark suite of sparse graphs. Tertiary graphs satisfy the property that each vertex has exactly three neighbors. The neighbors are picked at random by the *mkgraph* program such that all vertices have degree 3. Thus, each tertiary graph has *1.5n* edges. As with all graphs generated by *mkgraph*, no self-loops or duplicate edges are allowed.

We employed a number of other definitions for tertiary graphs, but the performance of our algorithms was not significantly affected. In particular, we created AD3 [KLCY94] graphs. Each vertex in an AD3 graph selects between 0 and 3 neighbors so that one vertex may end up being directly connected to many different nodes. Such graphs tend to have more components [KLCY94]. We also generated graphs in which the degree of each vertex lies between 0 and 6 (uniformly distributed). The performance of $\mathcal{A}_1$ and $\mathcal{A}_2$ on these graphs mirrored the results shown for tertiary graphs.

Nodes	$\mathcal{A}_2$ time (ms)	Comments
50,000	2,095.6	75,000 Edges
100,000	4,160.0	150,000 Edges
150,000	6,208.6	225,000 Edges
200000	8,246.1	300,000 Edges
250000	10,288.8	375,000 Edges

TABLE 4. **Tertiary Graphs**: These are highly sparse graphs. The degree of a node is fixed to 3, but the neighbors are selected randomly. If we let the degree vary from 0 to 6, the performance of the algorithms does not change noticeably.

We only present performance results from $\mathcal{A}_2$ on sparse graphs. There are two reasons for this. First, the data structures required by $\mathcal{A}_1$ become too large to fit in memory when the number of vertices gets beyond 9,000. Second, $\mathcal{A}_1$ is designed for dense graphs and doesn't perform well on these sparse graphs.

The times shown in Table 4 are considerably higher than those in the previous tables. The time taken by $\mathcal{A}_2$ to find the connected components of the tertiary graphs ranges from approximately 2.01 seconds to 10.29 seconds when the number of nodes varies from 50,000 to 250,000.

4.6. Grid Graphs. The other class of sparse graphs in our suite are the grids. We generated two dimensional (2D) and three dimensional (3D) grid graphs. For each possible edge of the grid, the probability that it exists in the graph was varied. The probabilities were 0.4, 0.6, 0.2, and 0.4 for graphs of classes 2D40, 2D60, 3D20 and 3D40 respectively.

Grids are highly sparse graphs. As Tables 5 and 6 indicate, $\mathcal{A}_2$ is not affected by the structure of these graphs as much as it is by their density. Most of these graphs have long chains in comparison with random or tertiary graphs. As the density of the graph increases, the average number of components and average length of a chain decreases. The impact of the longer chains is clearly reflected in the longer execution times of $\mathcal{A}_2$ in Tables 5 and 6.

Nodes	$\mathcal{A}_2$ 2D40 time(ms)	Edges	$\mathcal{A}_2$ 2D60 time(ms)	Edges
65536	4,218.6	52496	4,426.1	78517
262144	14,460.2	208893	17,557.2	313593
300000	17,916.7	239239	16,018.3	359047
400000	25,325.1	319397	27,274.1	479365

TABLE 5. **2D Grids**: Highly sparse two dimensional grids. The 2D40 and 2D60 graphs were constructed such that the probability of a grid edge's existence in the graph is 40% and 60% respectively.

	$\mathcal{A}_2$ 3D40		$\mathcal{A}_2$ 3D60	
65536	2,507.8	39174	2,807.2	78403
262144	12,110.6	156825	11,080.5	313934
300000	15,547.3	179656	14,865.2	359321
400000	20,432.3	239755	25,290.9	479458

TABLE 6. **3D Grids**: 3D20 and 3D40 are highly sparse three dimensional grids. The corresponding probability of the existence of a grid edge in the graph is 20% and 40% respectively.

5. SLOWER ALGORITHMS

While working with early versions of $\mathcal{A}_1$ and $\mathcal{A}_2$ we evaluated the possibility of performance gains using random mating techniques from the RM algorithm of [Ble90], a variation of which was presented as $cc\_RM2()$ in [Gre93]. Table 7 shows timing results of the NESL program $cc\_RM2()$ compared with the MPL implementations[1] of Algorithm 5.2 of [J92] and algorithm $\mathcal{A}_2$. We acknowledge that the comparison is not entirely fair since MPL programs are in general faster than NESL versions.

Greiner claims the RM algorithm has $O(\log n)$ time complexity and $O(m \log n)$ work complexity in the worst case. However, the RM algorithm relies on CRCW capabilities, and the MasPar doesn't provide such support in hardware. CRCW can be simulated using library routines as was done in [HRD92], but then the *constant* communication costs assumed in the PRAM analysis isn't constant in the implementation. Moreover, the NESL implementation of the RM algorithm uses calls to the router for the *mating*, which can take up to 100 times longer than a mesh oriented communication mechanism. Our attempts to remove calls to the router led to algorithms similar to $\mathcal{A}_2$, but less efficient. Next we attempted to use random mating techniques at selected points in the algorithm. However, the performance cost of simulating the CRCW requirements of RM outweighed the potential benefits. We have concluded that random mating will not improve the performance of $\mathcal{A}_1$ or $\mathcal{A}_2$. Algorithms $\mathcal{A}_1$ and $\mathcal{A}_2$ perform well on the MasPar

---

[1] All algorithms, except the NESL $cc\_RM2()$ program, were implemented using the language MPL.

because great care has been taken to eliminate calls to the router and they don't require CRCW capabilities.

Nodes, Edges	NESL RM seconds	Jájá's 5.2 seconds	$\mathcal{A}_2$ seconds	Density
4096,419328	229.380	13.72	0.1364	5% complete
4096,167731	52.650	14.23	0.1457	2% complete
4096,4096	3.73	4.1	0.12	0.05% complete
8192,81920	15.46	4.7	0.54	0.24% complete
16384,163840	32.34	68.0	16.97	0.12% complete
409600,409600	40.95	273.77	42.37	0.00005% complete

TABLE 7. **Random Graphs**: Comparisons of a NESL implementation of Random Mating to MPL implementations of sparse graph connected component algorithms.

We also implemented a simple sequential algorithm based on depth first search of the graph. This was implemented on an HP 9000-712/80, an 80MIPS machine. We found that for small[2] 2% random graphs the sequential implementation beat our MasPar algorithms. As the graph grows beyond 4K nodes, the sequential implementation starts getting slower. We observed that the sequential implementation exhibited about 2-7 times improvement in performance for sparse random graphs of up to 8K nodes over the MasPar routines. However, the sequential machine did not have sufficient memory to store larger graphs. Therefore, performance dropped considerably when the graphs were paged in and out of memory. The performance of the sequential machine was limited by memory even though it had a significantly faster processor than the type of processors used in the MasPar.

6. FASTER ALGORITHMS

The success of a parallel algorithm lies in how well it keeps the processors busy and how well the communication pattern can be mapped onto the structure of the machine. We used fast communication mechanisms, but load balancing remains an issue.

We found that cyclic (cut-and-stack) decomposition provides better all around performance than hierarchical (block) decomposition for the sparse graphs handled by $\mathcal{A}_2$, but both of these simple virtualization techniques can result in load imbalances among the processors. While first developing our graph creation tool (see Section 4.2) to build the benchmark graphs, we employed a bad random number generator and our *random graphs* were not very random. The resulting graphs produced a load imbalance that was worse than 50:1 (and we may find such graphs in practice). This type of load imbalance creates more work than our $O(m \log n)$ goal, but the overall execution times were still not far from the numbers reported in this paper — they were about 10–20% slower. With a more uniform random number generator in place, we see processor load is balanced quite well with a load imbalance on the order of 1.3:1 for 2% complete 8,000 node graphs. However, we have seen an imbalance as high as 5.4:1 for some graphs.

---

[2] 4000 vertices

We have identified three distinct methods of improving the performance of our connected components algorithms. The next three sections outline these ideas.

6.1. Load Balancing. Virtualizations based on random sampling may improve the load balance between processors when an imbalance exists. To come close to the best known PRAM complexity of $O(m \log n)$, we need to get the work distributed evenly. One way to achieve this goal would be to execute a fast graph *pre-conditioner* that determines load balance and sparsity of the graph before it is distributed. Our plan is to have each PE randomly select edges from the block it reads and execute the pre-conditioner. This sampling is sorted and then segmented scans count the degree of each node to determine the connectivity.

Load balancing can also be performed by creating new edges in under-loaded PEs and then mapping some of the edges from the overloaded PEs to these new edges. One can think of it as splitting graph G that contains a node u into two graphs G_1 and G_2 that contain nodes u_1 and u_2 respectively. For each edge (u, v) $\in$ G there exists either $(u_1, v) \in G_1$ or $(u_2, v) \in G_2$. In addition, the edge (u_1, u_2) is created. The resulting graph $G' = G_1 \cup G_2$ has the same connected components as G.

6.2. Graph Contraction. Graph contraction, which substitutes a smaller, simpler graph problem for the original graph, is another promising method for reducing the work complexity of our algorithm. In practice, after a couple of iterations, we get several trees that form rooted stars. Some of these rooted stars are actually stagnant trees while others are connected components that have already collapsed to a star. Building a new graph with single nodes representing the rooted stars and keeping only the vertices and edges necessary to continue the algorithm has the potential to greatly reduce the work complexity. However, graph contraction introduces its own set of problems. It can cause load imbalance, especially with vertices that have dense connections in the new graph. Another problem in implementing graph contraction is recognizing the duplicate edges that are no longer needed in the smaller graph. Duplicate edges arise when one node in the contracted graph represents a stagnant rooted star that has edges connecting multiple leaf vertices to a node in a chain of another tree. While both of these problems have been solved before, the solution employed must use only row or column communication primitives if we are to reduce the execution time of the algorithm as well as its work complexity.

6.3. Type of Graph. There exist a variety of algorithms that perform differently on different classes of graphs. If we could identify the best possible algorithm for a given class of graphs and given a graph, identify its class efficiently, we may be able to find components of any given graph efficiently.

In this enhancement, we choose one of the connected components algorithms based on the graph density in the sampled data. The hard part is finding the correct density thresholds for the sampled data. We hope to spend a small amount of time up front to select the proper algorithm and to create a balanced work load. For a large class of graphs, this overhead will be more than offset by the efficiency gained by selecting the correct algorithm and having the work evenly distributed.

We feel that this type of sophisticated virtualization is the key to finding connected components quickly. It provides the opportunity to select the best algorithm for the graph density and to distribute the work evenly.

7. Conclusion

We have shown how to implement pointer jumping and related CRCW PRAM operations using simple row and column operations to minimize communication time and thus speed up the total execution. We have encouraging performance results, and have shown the feasibility of efficient implementations on modest sized machines.

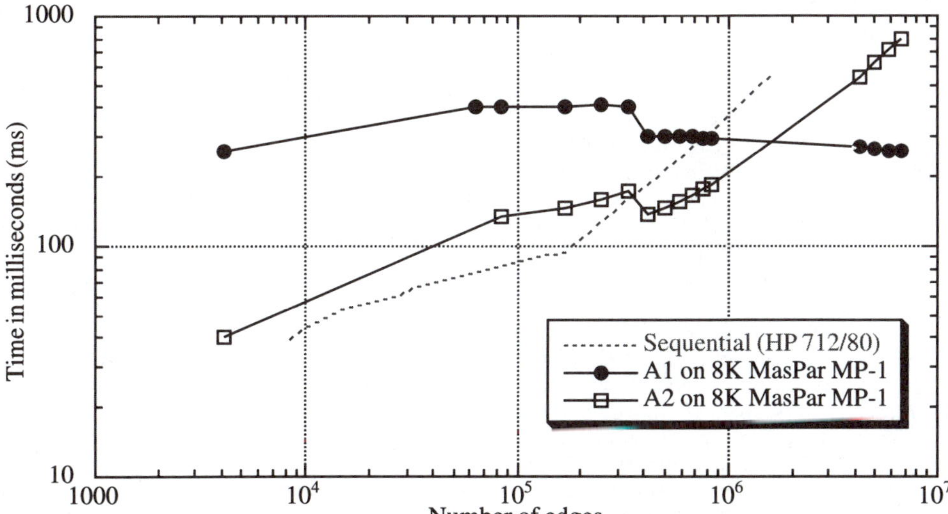

FIGURE 3. Performance Analysis: This graph plots the performance of algorithms $\mathcal{A}_1$ and $\mathcal{A}_2$ against a depth-first sequential algorithm for a 4096 vertex graph as we increase the graph density (i.e. the number of edges). Algorithms $\mathcal{A}_1$ and $\mathcal{A}_2$ were executed on a 8196 processor MasPar MP-1. The sequential algorithm was executed on a HP 712/80 workstation.

The graph in Figure 3 shows the effectiveness of our algorithms. The number of edges were varied while keeping the number of nodes constant at 4096. The performance of algorithms $\mathcal{A}_1$ and $\mathcal{A}_2$ have been compared with a sequential implementation on an HP 712/80 workstation. The size was kept small to accommodate the sequential implementation, but the general characteristics of $\mathcal{A}_1$ and $\mathcal{A}_2$ is reflected in this graph. (For larger graphs, the sequential implementation becomes less competitive at lower densities.) The time of $\mathcal{A}_1$, which uses the adjacency matrix explicitly, remains relatively constant, while the time of $\mathcal{A}_2$ increases with the number of edges. The shape of the graph for $\mathcal{A}_2$ tracks the sequential implementation much more closely since it uses an adjacency list like representation.

Not surprisingly, the key to getting good execution times for sparse graphs is the careful implementation of the row and column operations on the sparse adjacency matrix. We believe we can get results on highly sparse graphs that rival our random graph times by additional efforts in this area. With more data structure changes, we think we can increase the size of the graphs that we will be able to process and reduce the total time. We also believe that such changes will make it possible to do work at each step strictly proportional to the largest number of edges present on any processor. To this end, we believe there is a potential benefit in using sampling techniques to reduce the work balance problem to a manageable task.

Further work in this area includes the analysis and implementation of the row and column operations on other parallel machines to examine their performance relative to CRCW operations. If the results of that effort look promising, there are many other CREW and CRCW PRAM graph algorithms that employ pointer jumping and similar operations that could be implemented using the techniques we have described to make them more practical on current parallel machines.

REFERENCES

[AS87] B. Awerbuch and Y. Shiloach. New connectivity and MSF algorithms for Ultracomputer and PRAM. *IEEE Transactions on Computers*, 36(10):1258–1263, 1987.

[Ble90] G. Blelloch. Unpublished CVL Code, 1990.

[CLC82] F. Chin, J. Lam, and I. Chen. Efficient parallel algorithms for some graph problems. *Communications of the ACM*, 25(9):659–665, 1982.

[CV91] R. Cole and U. Vishkin. Approximate parallel scheduling. Part II: Application to optimal parallel graph algorithms in logarithmic time. *Information and Computation*, 92(1):1–47, 1991.

[Gre93] J. Greiner. A comparison of data-parallel algorithms for connected components. Technical Report CMU-CS-93-191, CMU, 1993.

[HCS79] D. Hirschberg, A. Chandra, and D. Saraswate. Computing connected components on parallel computers. *Communications of the ACM*, 22(8):461–464, 1979.

[Hir76] D. Hirschberg. Parallel algorithms for the transitive closure and the connected component problems. In *Eighth Annual ACM Symposium on theory of Computing*, pages 55–57, Hershey, Pennsylvania, 1976.

[HRD92] T. Hsu, V. Ramachandran, and N. Dean. Implementation of parallel graph algorithms on the MasPar. Technical Report TR-92-38, University of Texas at Austin, 1992.

[HRD94] T. Hsu, V. Ramachandran, and N. Dean. Parallel implementation of algorithms for finding connected components. In *DIMACS implementation challenge*, 1994.

[HW90] Y. Han and A. Wagner. An efficient and fast parallel-connected component algorithm. *JACM*, 37(3):626–642, 1990.

[Já92] J. Jájá. *An Introduction to Parallel Algorithms*. Addison Wesley, NewYork, 1992.

[KLCY94] A. Krishnamurthy, S. Lumetta, D. Culler, and K. Yelick. Connected components on distributed memory machines. In *DIMACS implementation challenge*, 1994.

[KRS86] C. Kruskal, L. Rudolph, and M. Snir. Efficient parallel algoritms for graph problems. In *1986 International Conference on Parallel Processing*, pages 278–284, St. Charles, Illinois, 1986.

[SV82] Y. Shiloach and U. Vishkin. An $O(\log n)$ parallel connectivity algorithm. *Journal of Algorithms*, 3(1):57–67, 1982.

[Vis84] U. Vishkin. An optimal parallel connectivity algorithm. *Discrete Applied Mathematics*, 9(2):197–207, 1984.

[Wyl79] J. Wyllie. *The Complexity of Parallel Computation*. PhD thesis, Cornell University, Department of Computer Science, Ithaca, NewYork, 1979.

DEPARTMENT OF COMPUTER SCIENCE, UNIVERSITY OF NORTH CAROLINA, CHAPEL HILL NC 27599-3175, USA,

E-mail address: goddard@cs.unc.edu

DIMACS Series in Discrete Mathematics
and Theoretical Computer Science
Volume **30**, 1997

Implementing Parallel Shortest-Paths Algorithms

Marios Papaefthymiou and Joseph Rodrigue

ABSTRACT. We have implemented two parallel versions of the Bellman-Ford-Moore algorithm for the single-source shortest-paths problem. Our software is written in C and runs on the CM-5 parallel supercomputer using CMMD communication primitives. We have compared the performance of our parallel programs with a serial implementation of the Bellman-Ford-Moore algorithm developed by Cherkassky, Goldberg and Radzik. In our experiments we used 50 randomly generated graphs with up to 2^{15} vertices and 2^{21} edges. Our fastest parallel program always achieved speedups greater than 1 when the average degree of the graphs exceeded 2^5 for the smaller and 2^3 for the larger inputs in our test suite. On dense graphs, we achieved speedups of up to 7.8 on a CM-5 with 32 processors.

1. Introduction

The shortest-paths problem is a classic combinatorial optimization problem that arises in a wide spectrum of applications including VLSI design, network routing, and commodity flow. Several serial and parallel algorithms have been proposed for computing shortest paths in graphs [**1, 4, 6, 9**]. The nature of most of these studies is theoretical, however. An empirical study of serial algorithms for shortest paths was only recently presented in [**3**]. Moreover, the efficient implementation and practical performance of parallel algorithms for computing shortest paths remains a largely unexplored field.

We recently embarked on an empirical comparison of serial and parallel shortest-paths algorithms. We implemented several parallel versions of the Bellman-Ford-Moore algorithm for single-source shortest paths. This algorithm is the asymptotically fastest polynomial-time scheme for the general shortest-paths problem on uniprocessors. We developed our code on the CM-5 parallel supercomputer platform using the C programming language and the CMMD communication primitives. In this paper we describe two of our implementations, and we present an empirical comparison of their performance with a serial Bellman-Ford-Moore code due to Cherkassky, Goldberg, and Radzik [**3**] that ran on a Sparc 2. The Cherkassky-Goldberg-Radzik code was the fastest public-domain implementation of the Bellman-Ford-Moore algorithm we were aware of. Achieving parallel speedups over this fast serial code was far more challenging than achieving speedups over uniprocessor executions of our parallel programs.

1991 *Mathematics Subject Classification.* Primary 90-04; Secondary 90C08.

This work was supported in part by a grant from DuPont Corporation. Access to the CM-5 supercomputer was provided through Project SCOUT.

The speedups achieved by our parallel programs depended on the sparsity and the size of the input graphs. Our test suite comprised directed graphs with integer edge-weights that were generated using the **sprand** random graph generator from [3]. The size of our graphs ranged between 2^{10} and 2^{15} vertices and between 2^{11} and 2^{21} edges. On the sparse inputs, neither of our two parallel programs matched the performance of the serial one. Even on the largest input graphs with millions of edges, the serial implementation terminated within a few seconds. On the dense inputs, however, our parallel programs were significantly faster than the serial one, achieving speedups of up to 7.8 on a CM-5 with 32 processors. Over the range of inputs tested, both parallel programs achieved speedups greater than 1 when the average degree of the graphs exceeded 2^6. On the inputs with more than 2^{11} vertices, our fastest parallel algorithm achieved speedups greater than 1 as soon as the average degree of the graphs exceeded 2^3.

The remainder of this paper is organized as follows. In Section 2 we briefly present the shortest paths problem and describe the Bellman-Ford-Moore procedure for solving it. We also describe the serial implementation of this procedure by Cherkassky, Goldberg and Radzik. In Section 3 we describe the two parallel programs we experimented with: A *coarse-grain* program that uses vector communication primitives and a *fine-grain* program that relies on scalar communication primitives. The coarse-grain program performs fewer communication operations than the fine-grain one. The fine-grain program communicates smaller messages, however, and relies on an edge-ordering heuristic to achieve high performance. In Section 4 we describe our input graphs and data partitioning schemes. We present our experimental results in Section 5 and conclude our paper with a discussion of ongoing work and directions for further research.

2. Shortest-paths and the serial Bellman-Ford-Moore algorithm

We begin this section with a brief review of the single-source shortest-paths problem. We then outline the Bellman-Ford-Moore algorithm for computing single-source shortest paths, and we discuss the Cherkassky-Goldberg-Radzik implementation of this algorithm that we used in our investigation.

In the single-source shortest-paths problem, given a directed graph $G = (V, E, w)$ with integer weights $w(u, v)$ for each edge $(u, v) \in E$, we wish to find a minimum-weight path from a specified source vertex $s \in V$ to each vertex $v \in V$. This problem is equivalent to computing an assignment $d : V \to \mathbf{Z}$ that maximizes $d(v)$ for each vertex $v \in V$, subject to the constraints that $d(s) = 0$, and that for each edge $(u, v) \in E$, we have

$$(2.1) \qquad\qquad d(v) \leq d(u) + w(u, v) \ .$$

A feasible assignment d exists if and only if there exists no directed cycle C in G with negative weight $w(C) = \sum_{(u,v) \in C} w(u, v)$. Given a feasible assignment d, the parent $\pi(v)$ of each vertex v in a shortest path from s to v is any vertex u such that $(u, v) \in E$ and $d(v) = d(u) + w(u, v)$.

The asymptotically fastest strongly-polynomial algorithm that is known for computing shortest paths was independently proposed by Bellman, Ford, and Moore [**2, 5, 8**]. The operation of this scheme is straightforward. Initially, all labels $d(v)$ are set to ∞ for $v \neq s$, and $d(s)$ is set to 0. Subsequently, the algorithm performs $|V| - 1$ passes over the edge-set E. In each pass, each edge $(u, v) \in E$ is *relaxed* once, that is, if the inequality $d(v) \leq d(u) + w(u, v)$ is violated, then the label $d(v)$

is set to $d(u) + w(u, v)$ and the parent $\pi(v)$ is set to u. Throughout the execution of the algorithm, each label $d(v)$ is an upper bound on the length of the shortest path from s to v. After each pass, the labels $d(v)$ monotonically decrease, approaching the lengths of the corresponding shortest paths. After i passes, for every vertex v whose shortest path from s has at most i edges, the label $d(v)$ equals the length of that path. Thus, after at most $|V| - 1$ passes, the algorithm has computed all shortest paths from the source s, or it has discovered a directed cycle with negative weight, in which case the problem is infeasible. The total running time of the Bellman-Ford-Moore algorithm is $O(|V||E|)$.

An interesting property of the Bellman-Ford-Moore algorithm is that during each pass the edges in G can be relaxed in any order without affecting correctness. Several heuristics have been proposed that improve the practical running time of the Bellman-Ford-Moore algorithm by relaxing edges in a specific order [4]. Although these heuristics do not improve the algorithm's asymptotic behavior, they seem to work well in practice.

The serial Bellman-Ford-Moore code we experimented with employs a *parent-checking* heuristic to determine a good order for relaxing the edges in a graph G [3]. In this implementation, vertices are maintained in a FIFO queue which initially contains only the source s. For each vertex u pulled off the queue, all outgoing edges (u, v) are relaxed only if u's parent $\pi(u)$ is not currently in the queue. Intuitively, if $\pi(u)$ is in the queue then the label $d(u)$ will be updated again, and so it is pointless to relax u's outgoing edges until that update takes place. Vertices are inserted into the queue if a relaxation updates their labels.

3. Parallelizing the Bellman-Ford-Moore algorithm

We have experimented with several different parallel implementations of the Bellman-Ford-Moore algorithm on the CM-5. In this section we describe our two most efficient programs, a coarse-grain program that uses vector communication primitives and a fine-grain program that uses scalar communication primitives.

Our two implementations have several common characteristics and a few major differences. In both programs, for example, we have an alternation of computation and communication phases. Moreover, both programs maintain on each processor local copies of the labels $d(u)$ for all $u \in V$. In the coarse-grain program, all labels $d(u)$ are updated with one global vector operation. In the fine-grain program, however, a global update is performed on a single $d(u)$, each time trying to pick the best u to update. Thus, the coarse-grain program terminates after at most $|V|$ vector updates, whereas the fine-grain program may require up to $|V|^2$ scalar updates.

3.1. The coarse-grain program. At the beginning of our coarse-grain program, each processor of the CM-5 is assigned a subset of the input graph's edges according to the data distribution scheme that we describe in Section 4. These subsets are disjoint and their assignments never change during the execution of the program. Our program proceeds by iteratively performing a computation phase followed by a communication phase. During the computation phase, each processor makes a pass over its edges and updates its local labels $d(v)$. After the end of the computation phase, all processors perform a global vector communication step that for each vertex $u \in V$ sets the local label $d(u)$ of each processor equal to the current minimum among all labels $d(u)$. This communication operation ensures that every

$f_g = f_l$ %% f_l is initially FALSE
f_l = FALSE
for each vertex u
    do if $d(u) > d_{min}(u)$
        then $d(u) \leftarrow d_{min}(u)$
            $\pi(v) \leftarrow \infty$
            f_g = TRUE
            if outdegree$(u) > 0$
                then mark u
for each vertex u in order
    do if u is marked
        then unmark u
            for each edge (u, v)
                do if $d(v) < d(u) + w(u, v)$
                    then $d(v) \leftarrow d(u) + w(u, v)$
                       $\pi(v) \leftarrow u$
                       f_l = TRUE
                       if outdegree$(v) > 0$
                          then mark v
if f_g = FALSE
    then terminate

FIGURE 1. The computation phase of the coarse-grain program.

processor begins the next computation phase with the best approximation that has been computed so far for every label $d(u)$. The vector communication has been implemented on the CM-5 using the vector **reduce** operation with the **min** operator.

Each iteration in the coarse-grain program corresponds to a pass of the serial Bellman-Ford-Moore algorithm over the edge-set E. The number of iterations in the two implementations is not the same, however, because in each computation phase of the parallel program the relaxations on each processor are based only on its local edges. Thus, the coarse-grain program may require more iterations to propagate vertex labels along shortest paths whose edges have been assigned to more than one processors.

We applied two heuristics to speed up our coarse-grain program by increasing the effectiveness of each computation phase. The first heuristic orders the edge relaxations on each processor so that a single pass brings the labels $d(u)$ as close as possible to the shortest-paths lengths. In the beginning of the program, each processor performs a breadth-first search on the graph. In each subsequent computation phase, each vertex u is visited in the order specified by the arrival times of the breadth-first search, and all its outgoing edges (u, v) are relaxed. Intuitively, this ordering propagates label changes in the graph as far as possible.

The second heuristic avoids unnecessary edge relaxations by ensuring that an edge (u, v) is relaxed only if the label $d(u)$ has been updated. To that effect, in the beginning of each computation phase, our program marks all vertices whose labels have changed after the preceeding communication phase. It also marks the vertices whose labels are updated during the computation phase. Each vertex u is visited in the order specified by the first heuristic, and its outgoing edges (u, v) are relaxed if and only if vertex u is marked.

Figure 1 gives pseudocode for the computation phase of the coarse-grain program. Initially, each processor marks all vertices u whose labels $d(u)$ exceed the minimum $d_{min}(u)$ that resulted from the vector **reduce** communication with the **min** operator. Subsequently, it visits its vertices in the breadth-first order specified in the beginning and relaxes all edges (u, v) emanating out of marked vertices u. Using a good ordering, the vertices v marked in the nested **for** loop will tend to be downstream from u, that is, they will come after the current vertex u in the order. Thus, their outgoing edges (v, v') will be relaxed before the next communication.

The computation terminates on the first iteration for which no vertices are marked on any processor. Processors reach consensus regarding termination without incurring a penalty in communication cost. To that effect, we use the flags f_g and f_l to keep track of updates due to global communication and local relaxations, respectively. The program tests f_g after each computation phase and terminates if it is **FALSE**. Intuitively, each processor terminates if its local copies of $d(u)$ are as good as the global minima and if none of its own $d(u)$'s has been updated on the previous iteration. The cost of this synchronization is only one global vector **reduce** communication.

The parents $\pi(u)$ in the shortest-paths tree are computed together with the labels $d(u)$. Each processor keeps a vector of labels $\pi(u)$ initialized to ∞ (except for $\pi(s) = 0$). When $d(v)$ is updated as the result of relaxing a local edge (u, v), then the parent $\pi(v)$ is set to u. Whenever $d(v)$ is updated after a communication, however, the parent $\pi(v)$ is reset to ∞. At the end of the computation, the parents $\pi(u)$ can be computed for all u by a global **reduce** on the vector π with the **min** operator.

3.2. The fine-grain program. In the Bellman-Ford-Moore algorithm, any effort spent relaxing edges emanating from a vertex u is wasted until the label $d(u)$ has attained its final value. One inefficiency of the coarse-grain algorithm is that each processor independently selects *any* vertex u whose label has been updated and relaxes only its local edges (u, v). In the fine-grain program we describe in this section, all processors heuristically select the *"best"* vertex u and relax all its outgoing edges (u, v).

The best vertices u are those whose labels $d(u)$ equal their shortest-paths lengths. Our fine-grain program makes a good guess in finding one of these vertices by selecting the vertex u with the minimum label $d(u)$ among the candidate vertices. If the graph contains no negative-weight edges, this scheme is identical to the selection scheme in Dijkstra's algorithm [4]. If there are edges with negative edge-weights, our scheme is still a reasonable heuristic.

Our fine-grain program operates as follows. Each processor maintains a heap of vertices to be relaxed, ordered by their labels $d(u)$. During each communication phase, each processor nominates the minimum element on its heap. (A processor sends ∞ if its heap is empty.) All processors select the vertex u with the minimum label $d_{min}(u)$ using a **reduce** communication with the **min** operator. They subsequently perform the local computation shown in Figure 2. During each such computation phase, each processor updates $d(u)$, deletes u from its heap and relaxes all edges (u, v) in its subgraph. For every label $d(v)$ that is updated in a relaxation, the processor adjusts the position of v on its local heap or inserts v into

if $d_{min}(u) = \infty$
   then terminate
if $d(u) > d_{min}(u)$
   then $d(u) \leftarrow d_{min}(u)$
      $\pi(v) \leftarrow \infty$
HEAP_REMOVE$(u, d(u))$
for each edge (u, v)
   do if $d(v) < d(u) + w(u, v)$
      then $d(v) \leftarrow d(u) + w(u, v)$
         $\pi(v) \leftarrow u$
         if IN_HEAP?$(v, d(v))$
           then HEAP_UPDATE$(v, d(v))$
           else HEAP_INSERT$(v, d(v))$

FIGURE 2. The computation phase of the fine-grain program.

the heap if it is not already there. The parents $\pi(u)$ are computed in exactly the same way as in the coarse-grain implementation. The program terminates when the label $d_{min}(u)$ equals ∞, in which case all heaps are empty and the shortest-paths lengths have been computed.

Although the fine-grain program communicates much more frequently than the coarse-grain version, it almost always outperformed it in our experiments. One explanation is that the fine-grain communication phase is much faster than the coarse-grain one, since each processor sends out only a vertex u and its label $d(u)$; in comparison, each processor in the coarse-grain program broadcasts $|V|$ labels. Another explanation is that the fine-grain program may perform fewer relaxations that the coarse-grain one, because it updates each local label $d(u)$ as few times as possible.

3.3. Implementation issues. An important implementation issue for both programs was whether to use the CM-5 vector units (parallel arrays). Our programs do not rely on these units, because the only communication operations they support are ordinary **send**'s and **receive**'s, and we preferred to use the more powerful **reduce** primitives instead.

For our coarse-grain program, we were mainly concerned with the efficient execution of its computation phase. In an early version of our program, we let each processor relax *all* marked vertices in each phase. To our surprise, we found that we achieved significantly better performance by making only one pass over the vertices, usually without increasing the number of iterations. The reason behind this phenomenon was that the first pass updated many more labels than subsequent passes.

Our main concern with the fine-grain program was the efficiency of its communication phase. In our implementation, we reduce the number of communications required during each communication phase by combining the vertex u and its label $d(u)$ in a single communication operation. Specifically, we view each heap element as a pair $(u, d(u))$ encoded into w-bit *cells*. In the $\lceil \log |V| \rceil$ low-order bits of each cell we store u, and in the remaining $b = w - \lceil \log |V| \rceil$ high-order bits we store $d(u)$. For the high-order bits, we reserve the values $\mathsf{OF} = 2^{b-1} - 1$ and $\mathsf{UF} = -2^{b-1}$

to denote overflow and underflow, that is, for $d(u) \geq$ OF and $d(u) \leq$ UF we store OF and UF, respectively. The min operation in the **reduce** communication treats the cells as w-bit signed integers. After a cell has been selected, each processor takes it apart and examines $d(u)$. If UF $< d(u) <$ OF, the processors continue with the computation phase. Otherwise, the processors communicate again to broadcast $d(u)$. In practice, unless b is very small, $d(u)$ is within bounds most of the time, and the second communication is unnecessary. This method will not yield the u with minimum $d(u)$ if there are several vertices u with $d(u) \leq$ UF. Unless b is small, however, any such vertex is likely to be as good a choice as any other vertex.

4. Input graphs and data partitioning

In our experiments, we concentrated on cyclic graphs that included edges with negative weights. We generated these graphs using the **sprand** random network generator of Cherkassky, Goldberg and Radzik [3] with the command **sprand V E 561 -lm 0 -ll 5 -pm 0 -pl 5**. The resulting graphs had edge-weights in the interval [-5, 10] and initially contained one connected cycle of length $|V|$. The other edges in the graph were inserted randomly. To facilitate data partitioning, we preprocessed the input graphs by sorting the edge-lists so that edges leaving the same vertex were grouped together.

To facilitate I/O on the CM-5, we converted each input into a binary format that presented each processor with a fixed and predictable number of bytes. In our format, the first word gave $|V|$, the second word gave $|E|$, and the remaining $3 \cdot |E|$ words gave the vertices u and v of the edge (u, v) and the weight $w(u, v)$. During a **read** operation, each processor read the first two words of the input file in CMMD_sync_bc mode and then switched to CMMD_sync_seq mode to read its block of the input file. In the CMMD_sync_seq mode, each processor p read B bytes starting at address $j + p \cdot B$, where B was equal to the total number of bytes in the input file divided by the number of processors in the CM-5 partition, and j was the position of the file pointer before the **read** operation.

We experimented with several data partitioning strategies, including "unshuffling", that is, dealing the input edges into M piles and then concatenating the piles. Unshuffling into M piles can be performed iteratively in $O(|E| \log M)$ steps. When the input of the coarse-grain program was unshuffled into 2 piles, we found that its performance was only marginally better than with the sorted input, and then only for very dense graphs. With its input unshuffled into 128 piles, the coarse-grain program performed significantly worse than with the original sorted input. Despite its poor performance with our coarse-grain program, unshuffling was well-suited to our fine-grain program. Intuitively, this result was not surprising. In each computation phase of the fine-grain program, all processors relax edges emanating from the same vertex. By spreading these edges evenly across the machine, unshuffling balances the computational load and results in better performance. In all our experiments with the fine-grain program, we unshuffled the input graphs into 32 piles, whereas with the coarse-grain program we did not unshuffle at all.

5. Experimental results

In this section we first describe our experimental procedure. We then present our results and discuss the performance of our parallel programs.

We ran our parallel programs on a 32-processor partition of a CM-5 parallel supercomputer. Each processing element of this CM-5 was a Sparc 2 with 32MB of main memory and attached vector units. We ran the Cherkassky-Goldberg-Radzik serial code on the front-end of the CM-5 which was a Sparc 2 with the same CPU speed as the CM-5 nodes and 64MB of main memory. To ensure the correctness of our parallel programs, we developed a serial and two other parallel implementations of the Bellman-Ford-Moore algorithm in addition to the programs we describe in this paper. For all test runs, the outputs of these programs were in accord with each other. Our programs were compiled using `gcc` with the `-O` flag.

Our experimental results are shown in Figure 3. Timings were obtained for graphs with vertex counts ranging between 2^{10} and 2^{15}. For each vertex-count $|V|$, the performance of the three programs was measured on a collection of graphs with edge-counts $|E|$ between $2 \cdot |V|$ and $|V|^2$ in powers of 2. All our timings are CPU seconds devoted to the execution of the shortest-paths programs and do not include I/O setup time, time spent on page faults, or time spent on other processes. Thus, our comparison focuses entirely on computing and communication costs and does not take into account virtual memory considerations.

In general, our fine-grain program performed better than the coarse-grain implementation and was outperformed by the serial code only on the sparse input graphs. For the smaller test graphs, the fine-grain program became faster than the serial code when the average degree exceeded 2^5. For the larger graphs in our test suite, the fine-grain program achieved speedups greater than 1 as soon as their average degree exceeded 2^3.

For graphs with $|E| \approx |V|$ (not shown), the execution time of the coarse-grain program blew up by a factor of 20. In these graphs the depth of the shortest-paths tree was almost $|V|$, and the program required many phases to update the labels all the way to the leaves of the tree. For dense graphs, however, shortest-paths trees were much shallower and labels propagated within a few iterations. For the larger of our graphs, the depth of the shortest-paths tree did not exceed 30 vertices, and the coarse-grain program terminated within five or six iterations.

We ran the serial Cherkassky-Goldberg-Radzik code on the input graphs exactly as they came out of their graph generator. For our parallel implementations, however, we relabeled vertices randomly, because the cycles produced by the generator were much too predictable to be difficult for our programs. Thus, our parallel algorithms were executing on more "difficult" inputs than the serial Cherkassky-Goldberg-Radzik code.

6. Future work

To date we have not been able to run our programs on graphs with more than 2^{21} edges due to lack of memory on the front-end of the CM-5 we have been using. Moreover, we have not experimented thoroughly with larger CM-5 configurations, due to access restrictions on the CM-5. Our preliminary results indicate that our programs scale well with larger inputs and larger numbers of processors, and our long-term goal is to perform a more thorough study of the scalability of our current implementations.

In the course of our work, we realized the importance of being able to gauge the difficulty of input graphs. We confirmed, for example, that bigger graphs are not necessarily more difficult graphs, and that adding random edges usually makes

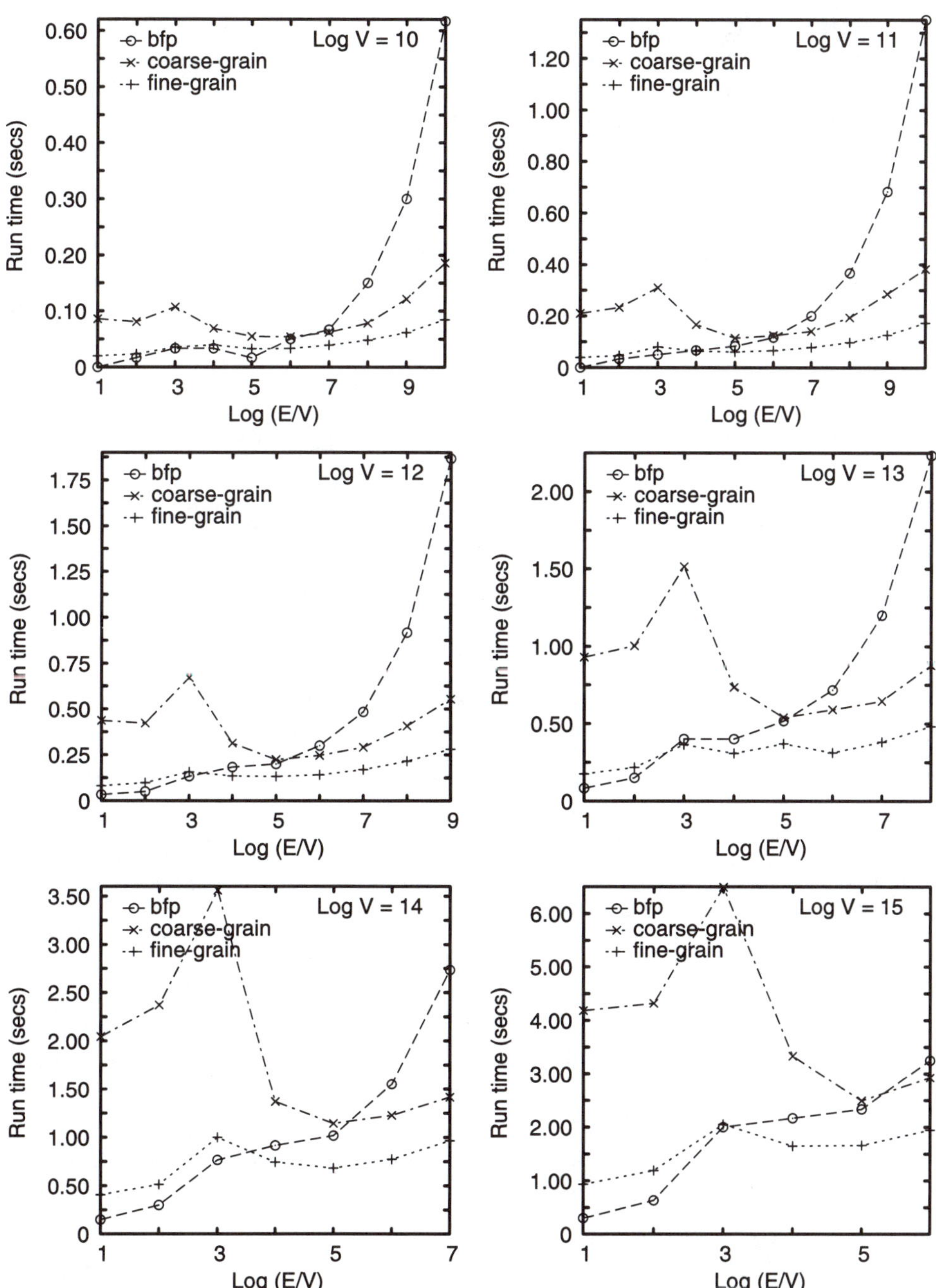

FIGURE 3. Performance of the serial shortest-paths program **bfp** by Cherkassky-Goldberg-Radzik running on a Sparc 2 and of our two parallel implementations running on a 32-processor CM-5.

the problem easier, not harder. Moreover, graphs with taller shortest-paths trees will probably make more difficult inputs. Before we go much farther with the implementation of new algorithms, we plan to design a graph generator that allows us to "shape" its output graphs with specific characteristics.

The static data partitioning schemes we described in this paper were the result of a compromise between programming ease and efficient execution. Based on the short running times of our programs, these simple data partitioning techniques seem to be working well. We thus feel that dynamic load balancing for shortest-paths problems with a few million edges is not essential for achieving high performance. An interesting area of further investigation would be the development of more sophisticated and effective static data partitioning schemes that rely on fast graph-separator techniques.

Acknowledgments

We would like to thank Charles Leiserson, Yossi Matias, and Uzi Vishkin for helpful discussions.

References

[1] D. P. Bertsekas and J. N. Tsitsiklis, *Parallel and Distributed Computation*, Prentice Hall, 1989.

[2] R. E. Bellman, *On a routing problem*, Quart. Appl. Math., 16:87–90, 1958.

[3] B. Cherkassky, A. Goldberg, and T. Radzik, *Shortest paths algorithms: theory and experimental evaluation*, Technical Report STAN-CS-93-1480, Stanford, 1993.

[4] T. H. Cormen, C. E. Leiserson, and R. L. Rivest, *Introduction to Algorithms*, McGraw-Hill, MIT Press, 1990.

[5] L. R. Ford, Jr. and D. R. Fulkerson, *Flows in Networks*, Princeton Univ. Press, Princeton, NJ, 1962.

[6] Y. Han, V. Pan, and J. Reif, *Efficient parallel algorithms for all-pairs shortest-paths in directed graphs*, Proc. 4th ACM Symposium on Parallel Algorithms and Architectures, July 1992.

[7] R. Harlan, *Searching in parallel: case study with single-source shortest-paths algorithms*, ACM SIG CS Education Bulletin, 23(1), March 1991.

[8] E. F. Moore, *The shortest path through a maze*, Proc. of the Int. Symp. on the Theory of Switching, pages 285–292, Harvard University Press, 1959.

[9] G. Pantziou, P. Spirakis, and C. Zaroliagis, *Efficient parallel algorithms for shortest paths in planar digraphs*, BIT, 32, 1992.

DEPARTMENTS OF ELECTRICAL ENGINEERING AND COMPUTER SCIENCE, YALE UNIVERSITY, NEW HAVEN, CONNECTICUT 06520
E-mail address: `marios@yale.edu`

DEPARTMENT OF COMPUTER SCIENCE, YALE UNIVERSITY, NEW HAVEN, CONNECTICUT 06520
Current address: IBM Israel, MATAM Adv Tech Ctr, Haifa 31905, Israel
E-mail address: `jrodrigue@vnet.ibm.com`

DIMACS Series in Discrete Mathematics
and Theoretical Computer Science
Volume **30**, 1997

Finding Friends-Of-Friends Clusters Quickly

BRENDAN MUMEY

ABSTRACT. This paper describes a new parallel algorithm for finding *friends-of-friends* clusters in point sets in Euclidean space. A new solution to a special case of the *bichromatic closest pairs problem* is used by the algorithm. An implementation was done on the Kendall Square Research KSR-2 multiprocessor and performance results are given.

1. Introduction

A popular method in the astrophysics community for finding clusters in large-scale particle simulations is the *friends-of-friends* approach. It is based on the bottleneck distance metric. The bottleneck distance between two points is defined to be the minimum possible length of the maximum length edge in a path between them in the distance graph of point set:

$$d_b(x, y) = \min_{\text{paths } P \text{ connecting } x \text{ and } y} \;\; \max_{\text{edges } e \in P} \text{length}(e)$$

Two points in a tightly clustered clump will be close under the bottleneck distance metric as there will be many nearby intermediate points to go through. Conversely, points which are isolated must incur large bottleneck costs to reach other points. Two points x and y are τ-*clustered* if and only if $d_b(x, y) \leq \tau$. The object is, for a given τ, to find all the τ clusters. One way of doing this is to construct a Euclidean minimum spanning tree (EMST) in the distance graph and remove all edges which are longer than τ. The remaining connected components constitute the τ clusters. Unfortunately, constructing an EMST in three dimensions is a difficult problem for the problem size of interest, $n > 10^6$. The best sequential algorithm seems to be Yao's $O((n \lg n)^{1.5})$ time method[**5**].

A natural compromise is to find a good approximation to the exact solution. We say an approximate cluster finding algorithm is ϵ-*close* if:

    (i) $\delta_b(x, y) > \tau(1 + \epsilon) \Rightarrow x$ and y are identified to be in different clusters.

    (ii) $\delta_b(x, y) \leq \tau \Rightarrow x$ and y are identified to be in the same cluster.

1991 *Mathematics Subject Classification.* Primary 68Q22, 68Q25; Secondary 68-04.

For many astrophysics clustering problems, ϵ as high as 0.1 is acceptable according to the practitioners the author has asked.

This papers presents a new parallel algorithm to find ϵ-close τ clusters. The worst case time is $O((\lg \frac{\Delta}{\epsilon\tau} + f(\epsilon))n/p)$ in the PRAM model, where Δ is the diameter of the point set and p is the number of processors. The function f depends on the dimension of the point set. For two dimensions we can show $f(\epsilon) = O(\sqrt{1/\epsilon})$ and for three dimensions we can show $f = O(1/\epsilon^{1.25})$. An overview of the algorithm is first described, followed by a discussion of its implementation for the Kendall Square KSR-2 shared memory multiprocessor and the performance achieved on astrophysical data.

2. The Algorithm

We present the serial version of the algorithm first. Parallelization issues are described subsequently. The algorithm is divided into two phases. In the first phase an *oblivious kd-tree* is constructed on the point set. This is an adaptation of standard kd-trees [1]. A bounding box for the point set is first found. We will assume that the sidelengths of this bounding box are equal (this is needed later in the proof of the running time bound). In general, the length of the largest dimension present in the current box is split exactly in half to form two child boxes. The process is repeated for each non-empty child box recursively. When the length of the longest dimension is less than $\theta = \epsilon\tau/4$, the box is no longer split. The value of θ is chosen so that estimating the maximum (minimum) distance between two points in θ-sized boxes by the maximum (minimum) distances between the box boundaries meets the approximation bounds above. The tree constructed is said to be *θ-resolved*. The maximum depth of a θ-resolved oblivious kd-tree is $O(\lg(\Delta/\epsilon\tau))$. It is easy to establish that the cost of building the tree is proportional to the depth of the tree times n, so the time cost of the first phase of the algorithm is $O(\lg(\Delta/\epsilon\tau)n)$. In the astrophysics application the cluster finder will typically be invoked at different time slices in the course of a particle simulation. It may not be necessary to completely rebuild the tree if not too many points have changed. In practice, the time to completely rebuild the tree and compute the clusters is small relative to the time needed to integrate the particles between time slices.

The second phase of the algorithm is more complicated. The basic idea is to start at a point x and determine which points are contained within a ball centered on x of radius τ. These points can be added to the cluster containing x. If a ball is expanded around every point it is fairly easy to argue that all the clusters will be found correctly: If two points x and y have a bottleneck distance less than the threshold τ, then there will be a path through points in the point set connecting them such that the distances between adjacent points in the path are all less than τ. Since we expand a ball around every point we will merge together all the points in this path, including x and y, into the same cluster.

The cluster-finding phase of the algorithm walks through the tree in a depth-first fashion, starting from the root and continuing until a node whose bounding box has diameter at most τ is reached. If this node's cluster has not yet been determined then a new cluster is formed and all the nodes rooted by this node are marked as belonging to the cluster. A local search through the neighbouring nodes is then performed to determine if any should be linked to the current cluster. This is accomplished by searching back up the tree to locate the neighbouring boxes and testing each in turn to find new points to merge into the cluster. A subroutine is used to check whether two nodes contain points which belong to the same cluster. It uses a filtering technique to reduce the work. The subroutine is described below and an analysis of its running time can be found in Appendix A. Pseudo-code is given in Figure 1. The findCluster procedure is invoked on the root node of the kd-tree. Subscripts l and r indicate the left or right child of a node respectively.

```
findClusters( treeNode N )
    if diameter( box(N) ) ≤ τ
        if cluster(N) = UNKNOWN
            startNewCluster( N );
        L = findNeighbours( N );
        for each n ∈ L
            if (cluster(n) ≠ cluster(N))
                and CPsubroutine( box(n), box(N) )
                    linkClusters( n, N );
    else
        findClusters( N_l );
        findClusters( N_r );
```

FIGURE 1. The main cluster building algorithm

2.1. The Comparison-Pair Subroutine. Given two nearby non-empty boxes, both having diameter less than τ, the problem is to determine whether they belong to the same cluster. This will happen if and only if there is some point in the first box, call it L, which is within distance τ from some point in the second box, call it R. This is a special case of the bichromatic closest-pairs problem discussed in [4].

Let m be the total number of points in both boxes. We present an $O(f(\epsilon) \cdot m)$ time method for this special case. Bounds on f are presented in Appendix A. The basic idea is to keep a queue of box pairs. The idea is that the queue will contain pairs of boxes, called *comparison-pairs*, which might contain points which link L and R, but further checking is necessary. The queue is initialized to the pair $< L, R >$. The general step is to pop a comparison-pair $< l, r >$ off the queue. If the maximum separation between boxes l and r (defined as the maximum distance between the surfaces of the two boxes) is at most $\tau(1 + \epsilon)$, we know that a pair of points separated by distance at most $\tau(1 + \epsilon)$ exists to link L and R. If the minimum separation is greater than τ then this particular comparison-pair cannot possibly contain points that link L and R and so can be ignored. If neither of these events occur, each box in the pair is subdivided into its two sub-boxes and the cross-product of the left sub-boxes with right sub-boxes is formed. This cross-product is pushed onto the tail of the queue. The next comparison-pair is popped off the head of the queue and the above process is repeated. This continues until a comparison-pair is found which links L and R or the queue is empty. Pseudo-code is given in Figure 2.

```
boolean CPsubroutine( box L, box R )
    boxPairQueue = {< L, R >}
    while boxPairQueue ≠ {}
        < l, r > = pop( boxPairQueue );
        if maxSeparation( l, r ) < τ(1 + ε)
            return true;
        if minSeparation( l, r ) ≤ τ
            push( boxPairQueue, < l_l, r_l > );
            push( boxPairQueue, < l_l, r_r > );
            push( boxPairQueue, < l_r, r_l > );
            push( boxPairQueue, < l_r, r_r > );
    return false;
```

FIGURE 2. The comparison-pairs subroutine

2.2. Parallelization Issues. The first major obstacle to confront in parallelizing this algorithm is the fact that the central data structure, the kd-tree must be distributed. If there is a single address space (as in the KSR-2) this is easy, but if not some means of locating parts of the tree residing in other processors address spaces must be provided. If the tree is to be constructed in parallel the underlying point set needs to be distributed among the processors first and they must collaborate in the building process. The approach taken is to replicate a top part of the tree in each processor. Each processor is responsible for one or more of the subtrees descending down from leaves of the top part. This is done so that each processor has approximately the same number of points. A processor can quicky determine on which other processor a non-local point lies by searching the top part of the tree to find out on which branch of the top part it lies.

Another issue arises in the cluster-building phase. As clusters may cross processor boundaries, some means of linking clusters across these boundaries must exist. This is accomplished with a global naming scheme for clusters. A cluster name is a tuple (`iPart, id`), where `iPart` is the number of a unique identified point in the cluster and `id` is the processor number where this point is located. As clusters are found in parallel, some means of merging clusters concurrently must be available. We use a locked version of the standard *union-find* data-structure [**2**] for this purpose.

3. Implementation and Performance

This section describes the current implementation of the algorithm for the KSR-2 and its performance on real data. The implementation differs from the algorithm presented in that a standard kd-tree is used, rather than an oblivious kd-tree. This was done because we had access to some debugged and optimized parallel code for standard kd-trees and it was easy to implement the cluster-finder using this existing code as a starting point. For most distributions, it was thought that performance would be comparable. The standard kd-tree also has the advantage that it is balanced and thus can be simply implemented without pointers, using arrays. The implementation also has the ability to handle *quasi-periodic* boundary conditions, a feature we do not describe.

The program was written on top of a system for managing distributed data structures called *MDL*. MDL was developed by Joachim Stadel in the Department of Astrophysics at the University of Washington. The idea of MDL (machine dependent layer) is to provide a common interface for accessing shared data across processors so the higher levels of the program are machine-independent. To port to a different multiprocessor, one just needs to rewrite the MDL part and recompile. In general each processor has a thread which sends and receives messages from similar threads on the other processors. This mechanism is used to access parts of the kd-tree which reside on nonlocal processors. These accesses include both reads and writes. There are functions for returning a local pointer to a node's data, given an `iPart` and `id`, returning the parent and children of a node, etc. The provision for locking a node is also provided. This is necessary for merging clusters, as discussed above.

The implementation performed quite well. Figures 3 and 4 summarize the performance achieved by the KSR-2 on a 10^6 particle file representing a globular cluster of galaxies from an astrophysical simulation[1]. The values of τ and ϵ were taken to be 10.0 and 0.1 respectively; typical numbers for this data set. Experiments on different particle distributions were conducted to ensure the one chosen was representative; this was the case. It is somewhat curious that the speed-up curve does not have steadily decreasing slope. Two explanations

---

[1]The author is grateful to Dr. R. Carlberg, Department of Astrophysics, University of Toronto for providing test data sets.

are offered: First, the KSR-2 used had two rings of 32 processors each. Inter-ring communication is about twice as slow as intra-ring communication; this would reduce efficiency most dramatically when most processors are on one ring but a couple are on the other. Another possible explanation that this is a data distribution effect. The tree which gets built depends on the number of processors used. There may be some variation in the efficiency of the tree which is built.

The reason for diminishing speed-up returns is that the proportion of nonlocal work increases with the number of processors used. Roughly speaking, this is because nonlocal work is proportional to the surface area of the region of space assigned to a processor, whereas local work is proportional to the volume. This ratio increases with more processors. In contrast to the PRAM model, the cost of nonlocal memory accesses is at least a factor of 10 more than the cost of local accesses. In this respect, a theoretical model which takes this phenomenon into account (eg. *LogP* [**3**]) would be more predictive. Inevitably it is more complicated to prove time bounds in such a model.

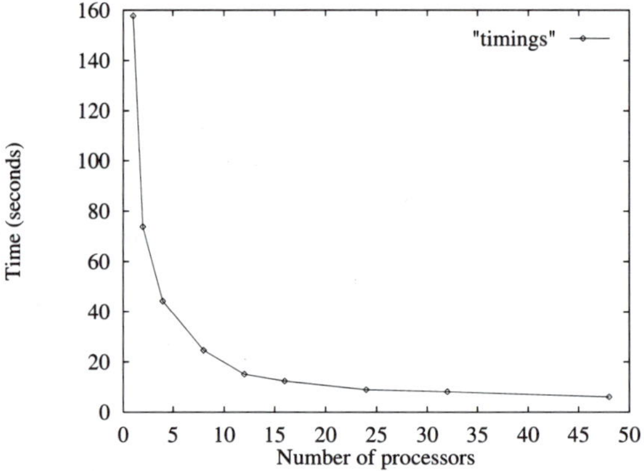

FIGURE 3. KSR-2 timings for a 10^6 particle globular cluster

4. Conclusions

We have developed a new parallel friends-of-friends cluster finder and have achieved good performance with a shared memory implementation on the Kendall Square KSR-2 multiprocessor. The implementation is current being used by the theoretical astronomy group at the University of Washington. The algorithm uses a new solution to a special case of the bichromatic closest pairs problem which may be of interest in its own right.

REFERENCES

1. J. Bentley, *Multidimensional binary search trees used for associative searching*, Comm. of the ACM **18** (1975), 509–517.

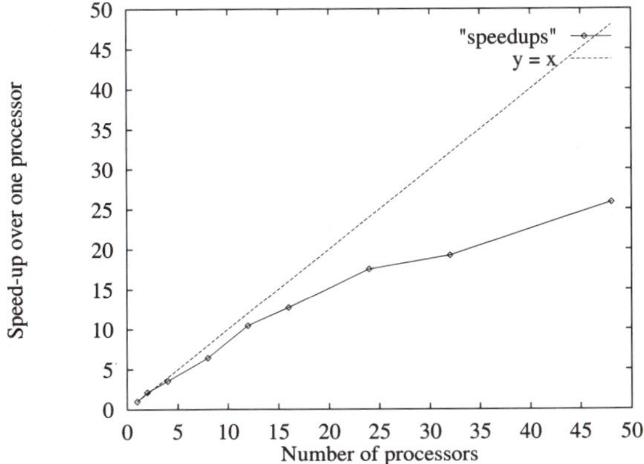

FIGURE 4. Plot of KSR-2 speed-ups

2. T. Cormen, C. Leiserson, and R. Rivest, *Introduction to algorithms*, MIT Press, Cambridge, 1990.
3. D. Culler, R. Karp, D. Patterson, A. Sahay, K. Schauser, E. Santos, R. Subramonian, and T. von Eicken, *LogP: Towards a realistic model for parallel computation*, Proc. 5th Symp. on Parallel Algorithms and Architectures (1993).
4. N. Katoh and K. Iwano, *Finding k farthest pairs and k closest/farthest bichromatic pairs for points in the plane*, Proc. 8th ACM Symp. on Computational Geometry (1992).
5. A. Yao., *On constructing minimum spanning trees in k-dimensional spaces and related problems*, SIAM Journal on Computing **11** (1982), 721–736.

Appendix A. Running time analysis

For any fixed dimension there are only a constant number of box pairs involving a particular box for which the comparison-subroutine could be invoked on. The following lemma shows that a particular invocation of the comparison-pair subroutine runs in time proportional to the number of points contained in the pair. Thus the amortized cost per point is a constant depending only on the dimensionality of the point set and the approximation tolerance, ϵ. We present the proof in two dimensions and mention how it generalizes to three dimensions.

LEMMA A.1. *Let the comparison-pair subroutine be invoked on two boxes, L and R, which contain a total of m points between them. For two dimensional point sets, the subroutine finishes in $O(\sqrt{1/\epsilon} \cdot m)$ time.*

Before we can prove the main lemma, we need some definitions and several auxiliary lemmas. Let P be the set of comparison-pairs examined during the execution of the subroutine. The time spent by the algorithm is proportional to $|P|$.

When the comparison-pair subroutine is initially invoked, the left and right boxes have the same dimensions. This is because because the bounding boxes at any given level in an oblivious kd-tree have the same size and shape. A technicality occurs when one of the boxes consists of singleton point. Rather than using its exact position in the calculations, we will assume that there is a hierarchy of smaller boxes surrounding it. The sizes of these boxes will correspond to the box sizes in the tree at the levels below the singleton box. In this way, comparisons-pairs will always be formed by boxes at the same level in the tree. Thus we can partition the set P by the tree level of each pair. In the context of the proof, we will say the initial comparison-pair on which the subroutine is invoked has level 0. It makes the analysis easier if we associate two spheres with each box i. Let c_i be the center of box i. We define R_l to be the radius of the smallest sphere which can enclose boxes at level l. Similarly r_l is defined to be the radius the largest sphere which fit inside boxes at level l. Note that $R_{l+2} = R_l/2$ and $r_{l+2} = r_l/2$. Since we are assuming the initial bounding box of the point set is chosen so that sidelengths are all equal, it easy to establish that for all $l \geq 0$,

$$(\text{A.1}) \qquad\qquad R_l/r_l \leq \sqrt{2}$$

and

$$(\text{A.2}) \qquad\qquad 2^{-(l/2+3)}\tau < R_l \leq 2^{-(l/2+1)}\tau.$$

Let P_l be the set of comparison-pairs at level l examined by the subroutine. We have

$$P = \bigcup_{l=0}^{2\lg(4/\epsilon)} P_l.$$

If $(i,j) \in P_l$ we observe that

$$(\text{A.3}) \qquad\qquad \tau - 2R_l < |c_i - c_j| < \tau + 2R_l.$$

(If the first inequality fails, this pair of boxes will be known to contain points to link L and R, and so the subroutine would have terminated. If the second inequality fails, the pair is separated too much to possibly contain such points.)

The strategy for bounding $|P|$ will be to bound each of $|P_l|$ by in terms of the number of number of non-empty sub-boxes of L and R at level l. Let the *neighbours of box i* be the set

$$N(i) = \{j : (i,j) \in P \text{ or } (j,i) \in P\}.$$

From now on we will interchangeably refer to comparison-pairs as edges and non-empty box centers as vertices. For each level $l \geq 0$, define a value K_l by

$$K_l = \frac{32\sqrt{\tau R_l}}{\pi r_l}.$$

We will charge each edge $(i,j) \in P_l$ to one or two vertices according to the following rule:

If $\quad |N(i)| \leq K_l \quad$ charge vertex c_i one,

else if $\quad |N(j)| \leq K_l \quad$ charge vertex c_j one,

else $\qquad\qquad\qquad$ charge vertex c_i and c_j one-half.

Denote the set of vertices at level l by V_l. It follows that

$$(A.4) \qquad\qquad |P_l| = \sum_{c_x \in V_l} \text{charge}(c_x).$$

LEMMA A.2. *For all vertices* $c_x \in V_l$, $\text{charge}(c_x) < K_l$.

Consider a vertex $c_i \in V_l$. If $|N(i)| \leq K_l$, $\text{charge}(c_i) \leq K_l$, so the only case to consider is when $N(i) > K_l$. Let $J = \{j : j \in N(i) \text{ and } N(j) > K_l\}$. We have $\text{charge}(c_i) = |J|/2$. We will show that $|J| > 2K_l$ leads to a contradiction and so $\text{charge}(c_i) \leq K_l$. To do this we need a couple more lemmas.

LEMMA A.3. *If* $|J| > 2K_l$ *then there exists vertices* $\{c_j, c_k, c_l\}$ *such that:*

(i) $c_k, c_l \in J$ *and* $c_j \in N(l)$

(ii) $|c_i - c_j|, |c_k - c_l| > \sqrt{8\tau R_l}$

(iii) *Edge* (c_j, c_l) *crosses edge* (c_i, c_k)

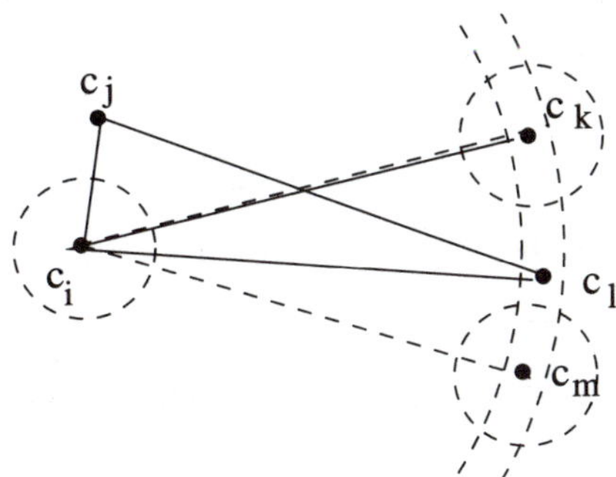

FIGURE 5. A possible configuration of the vertices $\{c_i, c_j, c_k, c_l\}$.

Proof: Since $J \subset N(i)$, by (A.3) we have $\tau - 2R_l < |c_i - c_x| < \tau + 2R_l$ for each $x \in J$. Thus c_x falls in an annulus around c_i of thickness $4R_l$ (see Figure 5). The set J exists in some section of this annulus. Let c_k and c_m be the extremal points bounding this section. Each vertex $c_x \in J$ has a ball around it of radius r_l which cannot contain other vertices. Within distance $\sqrt{8\tau R_l}$ of c_k or c_m, the volume available for points of J is less than $2 \cdot (8R_l \cdot \sqrt{8\tau R_l})$. Less than

$$\frac{2 \cdot 8R_l \cdot \sqrt{8\tau R_l}}{\pi r_l^2} \leq 2 \cdot K_l$$

points can fit in this space. Hence there must be a point $c_l \in J$ with $|c_l - c_k| > \sqrt{8\tau R_l}$ and $|c_l - c_m| > \sqrt{8\tau R_l}$. We know that $|N(l)| > K_l$ and $c_i \in N(l)$. Similar reasoning shows there must exist a point $c_j \in N(l)$ with $|c_i - c_j| > \sqrt{8\tau R_l}$.

The edge (c_j, c_l) must cross one of the edges (c_i, c_k) or (c_i, c_m). Without loss of generality, it crosses (c_i, c_k) (relabel c_k and c_m if necessary). The vertices $\{c_j, c_k, c_l\}$ have all properties listed in the lemma.

LEMMA A.4. *Such a configuration of vertices is impossible in Euclidean space.*

Proof: Referring back to Figure 5, we have the following constraints:

   (i) $\tau - 2R_l < |c_i - c_k|, |c_i - c_l|, |c_j - c_l| < \tau + 2R_l$
   (ii) Edge (c_j, c_l) crosses edge (c_i, c_k)
   (iii) $|c_i - c_j|, |c_k - c_l| > \sqrt{8\tau R_l}$

We show the first two constraints forbid the third. Assume the first two constraint hold. From the first constaint, the point c_l must fall in the intersection of annuli of thickness $4R_l$ centered at c_i and c_j respectively. As indicated in Figure 6, the point c_k must be located somewhere above the point c_l in order to maintain the second constraint. The first contraint also implies that c_k must fall in the annulus centered at c_i. We also know that $|c_j - c_k| > \tau - 2R_l$ at this point, because the subroutine would have terminated (by linking L and R) previously while processing comparison-pairs at level $l - 1$. This contrains c_k to lie in the shaded region shown in the figure. Thus $|c_k - c_l|$ is bounded above by the distance between the points where the outer boundary of one annulus meets the inner boundary of the other annulus. Let this distance be q. Some simple trigonometry shows that $|c_i - c_j| \cdot q = 8\tau R_l$, so

$$|c_i - c_j| \cdot |c_k - c_l| \le |c_i - c_j| \cdot q = 8\tau R_l.$$

But the second constraint implies that

$$|c_i - c_j| \cdot |c_k - c_l| > 8\tau R_l.$$

This contradiction completes the proof of this lemma, which in turn completes the proof of Lemma 2.

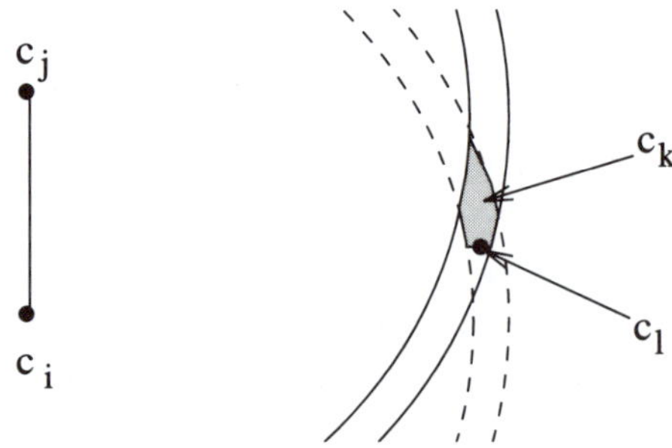

FIGURE 6. Locations of c_k and c_l permitted by constraint one.

PROOF OF LEMMA A.1: We make the observation that for any level l, $|V_l| \le m$. (Note the V_l includes the "imaginary" boxes around singletons, introduced to ensure comparison-pairs consist of boxes at the same level.) This is easy to see; if for some level l, $|V_l| > m$, there would be more than m pairwise-disjoint, non-empty boxes in the tree at this level and L and R would have to contain more than m points. We have:

$$|P| \;=\; \sum_{l=0}^{2\lg(4/\epsilon)} |P_l| \;=\; \sum_{l=0}^{2\lg(4/\epsilon)} \sum_{c_x \in V_l} \mathrm{charge}(c_x)$$

$$< \; \sum_{l=0}^{2\lg(4/\epsilon)} \sum_{c_x \in V_l} K_l \;<\; m \sum_{l=0}^{2\lg(4/\epsilon)} K_l.$$

Using (A.1) and (A.2) we derive $K_l \le \frac{256}{\pi} 2^{l/4}$. Evaluation of the K_l sum above gives

$$|P| \le 1025\sqrt{1/\epsilon} \cdot m.$$

As previously remarked, the running time of the subroutine is $O(|P|) = O(\sqrt{1/\epsilon} \cdot m)$.

A.1. Three dimensions. A proof similar to the above can given for three dimensions. We can show that no vertex is charged more than $K_l = O(2^{5/12\, l})$. The recurrence relation on R_l is now $R_{l+3} = R_l/2$. This changes the upper limit in the sum above to $3\lg(4/\epsilon)$. The bound on $|P|$ becomes $O(1/\epsilon^{1.25} \cdot m)$.

DEPARTMENT OF COMPUTER SCIENCE, UNIVERSITY OF WASHINGTON, SEATTLE, WASHINGTON 98195

E-mail address: brendan@cs.washington.edu

DIMACS Series in Discrete Mathematics
and Theoretical Computer Science
Volume **30**, 1997

A Practical Comparison of N-Body Algorithms

Guy Blelloch and Girija Narlikar

This work compares three algorithms for the three dimensional N-body problem, the Barnes-Hut algorithm, Greengard's Fast Multipole Method (FMM), and the Parallel Multipole Tree Algorithm (PMTA) to determine which of the algorithms performs best in practice. Although FMM has a better asymptotic running time ($O(N)$ instead of $O(N \log N)$ for uniform distributions), the algorithm is more complicated and it is not immediately clear above what values of N it performs better in practice. We studied the dependence of accuracy on the variable parameters θ, p and α, and then compared the floating point operation counts of the three algorithms at similar levels of accuracy, for both charged and uncharged random distributions. At a high level of accuracy (RMS-error $\approx 10^{-5}$), the FMM did the least number of operations for $N > 10^4$, assuming both charged and uncharged distributions of points. At a lower level of accuracy, (RMS-error $\approx 10^{-3}$) for uncharged distributions, the FMM did not outperform Barnes-Hut even for $N > 10^8$. For charged distributions of particles, both the FMM and PMTA were comparable at low accuracy. The algorithms were implemented in the parallel language NESL.

1   Introduction

The Classical N-body problem simulates the evolution of a system of N bodies, where the force exerted on each body arises due to its interaction with all the other bodies in the system. N-body algorithms have numerous applications in areas such as astrophysics, molecular dynamics and plasma physics. The simulation proceeds over time steps, each time computing the net force on every body and thereby updating its position and other attributes. If all pairwise forces are computed directly, this requires $O(N^2)$ operations at each time step. Hierarchical tree-based methods have been developed to reduce the complexity, such as the Barnes-Hut algorithm [4], which is $O(N \log N)$ for uniform distributions, or the more complex Fast Multipole Method [14], which is $O(N)$ for uniform distributions. The Parallel Multipole Tree algorithm [9] is a hybrid of the Barnes-Hut and the Fast Multipole method.

There have been several efforts to implement N-body code on parallel machines. The Stanford Splash benchmarks includes the Barnes-Hut algorithm as one of the

---

1991 Mathematics Subject Classification. Primary 70F10; Secondary 70-08, 68Q22, 68-06.

This research was sponsored in part by the Wright Laboratory, Aeronautical Systems Center, Air Force Materiel Command, USAF, and the Advanced Research Projects Agency (ARPA) under grant number F33615-93-1-1330. It was also supported in part by an NSF Young Investigator Award under grant number CCR-9258525, and by Finmeccanica.

applications [31]. They studied how to parallelize the code on a shared-memory model and derived speedups for up to 64 processors. Their algorithm has a serial bottleneck at the root of the tree, and is therefore not appropriate for a much larger number of processors. A similar version, for a distributed memory machine, was implemented by Salmon [27]. Several other researchers have implemented various N-body algorithms [6, 9, 13, 24, 30, 34]. These algorithms have been used extensively for applications in areas such as astrophysics [3, 19, 20, 21, 32] and molecular dynamics [10, 12, 17]. Error analysis of the algorithms has been performed both experimentally [5, 12, 18, 23] and analytically [14, 26, 33]. However, the analytical error bounds are pessimistic, and the algorithms give much lower errors in practice. Performance has been measured for specific implementations of N-body algorithms on specific platforms [6, 9, 13, 16, 18, 27]. Previous work has shown that it is possible to get close to peak floating point performance on parallel machines by being careful about the communication in these algorithms [6, 27].

However, there has been little work comparing the various N-body algorithms from a practical standpoint in terms of both error and running time. Board and others have compared their PMTA algorithm to the FMM [9, 10] based on running times for a particular implementation. Our work extends the above previous work in the following ways. Firstly, we compare all three algorithms, Barnes Hut, PMTA and FMM. Secondly, we consider both electrostatic and gravitational distributions of data, and show that the algorithms have quite different characteristics with the two types of forces. Thirdly, we use floating point operation counts to measure the work executed by the three algorithms in a manner independent of the machine and implementations. By deriving expressions for the operation counts of the algorithms we provide the ability to estimate their performances for large values of N without executing the code. This is particularly useful to help choose an algorithm and values for its parameters that will run well for a given level of accuracy and input distribution. Salmon [28] has given an upper bound for the number of interactions in the Barnes-But algorithm for both uniform and non-uniform distributions, but we give an exact expression for the expected number of interactions for uniform distributions that is much closer to the experimentally measured value. For example, at high accuracy, assuming a uniform distribution, Salmon's upper bound for $N = 10^5$ is about 4 times larger than the actual value, whereas our estimate is off by about 10%.

Our work involves the data-parallel implementation and comparison of the Barnes-Hut algorithm, the PMTA and the uniform FMM in three dimensions. We studied the dependence of the number of operations required by these algorithms and their accuracy on certain variable parameters, namely, θ in the Barnes-Hut algorithm, α in the PMTA and the number of terms p for all three algorithms. The goal was to compare the computational costs of the algorithms in practice, for various degrees of accuracy, for different sizes and distributions of input data. The FMM has two versions — a uniform version for uniform distributions of bodies, and a more complicated adaptive version for non-uniform distributions. Since we have tested the algorithms on points distributed randomly with uniform probability, we have restricted this work to the uniform version of the FMM. The Barnes-Hut and the PMTA, on the other hand, work well for both uniform and non-uniform distributions of data. We were interested in studying the trade-offs between the asymptotic complexity and the hidden constants, and this work should help decide weather it is worth implementing the more complex adaptive $O(N)$ FMM instead of the simpler Barnes-Hut or PMTA algorithms for different distributions of data.

Section 2 describes the Barnes-Hut, the PMTA and the FMM in detail. The experimental results are given in section 3, in which we describe how the algorithms were compared. Finally, the conclusions are given in section 4.

2 About the Algorithms

2.1 The Barnes-Hut Algorithm

The Barnes-Hut algorithm is based on a hierarchical octree representation of space in three dimensions. The algorithm has two phases. The first phase consists of constructing the octree by recursively subdividing the root cell containing all the particles into eight cubical subcells of equal size, until each subcell has at most one particle. Each cell contains the total mass and the position of the center of mass of all the particles in the subtree under it. In the second phase, the tree is traversed once per particle to compute the net force acting on it. We start at the root, and at each step, if the cell is *well separated* from the particle, we use the center of mass approximation to compute the force on the particle due to the entire subtree under that cell. Otherwise, each of its subcells is visited. A cell is considered well separated from a particle if its size, divided by the distance of its center of mass from the particle, is smaller than a parameter θ, which controls accuracy. In addition to the monopole (center of mass) approximation, higher order multipole terms can be used to increase accuracy.

A number of variants of the Barnes-Hut algorithms have been implemented, such as one by Barnes that allow better vectorization of the code at the cost of higher floating point operations counts [2]. Although we have restricted our analysis to the original version of the algorithm, it can be easily extended to simple variants.

2.2 The Fast Multipole Method (FMM)

The Fast Multipole Method (FMM) uses an octree similar to that of the Barnes-Hut algorithm. The uniform version builds a balanced octree. It distributes the particles into leaf cells, and computes their multipole expansions, followed by a bottom-up phase in which it constructs the multipole expansions of the parent cells by shifting and adding the expansions of its children. After the tree is built, it has a top-down phase in which the local expansion of the parent cell (which describes the potential field due to distant particles) is shifted to the center of each child, and added to the multipole expansions of the cells in the child's interaction list to form its local expansion. Finally, the local expansions at the leaf cells, along with direct interactions with particles in neighboring cells gives us the total force on each particle. The number of terms in the multipole expansions, p, controls the accuracy of the algorithm.

The primary difference between the FMM and the Barnes-Hut lies in the fact that the Barnes-Hut algorithm computes particle-cell interactions, whereas the FMM computes cell-cell interactions, thereby reducing its complexity.

2.3   Parallel Multipole Tree Algorithm (PMTA)

The PMTA is a hybrid of the Barnes-Hut and the FMM algorithms. It uses a rule similar to that of Barnes-Hut to determine the well-separatedness of two cells. Two cells are said to be well-separated from each other if the size of the bigger cell divided by the distance between the two cells is less than the parameter α. The tree is built as in the Barnes-Hut method, but a cell is recursively subdivided until it contains no more than m particles (instead of one particle as in the case of the Barnes-Hut algorithm). Then the tree is traversed top down for each leaf cell, and when a cell is found to be well-separated from the leaf cell, its multipole expansion is translated into a local expansion about the center of the leaf cell, and the rest of the subtree below that cell is not visited. All these translated local expansions are added and the gradient is found to get the force due to the far field on every particle in the leaf. The particles in the leaf cell interact directly with the particles in all the leaf cells that are not well separated from it. The number of terms in the multipole expansion, p, and the separation parameter α can both be varied to control accuracy. A theoretical error bound for this algorithm is not known.

3   Experimental Analysis

The goal of this work is to compare the constant factors in the computational work of the three algorithms and their variants; in particular to determine how the constants depend on the desired accuracy. We chose to use floating-point operation count as the measure of computational work since measuring the running time on a particular machine would be machine and implementation specific. Clearly results based purely on floating-point operations will not exactly correspond to the running times on a particular machine, however, they should be quite representative. This is because the non-computational overheads of the algorithms are approximately equal. They parallelize quite easily and can take advantage of locality to reduce communication overheads. Previous implementations on parallel machines have managed to reduce the non-computational overheads of these algorithms to 15% or less [6, 32, 34]. In this paper, we assume all floating point operations to have the same computational cost.

We have implemented two versions of the Barnes-Hut algorithm — one in rectilinear coordinates that uses quadrupole moments in addition to the center of mass (monopole) approximation, and one in spherical coordinates that can have an arbitrary number of terms in the expansion. Both these versions increase the accuracy at the cost of computing the additional terms. At all levels of accuracy we found that they outperform the monopole version, so the results reported here are for these versions only.

We have implemented the uniform version of the FMM. Greengard defines the *near field* of a cell (the cells that are not well-separated from a given cell) as its first and second nearest neighbors. We have also implemented a variant in which the near field is taken as just the first nearest neighbors. This reduces the maximum number of cells in the interaction list of a cell from 825 to 189, but also reduces the accuracy (making it necessary to use a larger p). As it turns out, the additional work required by the extra p terms approximately balances the work saved by using fewer neighbors, so that the two versions are competitive for all the levels of accuracies that we have studied. Hence we have used the original version for comparison with the other algorithms.

Our implementations have been carried out in NESL [7], a data parallel language that supports nested data parallelism. It presents to the programmer a uniform memory-cost model of computation. Therefore issues like load balancing and data distribution, which are critical to the efficiency of the algorithm, are left to the NESL compiler to handle.

Instead of using the existing theoretical error bounds, which turn out to be pessimistic in practice, we performed an experimental error analysis similar to previous work [5, 12, 18, 23]. The error we calculated is the RMS relative error in the force after a single time step, defined below.

$$ RMS\ error = \left[\frac{1}{N} \sum_{i=1}^{N} \left(\frac{|\vec{f}_{i,\,tree} - \vec{f}_{i,\,dir}|}{|\vec{f}_{i,\,dir}|} \right)^2 \right]^{1/2} $$

where

$\vec{f}_{i,\,dir}$ = force on particle i computed by the direct method, and,

$\vec{f}_{i,\,tree}$ = force on particle i computed by the tree-based method.

We found the dependence of error on the variable parameters in the algorithms, namely, θ in the case of Barnes-Hut, α in the case of the PMTA and the number of multipole terms p for all three algorithms. Figure 1 shows the variation of error with N for fixed values of these parameters. We calculated errors for N up to 100,000, as running the direct simulation above that value was not feasible. Since errors for values of N up to 100,000 varied in a similar manner for all three algorithms, we have assumed that the algorithms will behave in a similar fashion for higher values of N. We did an extensive search of the parameter space to find values that gave similar errors.

3.1 Operations as a Function of θ and N for the Barnes-Hut Algorithm

In this section we first derive an expression that approximates the number of interactions as a function of θ and N. The expression is of the form:

$$ b(\theta) N \log N - a(\theta) N $$

where $b(\theta) = O(1/\theta^3)$ and $a/b = O(\log \theta)$.

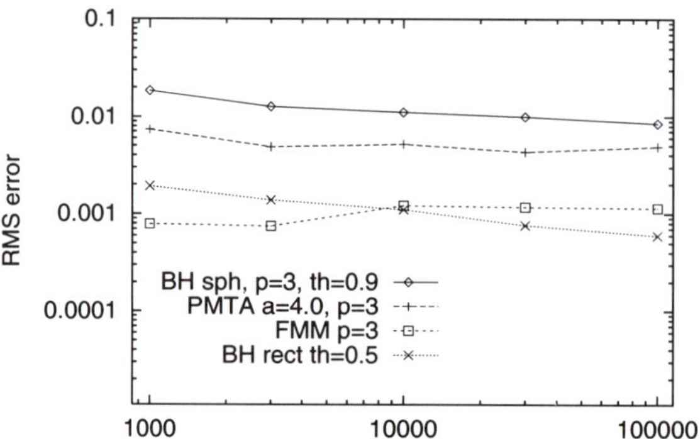

Figure 1: Experimental errors in gravitational forces on up to 100,000 randomly distributed points. Errors are shown for some fixed parameter values. Similar experiments were carried out for electrostatic forces. Errors for all the algorithms were found to vary in a similar manner. The errors shown here are not all for the same level of accuracy.

The interaction count derived in [23] is close to the one derived in this section, but our derivation is simpler and more precise. We have also run experiments to measure the number of interactions computed by the Barnes-Hut algorithms over different values of N and θ. Our measurements fit well with the derived expression. As it turns out, for higher accuracies (lower θ) the second term is significant for most values of N that would be used in practice (up to $\approx 10^7$), such that the $N \log N$ asymptotic behavior is not applicable over this range.

We now consider how many cells each particle interacts with as a function of θ and N. The total number of interactions is N times this result. We will make some approximations in the analysis. Remember that a cell can interact directly with a particle (it is well-separated) if the ratio of the cell size to its distance from the particle is less than θ. Our analysis is based on calculating how many cells in each level of the tree a particle will interact with. The number of interactions at each level is constant from the bottom of the tree up to a fixed level, at which point none of the cells are well-separated from the particle. This is what gives the $N \log N - N$ form of the equation.

Let us assume for the sake of simplicity that the space is unbounded, that is, it has no edges. In 3D the cell dimensions double at every level up the tree and the average number of particles in a cell increases 8-fold. If d is the distance between a particle and a cell of size s that is well-separated from it, then it follows that $d > s/\theta$. Similarly, the cells of size $2s$ (at the next higher level) that are well-separated from the particle lie at a distance $> 2s/\theta$ from it. Thus, the cells of size s that interact with the particle directly are more or less contained between spheres of radii s/θ and $2s/\theta$, centered around the particle (see figure 2). Hence the number of cells at that level (of size s) that interact with the particle are given by

$$f(\theta) = \frac{volume\ enclosing\ the\ cells}{volume\ of\ one\ cell} = \frac{4/3\pi[(2s/\theta)^3 - (s/\theta)^3]}{s^3} = 28\pi/3\theta^3$$

Given that a particle P interacts with $f(\theta)$ cells at each level, and that there are

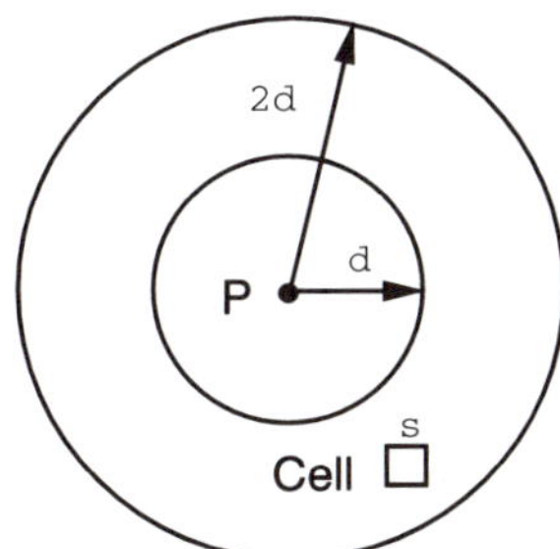

Figure 2:   A cell of size s that interacts with particle P. Cells of size s inside the inner sphere will be expanded further and cells outside the outer sphere that interact with particle P will be larger than size s. The total number of cells of size s which interact with P will be $\approx (28\pi/3) \cdot d^3/s^3$. Since $\theta = s/d$, this is $28\pi/3\theta^3$.

θ	$a(\theta)$	$b(\theta)$	$a(\theta)/b(\theta)$	
	measured	*measured*	*measured*	*derived*
1.0	40.9	26.8	1.526	1.624
0.7	169.1	78	2.168	2.139
0.6	276.4	120.6	2.29	2.36
0.5	551.6	209.8	2.63	2.624
0.3	3242.7	840	3.86	3.36
0.2	11278	3077.5	3.66	3.956

Table 1: Measured values of $a(\theta)$ and $b(\theta)$ for some values of θ, the measured ratio $a(\theta)/b(\theta)$ and the derived ratio $(=\log_8(28\pi/3\theta^3))$. The measured values of $a(\theta)$ and $b(\theta)$ shown here are averaged over values of N up to 25,000.

approximately 8^l particles in each cell at level l (l=0,1,... starting from the leaves), the total number of particles P interacts with up to level l (directly or indirectly) is $\sum_{i=0}^{i<=l} f(\theta) \times 8^i \approx f(\theta) \times 8^l$. Since there are totally N particles, all the particles will be covered upon reaching the level L given by

$$L \approx \log_8[N/f(\theta)]$$

This means that P interacts with $f(\theta)$ cells at each of the L levels, giving a total of $f(\theta) \times \log_8[N/f(\theta)]$ interactions per particle and a total of

$$\begin{aligned} I(N,\theta) &= N\,f(\theta)\log_8[N/f(\theta)] \\ &= f(\theta)N\log_8(N) - f(\theta)\log_8(f(\theta))N \end{aligned}$$

interactions across all particles. This explains why the number of interactions fits the $b(\theta)N\log N - a(\theta)N$ curve, with $a(\theta) = f(\theta)\log_8(f(\theta))$, $b(\theta) = f(\theta)$ and $a(\theta)/b(\theta) = \log_8(f(\theta))$.

Table 1 lists the values of $a(\theta)$ and $b(\theta)$ obtained from the measured number of interactions. They are close to the predicted values. It also lists the measured ratio of $a(\theta)/b(\theta)$ and the derived ratio $\log_8(f(\theta))$. Note that the slight deviation of the measured numbers from the derived expression can be explained by the following factors:

- The region containing the particles is bounded, so the above expression is not valid for interactions with particles near the edges.

- Some cells of size s may interact with the particle even though they are more than $2s/\theta$ away from it, since their siblings and parents are less than $2s/\theta$ away from the particle.

- The expression for the number of cells in the region between the two spheres is not exact, and some cells may be only partially within the region.

Figure 3 shows the variation of the measured number of interactions with N for some values of θ.

3.2   Comparison of Operation Counts

We have used the number of floating point operations to compare the work performed by the three algorithms. For the Barnes-Hut algorithm, we used the variation of the number of interactions with N for different θ (that was derived in the previous section), to estimate the number of interactions needed for larger numbers, and multiplied that by the number of floating point operations needed for each interaction. Note that the number of operations required for a particle-particle interaction and a particle-cell interaction are different, which we have included in our final expression to calculate the floating-point operation counts (see appendix A). Similarly, we use the number of operations required for particle-particle and particle-cell interactions in spherical coordinates to calculate the operation counts for Barnes-Hut in spherical coordinates. We obtained a similar estimate for the PMTA in terms of α, p and m. For the FMM we summed the number of floating point operations needed at each stage (for a given p), similar to the analysis carried out in [14, 26]. This is a reasonable estimate of the actual number since this is the uniform version of the algorithm and the distribution of points is random. The final expressions used for the floating point operation counts of the algorithms are listed in appendix A. In the case of the FMM, the optimum number of levels in the tree depends on N and p. The slope of the curve for the total work changes at values of N at which the optimal number of levels in the tree increases.

We compared the work performed by the algorithms for two different levels of accuracy. For uncharged distributions, at a lower level of accuracy (RMS error $\approx 10^{-3}$), where $\theta = 0.55$, $\alpha = 0.8$ and $p = 4$, all three do comparable work for practical values of N, with the Barnes-Hut in rectilinear coordinates doing the best for N as large as 10^8 million. Figure 4 shows the work done by the three algorithms at low accuracy for chargeless distributions. Figure 5 summarizes the results of the estimates for both levels of accuracy, for both charged(electrostatic) and uncharged(gravitational) distributions at $N \approx 10^7$. At lower accuracy (RMS error $\approx 10^{-3}$), the Barnes-Hut in rectilinear coordinates with the quadrupole moment

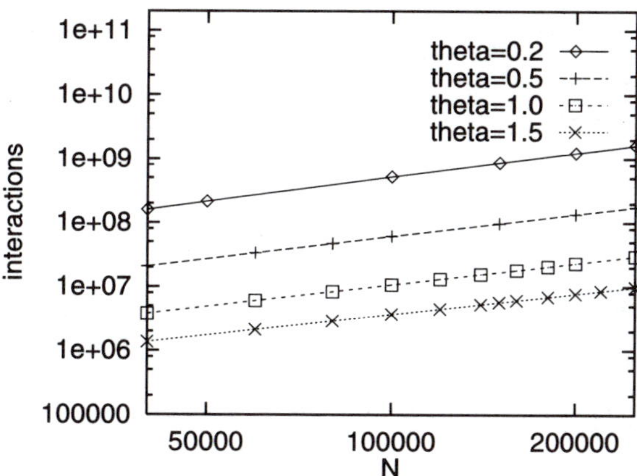

Figure 3: Measured number of interactions as a function of N in Barnes-Hut for four different values of θ.

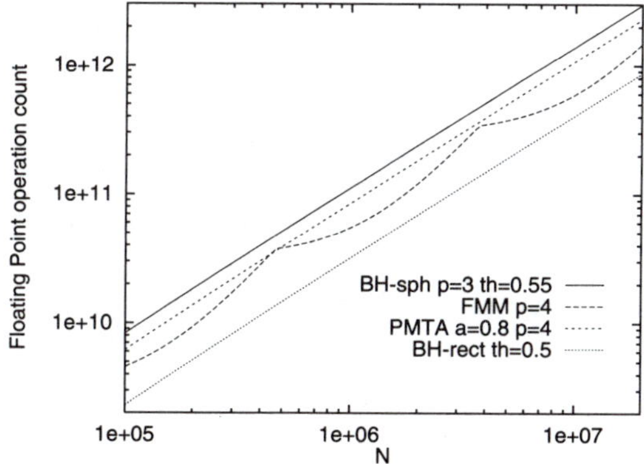

Figure 4: Floating point operation counts of the algorithms for gravitational (chargeless) distributions at low accuracy (RMS error $\approx 10^{-3}$). The bumps in the FMM curve occur due to the change in optimal number of levels in the FMM tree as N increases.

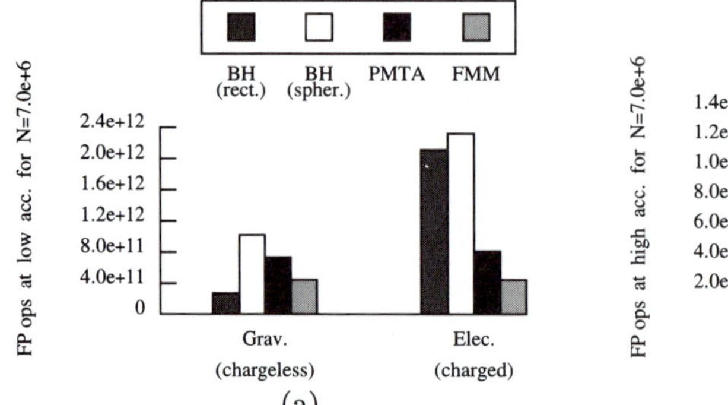

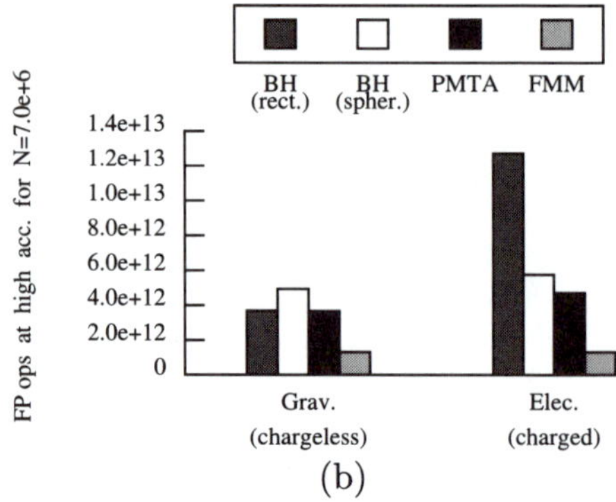

Figure 5: Floating point operation counts for the Barnes-Hut (in both rectilinear and spherical coordinates), the PMTA and the FMM for electrostatic and gravitational distributions. The figures show operation counts for $N = 7 \times 10^6$, at (a) low accuracy, and (b) high accuracy. The parameter values for the operation counts shown above are as follows. Low acc. (grav.): BH-rect. $\theta = 0.55$; BH-sph. $\theta = 0.55$, $p = 3$; PMTA $\alpha = 0.8$, $p = 4$, $m = 80$; FMM $p = 4$. Low acc. (elec.): BH-rect. $\theta = 0.28$; BH-sph. $\theta = 0.63$, $p = 6$; PMTA $\alpha = 1.5$, $p = 6$, $m = 190$; FMM $p = 4$. High acc. (grav.): BH-rect. $\theta = 0.2$; BH-sph. $\theta = 0.58$, $p = 8$; PMTA $\alpha = 0.4$, $p = 6$, $m = 170$; FMM $p = 7$. High acc. (elec.): BH-rect. $\theta = 0.135$; BH-sph. $\theta = 0.5$, $p = 7$; PMTA $\alpha = 0.4$, $p = 7$, $m = 220$; FMM $p = 7$.

performs the least number of operations for gravitational distributions. On the other hand, for electrostatic distributions, at low accuracy (RMS error $\approx 2 \times 10^{-3}$) both the FMM and PMTA do comparable amounts of work and do better than the Barnes-Hut versions. Finally, at high accuracy (RMS error $\approx 2 \times 10^{-5}$ for gravitational, $\approx 6 \times 10^{-5}$ for electrostatic), the FMM outperforms both the other algorithms. The rectilinear Barnes-Hut with quadrupole moments performs better for gravitational distributions because the lower order terms in the expansion dominate. Since this is not the case for electrostatic distributions, more than 3 terms are needed to accurately calculate the potential and force.

A few optimizations have been suggested for multipole-based algorithms, such as the use of FFTs to reduce the cost of translating expansions [15, 25, 29] at the cost of greater memory requirements. However, it has been reported that this optimization gives a overall speedup of less than 2 at a high level of accuracy ($p = 12$), and little or no speedup at lower accuracy ($p = 4$) [8]. Hence we have not included the FFT version in our experiments. Another optimization suggested is to reduce the number of multipole-to-local translations in the FMM by using what is called *parental conversion* [22]. This optimization uses the multipole expansion of the parent cell for translation into a local expansion if all eight of its children are in the interaction list. This reduces the maximum size of the interaction list from 825 to 189 at the loss of some accuracy. This loss of accuracy is compensated for by using one extra term in the expansion [22]. We found that at low accuracy ($p=4$) this gave a speedup of about $1.3 - 1.4$ and less at higher accuracy (higher p). Hence this optimization too has not been included in our experiments.

4 Conclusions

The conclusions of this work can be summarized as follows.

- The FMM always performs better than the other two algorithms, except for gravitational distributions at low accuracy, for which it performs less than twice the work performed by the Barnes-Hut algorithm.

- At low accuracy, for gravitational distributions, the operation counts of all three algorithms are nearly equivalent, with the Barnes-Hut in rectilinear coordinates doing the best for values of N up to 10^8 and more. For electrostatic distributions at low accuracy, the PMTA and the FMM do nearly equivalent amounts of work and outperform the Barnes-Hut versions.

- The negative linear term plays a significant role in the complexity of the Barnes-Hut algorithm. Hence Barnes-Hut does not perform strictly as $N \log N$ for reasonable values of N and θ.

- Although the two algorithms are competitive at low accuracy, the FMM always outperforms the PMTA.

- Barnes-Hut performs better for gravitational distributions using rectilinear coordinates. On the other hand, spherical coordinates prove to be more useful for electrostatic distributions at high accuracy. This is because we have used only up to the quadrupole moment in rectilinear coordinates. Quadrupole approximation works well for gravitational distributions since the first few multipole terms dominate, which is less true in the case of electrostatic distributions. For electrostatic distributions, opposite charges may cancel each other in the calculation of the monopole term, making the higher order terms more significant.

- Electrostatic distributions require more work to achieve the same level of accuracy as compared to gravitational distributions.

All three algorithms are highly parallel in nature. They have high memory requirements if we exploit all the available parallelism, hence timing fully parallel versions for large data sets was beyond the scope of this work. Even for moderately sized data sets, especially at high accuracy, some of the parallelism had to be reduced. Time has not yet permitted us to study the performance of the algorithms on non-uniform distributions, such as the Plummer model [1]. The PMTA and Barnes-Hut, being adaptive, work well on non-uniform distributions, whereas the uniform FMM does not. To make a fair comparison for non-uniform distributions, the more complicated adaptive FMM, or the algorithm by Callahan [11] will have to be implemented. The Barnes-Hut in rectilinear coordinates was the simplest to code. In spherical coordinates, all three algorithms were comparable in terms of difficulty of coding.

References

[1] S.J. Aarseth, M. Henon, and R. Wielen. Numerical methods for the study of star cluster dynamics. *Astronomy and Astrophysics*, 37(2):183–187, 1974.

[2] J.E. Barnes. A modified tree code: don't laugh; it runs. *Journal of Computational Physics*, 87(1):161–70, March 1990.

[3] J.E. Barnes. *N-Body Models of Collisionless Systems*, volume 1, chapter 8. Springer-Verlag, 1996.

[4] J.E. Barnes and P. Hut. A hierarchical $O(N \log N)$ force calculation algorithm. *Nature*, 324(4):446–449, December 1986.

[5] J.E. Barnes and P. Hut. Error analysis of a treecode. *Astrophysical Journal Supplement Series*, 70:389–417, June 1989.

[6] S. Bhatt, M. Chen, C.Y. Lin, and P. Liu. Abstractions for parallel N-body simulations. In *Proceedings Scalable High Performance Computing Conference*, pages 26–29, 1992.

[7] Guy E. Blelloch. Nesl: A nested data-parallel language. Technical Report CMU-CS-93-129, CMU, School of Computer Science, April 1993.

[8] J.A. Board and W.S. Elliot. Fast fourier transform accelerated fast multipole algorithm. Technical Report 94-001, Duke University Dept of Electrical Engineering, 1994.

[9] J.A. Board, Z.S. Hakura, W.S. Elliot, D.C. Gray, W.J. Blanke, and J.F. Leathrum Jr. Scalable implementations of multipole-accelerated algorithms for molecular dynamics. Technical Report 94-002, Duke Univaersity, 1994.

[10] J.A. Board, Z.S. Hakura, W.S. Elliot, and W.T. Rankin. Scalable variants of multipole-accelerated algorithms for molecular dynamics. Technical Report 94-006, Duke University Dept of Electrical Engineering, 1994.

[11] P.B. Callahan. Optimal parallel all-nearest-neighbours using the well-separated pairs decomposition. In *34th Annual Symposium on Foundations of Computer Science*, pages 332–340, Palo Alto, 1993. IEEE.

[12] H. Ding, N. Karasawa, and W. Goddard. Atomic level simulations of a million particles: The cell multipole method for coulomb and london interactions. *Journal of Chemical Physics*, 97:4309–4315, 1992.

[13] A.Y. Grama, V. Kumar, and A. Sameh. N-body simulations using message passing parallel computers. In *Proceedings of the Seventh SIAM Conference on Parallel Processing for Scientific Computing*, pages 355–60, San Francisco, February 1995.

[14] L. Greengard. *The rapid evaluation of potential fields in particle systems*. The MIT Press, 1987.

[15] L. Greengard and V. Rokhlin. A fast algorithm for particle simulation. *Journal of Computational Physics*, 73(325), 1987.

[16] L. Greengard and V. Rokhlin. On the efficient implementation of the fast multipole algorithm. Technical Report RR-602, Yale University Dept of Computer Science, 1988.

[17] L. Greengard and V. Rokhlin. On the evaluation of electrostatic interactions in molecular modeling. *Chemica Scripta*, 29A:139–144, 1989.

[18] L. Hernquist. Performance characteristics of tree codes. *Astrophysical Journal Supplement Series*, 64:715–734, August 1987.

[19] J.Dubinski and R.G.Carlberg. The structure of cold dark matter halos. *Astrophysical Journal*, 378:496, 1991.

[20] N. Katz, L. Hernquist, and D.H. Weinberg. galaxies and gas in a cold dark matter universe. *Astrophysical Journal*, 399:L109, 1992.

[21] G. Lake, N. Katz, T. Quinn, and J.A. Stadel. Cosmological n-body simulation. In *Proceedings of the Seventh SIAM Conference on Parallel Processing for Scientific Computing*, pages 307–12, San Francisco, February 1995.

[22] J.F. Leathrum, Jr., J.A. Board, and W.S. Elliot. The parallel fast multipole algorithm in three dimensions. Technical report, Duke University Dept of Electrical Engineering, 1992.

[23] J. Makino. Comparison of two different tree algorithms. *Journal of Computational Physics*, 88:393–408, 1990.

[24] P.H. Mills, L.S. Nyland, J.F. Prins, and J.H. Reif. Prototyping N-body simulation in proteus. In *Proceedings Sixth International Parallel Processing Symposium*, pages 476–482, 1992.

[25] V.Y. Pan, J.H. Reif, and S.R. Tate. The power of combining the techniques of algebraic and numerical computing. In *32nd Annual IEEE Symposium on Foundations of Computer Science (FOCS 92)*, pages 703–713, 1992.

[26] G.J. Pringle. *Numerical Study of Three-Dimensional Flow using Fast Parallel Particle Algorithms*. PhD thesis, Napier University, 1994.

[27] J. Salmon. Parallel $N \log N$ N-body algorithms and applications to astrophysics. In *COMPCON Spring '91, Digest of Papers*, pages 73–78, 1991.

[28] J.K. Salmon. *Parallel hierarchical N-body methods*. PhD thesis, Caltech University, 1991.

[29] K.E. Schmidt and M.A. Lee. Implementing the fast multipole method in three dimensions. *Journal of Statistical Physics*, 63(5):1223–1235, 1991.

[30] J.P. Singh, J.L. Hennessy, and A. Gupta. Implications of hierarchical n-body methods for multiprocessor architecture. *ACM Transactions on Computer Systems*, 13(2):141–202, May 1995.

[31] J.P. Singh, W.D. Weber, and A. Gupta. Splash: Stanford parallel applications for shared-memory. *Computer Architecture News*, 20(1):5–44, March 1987.

[32] M. Warren and J. Salmon. Astrophysical n-body simulations using hierarchical tree data structures. In *Proceedings of Supercomputing*, pages 570–6, 1992.

[33] M. Warren and J. Salmon. Skeletons from the treecode closet. *Journal of Computational Physics*, 111(1):136–55, March 1994.

[34] F. Zhao and S.L. Johnsson. The parallel multipole method on the connection machine. *SIAM Journal on Scientific and Statistical Computing*, 12(6):1420–1437, November 1991.

A   Expressions used to estimate the floating point operations counts

Let

$$
\begin{aligned}
W(x_1, x_2, \ldots) &= \text{Number of floating point operations performed by the} \\
&\quad\text{algorithm to calculate force on each particle in terms of} \\
&\quad\text{variable parameters } x_1, x_2, \ldots, \\
\theta &= \text{separation parameter for Barnes-Hut,} \\
\alpha &= \text{separation parameter for PMTA,} \\
p &= \text{number of terms in the multipole expansion} \\
&\quad (= 1, 2, 3, \ldots), \\
l &= \text{number of levels in the FMM tree} \\
&\quad (= 0, 1, 2, \ldots \text{ starting from the root), and,} \\
N &= \text{number of particles.}
\end{aligned}
$$

$W(x_1, x_2, \ldots)$ does not include the cost of building the octree, which is negligible compared to the cost of force calculation.

A.1   Barnes-Hut in rectilinear coordinates

$$
W(N, \theta) = C_q \cdot N \cdot f(\theta) \cdot \left(\log_8 \frac{N}{f(\theta)} - 1 \right) + d \cdot N \cdot f(\theta)
$$

where $f(\theta)$ is defined in section 3.1 and C_q is the cost of evaluating the gradient using up to quadrupole moments.

$$
\begin{aligned}
C_q &= \text{cost of gradient for uncharged distributions using only monopole and} \\
&\quad\text{quadrupole moments (the dipole moment vanishes if} \\
&\quad\text{evaluated about center of mass)} = 50 \text{ ,} \\
C_q &= \text{cost of gradient for charged distributions using monopole, dipole and} \\
&\quad\text{quadrupole moments} = 70 \text{, and,} \\
d &= \text{cost of a direct interaction} = 13.
\end{aligned}
$$

A.2   Barnes-Hut in spherical coordinates

$$
W(N, \theta, p) = g(p) \cdot N \cdot f(\theta) \cdot \left(\log_8 \frac{N}{f(\theta)} - 1 \right) + d \cdot N \cdot f(\theta)
$$

where $g(p)$ = cost of gradient for a multipole expansion of p terms
$$= 15p(p + 1) + 5p + 4.$$

A.3 PMTA

$$W(N, \alpha, p, m_{avg}) \;=\; t(p) \cdot \frac{N}{m_{avg}} \cdot f'(\alpha) \cdot \log_8\left(\frac{N}{m_{avg} f'(\alpha)}\right)$$
$$+\; d \cdot \frac{N m_{avg}}{7} \cdot f'(\alpha) \;+\; g(p) \cdot N$$

where

$t(p)$ = cost of translating a multipole expansion having p terms into a local expansion $= 3p^2(p+1)^2 + 5p(p+1)$,

m_{avg} = average population of leaf cells ($\approx m/2$), and,

$f'(\alpha)$ = average number of cells a leaf cell interacts with at each level (measured).

We have assumed that a leaf interacts with a constant $f'(\alpha)$ cells at each level, and the average radius of the sphere around the leaf cell containing all the cells that have interacted with it so far doubles at every level up the tree. This means that the volume of cells interacting with it at each level increases 8-fold. Hence the number of leafs it directly interacts with at the lowest level is $\approx (8/7 - 1) \cdot f'(\alpha) = f'(\alpha)/7$. This estimate agrees with the numbers we have measured experimentally for moderate values of N. We used $f'(1.5) = 374$, $f'(0.8) = 642$ and $f'(0.4) = 1910$.

A.4 FMM

$$W(N, p, l) = d \cdot near(l) \cdot \left(\frac{N}{8^l}\right)^2 + g(p) \cdot N + t(p) \cdot \sum_{i=2}^{l} trans(i)$$

where

$near(l)$ = total number of leaf pairs that interact directly in a tree with l levels.

= 1   for $l = 0$,

= $63 \cdot 2^{3l} - 225 \cdot 2^{2l} + 270 \cdot 2^l - 108$ for $l \geq 1$, and,

$trans(l)$ = the total number of local-to-local and multipole-to-local translations at the level l in the tree.

= 1352   for $l = 2$,

= $(1 + 875) \cdot 2^{3l} - 6750 \cdot 2^{2l} + 16740 \cdot 2^l - 13608$ for $l \geq 3$.

(Guy Blelloch) Computer Science Department, Carnegie Mellon University, Pittsburgh, PA 15213.
E-mail address: guyb@cs.cmu.edu

(Girija Narlikar) Computer Science Department, Carnegie Mellon University, Pittsburgh, PA 15213.
E-mail address: girija@cs.cmu.edu

DIMACS Series in Discrete Mathematics
and Theoretical Computer Science
Volume **30**, 1997

Parallel Algorithms for Geometric Dominance Problems

Jan Petersson

ABSTRACT. Consider a set S of n points in real d-dimensional space ($d \geq 2$). A point p is said to dominate another point q if the j:th coordinate of p is larger than that of q, for all $1 \leq j \leq d$. We present efficient parallel algorithms for the following problems. *Dominance Counting*: determine for each point $p \in S$ the number of points in S that are dominated by p. *Maxima*: determine for each point $p \in S$ whether it is dominated by any other point in S.

Our algorithms are for the mesh-connected SIMD computer. In the planar case the running time is $O(\sqrt{n})$ on a mesh of size $\sqrt{n} \times \sqrt{n}$, which is optimal in this model of computation. In the multidimensional case the running time is $O(d\,(2 + \sqrt{2}\,)^d \sqrt{n}\,)$, which is optimal for any fixed dimension $d \geq 2$.

Our algorithms are based on the (multidimensional) divide-and-conquer technique, and are given at a high level of detail. In addition to the standard asymptotic analysis, communication costs are closely examined. Virtualization is also discussed. In the planar case, specifically, our algorithms run in time $O(m \log m + m\sqrt{N}\,)$ on a mesh of size $\sqrt{N} \times \sqrt{N}$, where $m = n/N \geq 1$.

All algorithms have been implemented on a massively parallel computer, the MasPar MP–2. Experimental results, including comparisons with efficient sequential algorithms, are presented too.

1. Introduction

Parallel computational geometry is the study of efficient parallel algorithms for combinatorial problems dealing with collections of simple geometric objects. Research in this area has focused on the single instruction stream, multiple data stream model of computation. Most efforts have been directed towards shared-memory computers, but various interconnection-network models have also received attention (for a survey, see [**11**]). In this paper we consider the mesh-connected computer, which has turned out to be suitable for geometric computation (see e.g. [**14, 19**]). The problems treated concern dominance properties of points in real d-dimensional space ($d \geq 2$). The algorithms reported are based on the (multidimensional) divide-and-conquer technique [**3**], and are given at a high level of detail. In addition to the standard asymptotic analysis, communication costs are closely examined. Virtualization is briefly discussed. All algorithms have been implemented on a massively parallel computer, the MasPar MP–2. Experimental results, including comparisons with efficient sequential algorithms, are presented too.

1991 *Mathematics Subject Classification.* Primary 68Q22, 68Q25, 68U05; Secondary 68–04.

This section is organized as follows. Problem definitions and an overview of previous work are given in Subsection 1.1. The model of computation is described in Subsection 1.2. Additional concepts and fundamental operations are introduced in Subsection 1.3. As to the remainder of this paper, algorithms for the planar case are presented in Section 2, and the multidimensional case is treated in Section 3. (Further pointers to these sections are given below.) Virtualization is discussed in Section 4, and experimental results are presented in Section 5. Section 6 contains some final remarks.

1.1. Problem definitions and previous work. Let $x_j(p)$ denote the j:th coordinate of a point p in real d-dimensional space, $\boldsymbol{R}^d$. Then p *dominates* another point q in $\boldsymbol{R}^d$ if and only if $x_j(p) > x_j(q)$, for all $1 \leq j \leq d$. From this definition the following problem can be formulated.

PROBLEM 1. *Dominance Counting* (DOMd). Given a point set $S = \{p_1, p_2, \ldots, p_n\} \subset \boldsymbol{R}^d$ ($d \geq 2$), determine for each point $p \in S$ the number of points in S that are dominated by p, $dom(p, S)$.

This problem is often referred to as the *empirical cumulative distribution function*, and arises in a number of statistical applications [6]. A closely related concept is as follows. A point p is *maximal* in a point set S if and only no other point in S dominates p. The following problem arises in various applications, such as pattern classification and operations research [16].

PROBLEM 2. *Maxima* (MAXd). Given a point set $S = \{p_1, p_2, \ldots, p_n\} \subset \boldsymbol{R}^d$ ($d \geq 2$), determine for each point $p \in S$ whether it is maximal in S, $max(p, S)$.

The dimension d is usually regarded as a (small) constant. Both problems require sequential time $\Omega(n \log n)$ already in the planar case (see [3] and further references given therein).[1] A trivial parallel time lower bound is given in Subsection 1.2. But let us first give an overview of previous work, beginning with sequential algorithms.

The above problems can be efficiently solved by means of (multidimensional) divide-and-conquer. An $O(n \log^{d-1} n)$ solution for DOMd is presented in [6], and an $O(n \log^{\max\{1,d-2\}} n)$ solution for MAXd in [16]. Simpler descriptions of these algorithms, which are of particular interest for the present paper, are given in [3]. (Asymptotically faster algorithms, relying on elaborate data structuring techniques, can be found in [13, 25].) The number of maxima is usually much smaller than n. By this observation, the MAXd algorithm of [16] can be adapted to run in expected time $O(n \log n)$ [3], or even $O(n)$ [5, 7], under conditions that are quite general. (Another linear expected-time algorithm, based on an entirely different approach, is given in [4].) We return to this question in Section 6.

The above problems have also been studied for various models of parallel computation. Most algorithms proposed are based on some form of divide and conquer. Shared-memory computers and hypercubes are considered in [1, 2, 9, 15] and [8, 17, 18, 23], respectively. These papers deal mainly with DOMd and MAXd in lower dimensions. (The former problem is, on the other hand, often studied in a more general setting known as two-set planar dominance counting.) Algorithms for the mesh-connected computer are given in [10, 12, 21]. The last two papers, notably, address the multidimensional problems (and so does [9]). In Section 6, we briefly discuss these algorithms.

---

[1]All logarithms are taken to the base 2; $\log^k m$ is used as a shorthand for $(\log m)^k$.

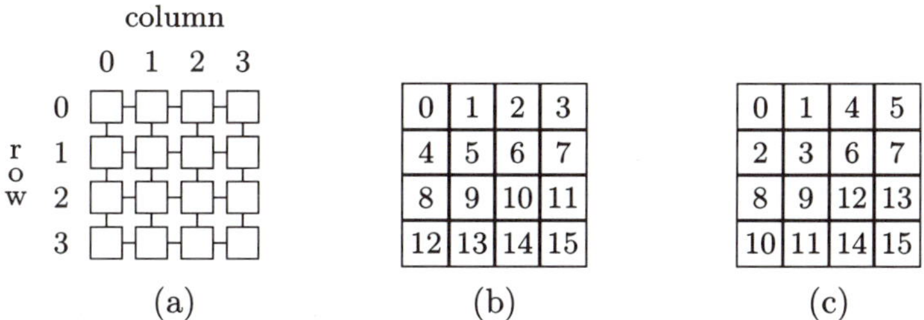

FIGURE 1. An MCC with 16 PEs (a), indexed according to row major order (b), and shuffled row major order (c).

· As already indicated, the parallel algorithms to be presented are essentially based on the (multidimensional) divide-and-conquer technique as described in [3]. The sequential algorithms given therein have also been used to develop virtualized versions of our algorithms (Section 4), and for experimental evaluation (Section 5). In the following two sections, we therefore in addition to our own work consider these sequential algorithms. The planar case is treated in Section 2. The DOM*2* algorithm of [3] is outlined in Subsection 2.1, and the corresponding parallel algorithm is given in Subsection 2.2. The MAX*2* problem is discussed in Subsection 2.3. Section 3 deals with the multidimensional case, and is organized in a similar way.

1.2. Model of computation. The mesh-connected computer (MCC) is a *single instruction* stream, *multiple data* stream (SIMD) computer, with $N = 4^k$ simple processing elements (PEs) arranged in a square grid and interconnected by horizontal and vertical communication links (see Figure 1(a)). Each PE has a local memory consisting of a fixed number of registers (words) of size at least $\log N$, and can perform standard arithmetic and logical operations on the contents of these registers in time $O(1)$. Each PE can also send or receive the contents of a register from a neighbor in time $O(1)$. (Concurrent communication must, however, go in the same direction: *north*, *east*, *south*, or *west*.)

Each PE stores its row and column indexes. In addition there is a designated register storing a scalar index. The indexing schemes used in this work are shown in Figure 1(b) and (c), and can be obtained from row and column indexes in time $O(1)$ and $O(\log N)$, respectively. In the latter case, the first quarter of the PEs forms one quadrant (*northwest*) of the mesh, the next quarter forms another quadrant (*northeast*), and so on, with this property holding recursively within each quadrant.

To provide some branching facilities, PEs may be programmed to ignore any particular instruction. Each PE can also resolve local indirect address references, independently of other PEs. (This feature, known as *addressing autonomy*, is really not part of the SIMD model, but is available on the MasPar MP–2. It is used only for the purpose of virtualization.)

To simplify exposition, we assume that $N = n$, that is, the number of PEs is equal to the number of input points, which hence is a power of four. (In Section 4, this assumption is relaxed.) At the outset, PEs are indexed in shuffled row major order, and input points are evenly (but randomly) distributed over the mesh, that is, one (arbitrary) point per PE. It is also assumed that no two input points share coordinate value x_j, for any $1 \leq j \leq d$. Obviously, to solve our problems we may have to combine point data stored at opposite corners of the mesh. Hence, both problems require time $\Omega(\sqrt{n})$ on the MCC already in the planar case.

FIGURE 2. An MCC with 16 PEs divided into 2-ranges (a), and 3-ranges (b). k-leftleaders are denoted by L, k-rightleaders by R, and k-neighbors by N. Within each k-range, PEs are indexed by row major order.

1.3. Fundamental operations. The core of MCC algorithms is the physical arrangement of data as provided by various data movement operations. (Hence, communication costs become a major concern.) The operations used in this paper are described below. However, for ease of reference, we first introduce som concepts (see Figure 2). A k-range, $0 \le k \le \log n$, is a sequence of PEs with shuffled row major indexes $i = i_0, i_0+1, \ldots, i_0+2^k-1$ such that $i_0 \bmod 2^k = 0$ (cf. Figure 1(c)). Thus, taken together k-ranges form a subdivision of the mesh into $n/2^k$ submeshes of size $2^{\lfloor k/2 \rfloor} \times 2^{\lceil k/2 \rceil}$. The two submeshes forming a $(k+1)$-range, $0 \le k \le \log n-1$, are distinguished as a k-leftrange and a k-rightrange according to the conditions $i \bmod 2^{k+1} < 2^k$ and $i \bmod 2^{k+1} \ge 2^k$, respectively. The smallest-indexed PE in a k-range is referred to as a k-leader; k-leftleaders and k-rightleaders are defined analogously. The k-neighbor of a k-rightleader, finally, is its neighbor from the corresponding k-leftrange. That is, for even k it is the PE to the west, for odd k the PE to the north.

The following data movement operations are restricted to k-ranges, and can be implemented to run in time $t(k) = O(2^{k/2})$, using a number of routing steps $c(k)$ to be specified for each operation separately. The row major ordering referred to below is shown in Figure 2. (In the algorithms to be presented, k-ranges are considered by increasing values of k. This additional indexing scheme can then simply be stored as local data, and be maintained in time $O(1)$ whenever the value of k is increased.) For the first three operations, the parameter a refers to a local word of memory, and upon completion this variable will contain the result.

$maximum(a, k)$: Compute the maximum value of a, and store the result at the k-leader. $c(k) = 2 \cdot 2^{k/2} - 2$ for even k, and $c(k) = 3 \cdot 2^{(k-1)/2} - 2$ for odd k.

$broadcast(a, k)$: Copy the value of a that is stored at the northeast corner (even k) or at the southwest corner (odd k). (These positions correspond to the position of a k-neighbor.) $c(k)$ is the same as for $maximum$.

$prefix\_sum(a, k)$: Compute the prefix sum of a with respect to row major order.[2] $c(k) = 3 \cdot 2^{k/2} - 3$ for even k, and $c(k) = 5 \cdot 2^{(k-1)/2} - 3$ for odd k.

For the last two operations, the parameter p is a local variable of *point* type.

$sort(p, j, k)$: Sort p by coordinate x_j into row major order. $c(k) = 14 \cdot 2^{k/2} - 4k - 14$ for even k, and $c(k) = 20 \cdot 2^{(k-1)/2} - 4k - 14$ for odd k.

$shuffled\_sort(p, j, k)$: Sort p by coordinate x_j into shuffled row major order. $c(k)$ is the same as for $sort$.

---

[2] The prefix sum s_i of a sequence $a_0, a_1, \ldots, a_{m-1}$ is defined by $s_i = \sum_{j=0}^{i} a_j$ $(0 \le i \le m-1)$.

To implement these operations we have used the *bitonic sort* algorithms of [20] and [24], respectively. The values of $c(k)$ are derived from the original papers. However, to reflect the true costs in our applications, $c(k)$ should be taken times the number of words that are required to store a point (and any associated information).

In addition to these range operations, we assume there is a routine for sorting the entire point set S into shuffled row major order. According to the characteristics given above, this can be done in time $O(\sqrt{n})$ for a total cost of $14\,(\sqrt{n}-1)-4\log n$ routing steps (within a constant factor). Observe that by sorting S into shuffled row major order by some coordinate x_j, we are guaranteed that the points residing in a k-leftrange have smaller x_j-values than the points residing in the corresponding k-rightrange, for any $0 \le k \le \log n - 1$.

2. Algorithms for the planar case

A sequential divide-and-conquer algorithm for DOM*2* is outlined in Subsection 2.1, and the corresponding parallel algorithm is presented in Subsection 2.2. The MAX*2* problem is treated in Subsection 2.3.

2.1. Divide and conquer for DOM*2*. Using divide and conquer, DOM*2* can be solved as follows. In the *division step*, the point set S is divided into a left subset S_1 and a right subset S_2 according to the median x_2-value in S, $\bar{x}_2$. In the *recursive step*, DOM*2* is solved for S_1 and S_2 separately. This process continues recursively until the current problem instance can be efficiently solved by brute force. (For the singleton set, specifically, the associated dominance value is zero.) In the *merge step*, finally, the solutions for S_1 and S_2 are combined to a solution for S.

We then use the following facts, both following immediately from the definition of dominance and the construction of S_1 and S_2.

    i. For any point $p \in S_1$: $dom(p, S) = dom(p, S_1)$.

    ii. For any point $q \in S_2$: $dom(q, S) = dom(q, S_2) + |\{\, p \in S_1 \mid x_1(q) > x_1(p)\,\}|$.

These facts transform readily into the following merge procedure (see Figure 3). First we project the input points perpendicularly onto the vertical line Λ defined by $\bar{x}_2$. Then we sweep Λ from below, maintaining an accumulator *count* (initialized to zero) as follows.

    i. When the projection of a point p lying to the left of Λ is encountered, the value of *count* is incremented by one.

    ii. When the projection of a point q lying to the right of Λ is encountered, the value of *count* is added to the dominance value associated with q.

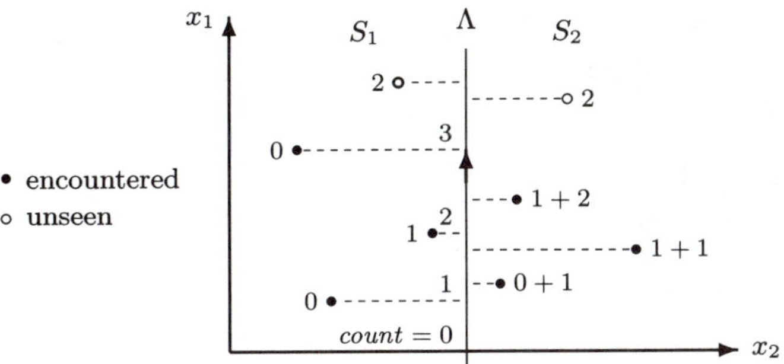

FIGURE 3. Merge procedure for DOM*2*.

A straightforward implementation of this scheme, where S is by x_1-coordinate in the merge step, yields $O(n \log^2 n)$ performance. This sequential algorithm is henceforth referred to as SDOM2. However, by using the *presorting* technique (see [**3**] for details), the merge step can be accomplished in linear time, resulting in optimal $O(n \log n)$ performance. Another, and perhaps more convenient, way to obtain this improvement is to make use of the fact that S_1 and S_2 are already sorted by x_1-coordinate when the recursive step is completed. That is, the desired x_1-sorted order of S can be established by means of a *sorted merge* operation. This faster version of SDOM2 is referred to as SFDOM2.

2.2. Parallel algorithm for DOM2. The algorithm, PDOM2, consists of two phases. In the *preprocessing phase*, the entire point set S is first sorted by x_2-coordinate into shuffled row major order. By this operation S is in effect divided into n singleton sets, each of which is contained in a 0-range. Then the dominance value, $dom(p)$, associated with each input point p is set to zero. This phase runs in time $O(\sqrt{n})$, and requires $28(\sqrt{n}-1) - 8\log n$ routing steps, since only coordinate values need to be effected by the sorting step.

To describe the *merging phase*, we use the notion of k-solutions in accordance with that of k-ranges. The output of the previous phase is thus n 0-solutions, and it remains to combine these subsolutions to a $(\log n)$-solution, that is, a solution for S. The computation is organized into $\log n$ stages. At each stage $k = 0, 1, \ldots, \log n - 1$, k-leftsolutions are merged with k-rightsolutions into $(k+1)$-solutions. Basically, this is accomplished by first sorting points stored in k-leftranges (left subsets) and points stored in k-rightranges (right subsets) jointly by x_1-coordinate into $(k+1)$-ranges (cf. Figure 3). Then, within each $(k+1)$-range, the "running total" of points originating from the left subset is calculated by means of a prefix sum operation, and dominance values for points originating from the right subset are updated accordingly. Details are given in Algorithm 1.

ALGORITHM 1. Merge procedure for PDOM2.

procedure *merge_dom*(**local** *point p, int k*);
local *int count*;
begin
0. **for** $i : i \bmod 2^{k+1} < 2^k$ **pardo**
        $origin(p) := L$;
    odpar;
    for $i : i \bmod 2^{k+1} \geq 2^k$ **pardo**
        $origin(p) := R$;
    odpar;
1. $sort(p, 1, k + 1)$;
2. **for** $i : origin(p) = L$ **pardo**
        $count := 1$;
    odpar;
    for $i : origin(p) = R$ **pardo**
        $count := 0$;
    odpar;
3. $prefix\_sum(count, k + 1)$;
4. **for** $i : origin(p) = R$ **pardo**
        $dom(p) := dom(p) + count$;
    odpar;
end

To analyze this phase, let us first decide the time, $t(k)$, and the number of routing steps, $c(k)$, that are required for merging at stage k. Steps 0, 2, and 4 can be accomplished in time $O(1)$, and no communication is involved. Hence, we can focus on steps 1 and 3. For step 1, specifically, we assume that the information associated with each input point p, i.e. $dom(p)$ and $origin(p)$, can be fit into one word of memory. (The $origin$ information needs only one bit.) That is, three words are required for p. The following characteristics can then be obtained from the performance figures provided in Subsection 1.3.

$$t(k) = O(2^{k/2}).$$

$$c(k) = \begin{cases} 65 \cdot 2^{k/2} - 12k - 57 & \text{for even } k, \\ 90 \cdot 2^{(k-1)/2} - 12k - 57 & \text{for odd } k. \end{cases}$$

To complete the analysis, it remains to decide the total time, $T(n)$, and the total number of routing steps, $C(n)$, that are required by the merging phase. These quantities can be computed according to the following formulae.

$$(1) \qquad T(n) = \sum_{k=0}^{\log n - 1} t(k)$$

$$(2) \qquad C(n) = \sum_{k=0}^{\log n - 1} c(k)$$

Simple calculations give $T(n) = O(\sqrt{n})$ and $C(n) = 155\,(\sqrt{n}-1) - 6\log^2 n - 51\log n$. To summarize, PDOM2 runs in optimal time $O(\sqrt{n})$, and the communication costs amount to $183\,(\sqrt{n}-1) - 6\log^2 n - 59\log n$.

Let us finally consider how the communication costs can be reduced. Similarly to the sequential case, we notice that k-ranges are already sorted by x_1-coordinate at each invocation of the merge procedure. That is, step 1 can be accomplished by means of a sorted merge operation. To this end, we have used the *bitonic merge* algorithm of [20], that is, a subroutine of the *sort* operation. According to [20], the number of routing steps required for merging two adjacent k-ranges is $6 \cdot 2^{k/2} - 4$ for even k, and $8 \cdot 2^{(k-1)/2} - 4$ for odd k. However, to make this subroutine applicable, k-rightranges must first be rearranged from ascending into descending x_1-sorted order. This takes $4 \cdot 2^{k/2} - 4$ routing steps for even k, and $6 \cdot 2^{(k-1)/2} - 4$ for odd k. (Again, these figures should be taken times three.) To summarize, we now have the following characteristics.

$$c(k) = \begin{cases} 35 \cdot 2^{k/2} - 27 & \text{for even } k, \\ 48 \cdot 2^{(k-1)/2} - 27 & \text{for odd } k. \end{cases}$$

By Formula 2, then, $C(n) = 83\,(\sqrt{n}-1) - 27\log n$. Hence, for this faster version of PDOM2, PFDOM2, the communication costs add up to $111\,(\sqrt{n}-1) - 35\log n$.

2.3. Parallel algorithm for MAX2. In order to use divide and conquer, we may rephrase the facts stated in Subsection 2.1 as follows (see Figure 4).

   i. For any point $p \in S_1$: $max(p, S) = max(p, S_1) \wedge x_1(p) \geq \max\{x_1(q) \mid q \in S_2\}$.
   ii. For any point $q \in S_2$: $max(q, S) = max(q, S_2)$.

Furthermore, for the singleton set the associated maxima status is 1. Given these facts, it is a simple matter to devise a sequential algorithm, SMAX2, with optimal $O(n \log n)$ performance. Let us therefore turn our attention to the parallel analogue, PMAX2, immediately.

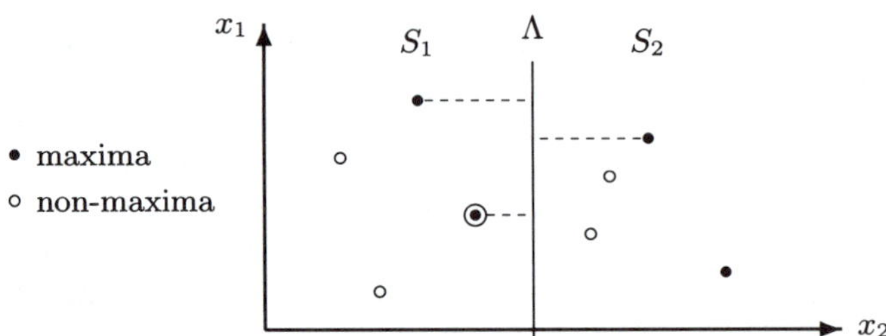

FIGURE 4. Merge procedure for MAX2.

The overall structure of PMAX2 is similar to that of PDOM2. (In this case, of course, preprocessing involves setting the Boolean attribute, $max(p)$, associated with each input point p to 1.) The merge procedure is given as Algorithm 2.

ALGORITHM 2. Merge procedure for PMAX2.

procedure $merge\_max(\mathbf{local}\ point\ p,\ int\ k)$;
local $real\ x1 = x_1(p)$;
begin
1. **for** $i : i\ \mathbf{mod}\ 2^{k+1} \geq 2^k$ **pardo**
        $maximum(x1,\ k)$;
    odpar;
2. **for** $i : i\ \mathbf{mod}\ 2^{k+1} = 2^k$ **pardo**
        if $odd(k)\ north.x1 := x1$; **else** $west.x1 := x1$; **fi**;
    odpar;
3. **for** $i : i\ \mathbf{mod}\ 2^{k+1} < 2^k$ **pardo**
        $broadcast(x1,\ k)$;
    odpar;
4. **for** $i : i\ \mathbf{mod}\ 2^{k+1} < 2^k$ **pardo**
        $max(p) := max(p)\ \mathbf{and}\ (x_1(p) \geq x1)$;
    odpar;
end

First, the largest x_1-value within each k-rightrange is reported to the k-rightleader. Next, these values are passed to the corresponding k-neighbors. In step 3, then, each k-neighbor broadcasts this value within its k-leftrange. By these three steps, each point p in a left subset has received the largest x_1-value from the corresponding right subset. Hence, it remains only to examine whether the maxima status for p should be changed (cf. Figure 4).

As to the analysis, steps 2 and 4 can be performed in time $O(1)$, and only one routing step is needed (in step 2). Performance figures for steps 1 and 3 are given in Subsection 1.3. To summarize, Algorithm 2 has the following characteristics.

$$t(k) = O(2^{k/2}).$$
$$c(k) = \begin{cases} 4 \cdot 2^{k/2} - 3 & \text{for even } k. \\ 6 \cdot 2^{(k-1)/2} - 3 & \text{for odd } k, \end{cases}$$

Then, according to Formulae 1 and 2, $T(n) = O(\sqrt{n})$ and $C(n) = 10\,(\sqrt{n}-1) - 3\log n$. Recalling the costs for preprocessing (cf. Subsection 2.2), we conclude that PMAX2 runs in optimal time $O(\sqrt{n})$, for a total cost of $38\,(\sqrt{n}-1) - 11\log n$ routing steps.

3. Algorithms for the multidimensional case

In Subsection 3.1, we consider how the sequential DOM*2* algorithm can be extended for the multidimensional problem. A parallel algorithm for DOM*d* is then presented in Subsection 3.2. Algorithms for MAX*d* are discussed in Subsection 3.3.

3.1. Divide and conquer for DOM*d*. Let us first consider how DOM*3* can be solved by divide and conquer. Assume that the point set S has been divided into a left subset S_1 and a right subset S_2 according to the median x_3-value in S, $\bar{x}_3$, and that DOM*3* has been solved for S_1 and S_2 separately. For each point $q \in S_2$, it then remains to decide the number of points $p \in S_1$ such that $x_1(q) > x_1(p)$ and $x_2(q) > x_2(p)$ (cf. Subsection 2.1). Thus, the problem encountered in the merge step is a slightly different version of DOM*2*.

By this observation, the final dominance values for the points in S_2 can be computed as follows (see Figure 5). Let Π be the plane orthogonal to the x_3-axis defined by $\bar{x}_3$. First, we project the input points perpendicularly onto Π. Let $P = \{\bar{p}_1, \bar{p}_2, \dots, \bar{p}_n\}$ be the set of projected points. Then, we solve the planar problem for P by divide and conquer, using the following slightly modified rules in the merge step (cf. Subsection 2.1).

i. When the projection (onto Λ) of a point $\bar{p}$ lying to the left of Λ is encountered, the value of *count* is incremented by one if and only if $p \in S_1$.

ii. When the projection (onto Λ) of a point $\bar{q}$ lying to the right of Λ is encountered, the value of *count* is added to the dominance value associated with q if and only if $q \in S_2$.

Informally, compared to the rules for the original planar problem, the restriction added in (i) prevents a point $q \in S_2$ from being considered by other points in S, hence from being reconsidered by other points in S_2. Similarly, the restriction added in (ii) prevents a point $p \in S_1$ from considering other points in S, hence from reconsidering other points in S_1. If any of these restrictions is violated, the input point concerned is simply ignored in the merge step.

The solution outlined above is an instance of multidimensional divide-and-conquer: *To solve a problem of size n in d dimensions, we first solve recursively two problems of size $n/2$ in d dimensions, and then recursively one problem of size n in $d-1$ dimensions.* For our particular application, we only have to incorporate some "bookkeeping" into this general scheme, to keep track of which input points are "active" when the planar case is reached by the recursive calls through dimensions (cf. Figure 5). Let us discuss this bookkeeping somewhat in detail.

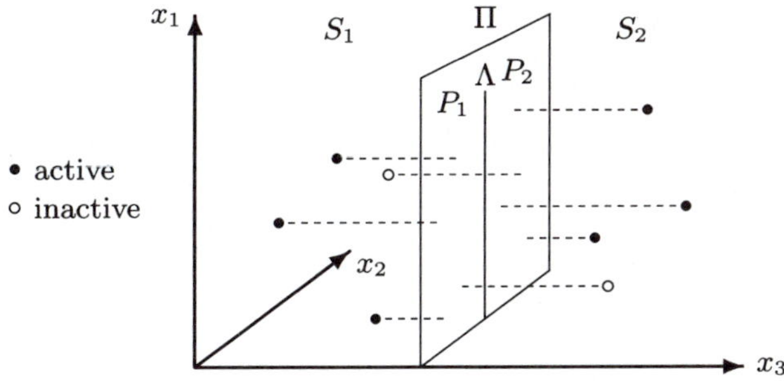

FIGURE 5. Merge procedure for DOM*3*.

Generalizing the three-dimensional case, a point $p \in S_1$ is active if and only if each of its successive projections $\bar{p}^j$ in j-dimensional space, $j = d - 1, \ldots, 3, 2$, lies to the left of the hyperplane Π^j dividing the input points currently considered in dimension j. Similarly, a point $q \in S_2$ is active if and only if $\bar{q}^j$ lies to the right of Π^j, for $j = d - 1, \ldots, 3, 2$. (Cf. Figure 5, where Π^2 is the dividing line Λ.)

This information can be passed through dimensions via a d-dimensional Boolean attribute, $active(p)$, associated with each input point p, and maintained as follows.

$$active(p, j) = \begin{cases} 1 & \text{if } j = d, \\ active(p, j+1) \wedge p \in S_1 & \text{if } j < d \text{ and } \bar{p}^j \text{ lies to the left of } \Pi^j, \\ active(p, j+1) \wedge p \in S_2 & \text{if } j < d \text{ and } \bar{p}^j \text{ lies to the right of } \Pi^j. \end{cases}$$

The restrictions posed by the modified planar merge procedure are then captured by the condition $active(p, 2) = 1$. Moreover, at the expense of a slightly increased running time, this procedure can be used also for the original planar problem, since the above condition then will be satisfied for all input points.

A straightforward implementation of the above scheme, where input points are sorted by x_1-coordinate in the modified planar merge procedure, yields $O(n \log^d n)$ performance (for any fixed dimension $d \geq 2$). Moreover, by using the techniques discussed in Subsection 2.1, the running time of this sequential algorithm, SDOMd, can be improved by a logaritmic factor. That is, the faster version thus obtained, SFDOMd, exhibits $O(n \log^{d-1} n)$ performance. (See [3] for details and analysis.)

3.2. Parallel algorithm for DOMd. The algorithm for the general case, PDOMd, resembles the algorithm for the planar case, PDOM2. The modifications required are mainly located to the merge procedure (Algorithm 1), which becomes recursive with respect to dimension. For each input point p, we will also maintain a d-dimensional Boolean attribute, $active(p)$, as explained in Subsection 3.1. For the purpose of analysis, it is assumed that this attribute can be fit into one word of memory. Thus, the information associated with p now requires two words.

In the preprocessing phase, sorting is done by x_d-coordinate, and initialization involves setting $active(p, d)$ to 1, for all input points p. This phase runs in time $O(d\sqrt{n})$, and requires $14d\sqrt{n} - O(d \log n)$ routing steps.

Similarly to the planar case, the merging phase is organized into $\log n$ stages. At each stage $k = 0, 1, \ldots, \log n - 1$, k-leftsolutions and k-rightsolutions for the d-dimensional problem are merged into $(k+1)$-solutions by means of an extended merge procedure (see Algorithm 3). Prior to each invocation, input points have their origin recorded, as was done in step 0 of Algorithm 1. Steps 1 to 4 of these two algorithms are basically the same, but now input points may be "ignored" on certain occasions. Steps 5 and 6 implement the recursive calls through dimensions. Substep 6.1, specifically, maintains the $active$ information according to the rule stated in Subsection 3.1.

To simplify analysis of this phase, the costs for prefix sum computations are excluded. Moreover, the number of routing steps needed for sorting n items when n is an odd power of two, $20\sqrt{n/2} - O(\log n)$, is approximated by $14\sqrt{n} - O(\log n)$. The total time, $T(n, d)$, that is required by the merging phase is then given by the following recurrence, where $2 \leq j \leq d$.

$$(3) \qquad T(n, j) = \begin{cases} O(1) & \text{if } n = 1; \\ T(n/2, j) + O(d\sqrt{n}) & \text{if } n \geq 2, j = 2; \\ T(n/2, j) + O(d\sqrt{n}) + T(n, j-1) & \text{if } n \geq 2, j \geq 3. \end{cases}$$

ALGORITHM 3. Merge procedure for PDOMd.

procedure $merge\_dom(\textbf{local }point\ p,\ int\ d,\ int\ k)$;
var $int\ l$;
local $int\ count$;
begin
    if $d = 2$
1. $sort(p,\ 1,\ k+1)$;
2.   **for** $i : origin(p) = L$ **pardo**
        if $active(p, 2)$ $count := 1$; **else** $count := 0$; **fi**;
      odpar;
      for $i : origin(p) = R$ **pardo**
        $count := 0$;
      odpar;
3. $prefix\_sum(count,\ k+1)$;
4.   **for** $i : origin(p) = R$ **pardo**
        if $active(p, 2)$ $dom(p) := dom(p) + count$; **fi**;
      odpar;
    else /* $d \geq 3$ */
5. $shuffled\_sort(p,\ d-1,\ k+1)$;
6.   **for** $l = 0$ **to** k **do**
6.1.   **for** $i : i \bmod 2^{l+1} < 2^l$ **pardo**
        $active(p, d-1) := active(p, d)$ **and** $(origin(p) = L)$;
      odpar;
      for $i : i \bmod 2^{l+1} \geq 2^l$ **pardo**
        $active(p, d-1) := active(p, d)$ **and** $(origin(p) = R)$;
      odpar;
6.2. $merge\_dom(p,\ d-1,\ l)$;
      od;
    fi;
end

Similarly, the total number of routing steps, $C(n, d)$, that is required by this phase is given by the following recurrence.

$$(4)\quad C(n, j) = \begin{cases} 0 & \text{if } n = 1; \\ C(n/2, j) + 14\,(d+2)\sqrt{n} - O(d \log n) & \text{if } n \geq 2,\ j = 2; \\ C(n/2, j) + 14\,(d+2)\sqrt{n} - O(d \log n) + C(n, j-1) & \text{if } n \geq 2,\ j \geq 3. \end{cases}$$

The solutions to Equations 3 and 4 are as follows.

$$T(n, d) = O(d\,(2 + \sqrt{2}\,)^d \sqrt{n}\,),$$

$$C(n, d) = 14\,(d + 2)\left(\sqrt{2}\,(2 + \sqrt{2}\,)^{d-1} - \sqrt{2}\right)\sqrt{n} - O(d \log^d n).$$

To conclude, PDOMd runs in time $O(d\,(2+\sqrt{2}\,)^d\sqrt{n}\,)$, which is asymptotically optimal for any fixed dimension $d \geq 2$, and the communication costs amount to $14\,(d+2)\left(\sqrt{2}\,(2+\sqrt{2}\,)^{d-1} - \sqrt{2} + 1\right)\sqrt{n} - 28\sqrt{n} - O(d \log^d n)$.

To reduce the communication costs, finally, we can replace the *sort* operation in step 1 of Algorithm 3 by a sorted merge operation, as described in Subsection 2.2. For this faster version of PDOMd, PFDOMd, the total number of routing steps is $14\,(d+2)\left(\frac{3+\sqrt{2}}{2+\sqrt{8}}(2+\sqrt{2}\,)^{d-1} - \sqrt{2} + 1\right)\sqrt{n} - 28\sqrt{n} - O(d \log^{d-1} n)$. Depending on the dimension d, the communication costs are hence reduced by at least 35 % (for large n). For the case $d = 2$, specifically, the improvement is about 45 %.

3.3. Parallel algorithms for MAXd. By now, it should be easy to see how the MAX2 algorithms discussed in Subsection 2.3 can be adapted for the general case. The parallel MAXd algorithm, PMAXd, runs in time $O(d\,(2+\sqrt{2}\,)^d\sqrt{n}\,)$, which is asymptotically optimal for any fixed dimension $d \geq 2$, and requires roughly the same number of routing steps as PDOMd does in one dimension less (for $d \geq 3$). The sequential analogue, SMAXd, runs in time $O(n\log^{d-1} n)$. However, according to the overview given in Subsection 1.1, we can obtain $O(n\log^{d-2} n)$ performance for $d \geq 3$, still using multidimensional divide-and-conquer. Let us investigate this for the three-dimensional case (see Figure 5).

More precisely, assume that MAX3 has been solved for S_1 and S_2 separately. For each (maximal) point $p \in S_1$, it then remains to examine whether there are points $q \in S_2$ such that $x_1(q) > x_1(p)$ and $x_2(q) > x_2(p)$ (cf. Subsection 2.3). To this end, we first sort S by x_2-coordinate. (Actually, either presorting or the alternative technique discussed in Subsection 2.1 should be used here to obtain the stated improvement.) Then, we scan the sorted list from right to left, keeping track of the largest x_1-value in S_2 encountered so far, $\hat{x}_1$. When a (maximal) point $p \in S_1$ is encountered, we now only have to examine whether $x_1(p) \geq \hat{x}_1$.

The parallel analogue of the sequential MAX3 algorithm outlined above closely resembles PFDOM2. Basically, we only have to replace the prefix sum operation used by the merge procedure (i.e. Algorithm 1) with a "postfix" maximum. Hence, following the pattern in Subsection 3.2, we can obtain a faster parallel algorithm for MAXd, PFMAXd, that runs in time $O(d\,(2+\sqrt{2}\,)^d\sqrt{n}\,)$ for $d \geq 3$, and requires roughly the same number of routing steps as PFDOMd does in one dimension less. Moreover, compared to PMAXd, the communication costs are reduced by (at least) 35 %. (Similar remarks apply in the sequential case.)

4. Virtualization

So far we have assumed that $N = n$, that is, the number of PEs is equal to the number of input points. Clearly, by the property of shuffled row major indexing, our results are valid also when $n < N$. The problems treated in this paper arise, however, in contexts where the problem size by far may exceed the size of existing parallel computers. In this section, we briefly discuss virtualization, that is, how to handle the case when there are $m = n/N \geq 1$ input points stored at each PE. More precisely, we sketch how PDOM2 can be adapted for this situation, so as to run in time $O(m\log m + m\sqrt{N}\,)$, provided that addressing autonomy is available.[3] (Communication costs will increase approximately by a factor m.)

Let us first say a few words about the fundamental operations involved, assuming an underlying virtual indexing scheme being (implicitly) defined by PE indexes and local indexes in the indicated lexicographic order. The bitonic sort algorithms of [20, 24] can be adapted for our current needs so as to run in time $O(m\sqrt{N}\,)$ simply by changing the interpretation of what constitutes an item in the so-called compare-exchange steps performed by these algorithms, provided that local sorted order is initially established (see [22] for details.) Virtualization of the prefix sum operation is straightforward; running time $O(m + \sqrt{N}\,)$ is then obtainable. The above performance figures apply in a "global" setting; when restricted to k-ranges, these operations can be completed in time $O(m \cdot 2^{k/2})$ and $O(m+2^{k/2})$, respectively.

---

[3]By this feature, merging and sorting can be locally performed in time $O(m)$ and $O(m\log m)$, respectively. This also suggests that DOM2 can be locally solved in time $O(m\log m)$.

Now, let us consider PDOM2 (cf. Subsection 2.2). The preprocessing phase can be adapted as follows. To prepare for sorting the entire point set S, input points are first locally sorted by x_2-coordinate. Once S is sorted, SFDOM2 is executed on each PE separately. (As a result, each 0-range stores a subsolution of size m.) To facilitate further sorting in the merging phase, finally, input points are locally sorted by x_1-coordinate. Hence, this phase runs in time $O(m \log m + m\sqrt{N})$.

The merging phase proceeds in $\log N$ stages. At each stage $k = 0, 1, \ldots, \log N - 1$, k-leftsolutions and k-rightsolutions, corresponding to subsolutions of size $m \cdot 2^k$, are merged into $(k+1)$-solutions by means of a slightly modified merge procedure (cf. Algorithm 1). Since the minor changes required are fairly obvious, we simply state that steps 0, 2, and 4 can be performed in time $O(m)$, step 1 in time $O(m \cdot 2^{k/2})$, and step 3 in time $O(m + 2^{k/2})$. Hence, this phase runs in time $O(m\sqrt{N})$.

The virtualization technique outlined above can also be applied to PDOMd. The analysis becomes, however, quite complicated since a local merge procedure, similar to SFDOMd, has to be taken into service (cf. steps 5 and 6 of Algorithm 3.) Let us therefore simply refer to experimental results presented in the next section.

5. Experimental results

The algorithms presented were implemented on a massively parallel computer, the MasPar MP–2, and experimentally evaluated. Some results, including comparisons with the corresponding sequential algorithms, are presented in this section. But let us first provide a background.

The MP–2 is a mesh-connected computer of SIMD type with $N = 16,384$ simple processing elements, providing additional features such as *global communication* and *addressing autonomy* (cf. Subsection 1.2). Our algorithms (see Table 1), including the fundamental operations listed in Subsection 1.3, were coded in MPL, a C-based language extended with data parallel constructs. As far as possible, we have only used features of MPL/MP–2 that comply with the MCC model of computation.[4] Thus, it has not been our ambition to develop fast algorithms for this particular machine. (Besides, shuffled row major indexing is not supported.)

TABLE 1. Time complexity of parallel algorithms.

PDOMd	$O(d\,(2+\sqrt{2}\,)^{d}\,\sqrt{n}\,)$	$d \geq 2$
PFDOMd	$O(d\,(2+\sqrt{2}\,)^{d}\,\sqrt{n}\,)$	$d \geq 2$
PMAXd	$O(d\,(2+\sqrt{2}\,)^{d}\,\sqrt{n}\,)$	$d \geq 2$
PFMAXd	$O(d\,(2+\sqrt{2}\,)^{d}\,\sqrt{n}\,)$	$d \geq 3$

The corresponding sequential algorithms (see Table 2) were implemented in C, and executed on a common workstation, the SUN SPARCstation 5/70. Sorting is performed by means of quicksort with median-of-three partitioning.[5] In addition, SFDOMd and SFMAXd rely on the alternative technique advocated in Subsection 2.1, rather than the presorting technique suggested in e.g. [**3**].

---

[4] The system supports no automatic virtualization; instead the physical machine is exposed to the user. That is, one can actually implement the virtualization strategy outlined in this paper.

[5] For the purpose of virtualization, the sequential algorithms were also implemented as local procedures on the MP–2. In this case, mergesort rather than quicksort is employed.

TABLE 2. Time complexity of corresponding sequential algorithms.

SDOMd	$O(n \log^d n)$	$d \geq 2$
SFDOMd	$O(n \log^{d-1} n)$	$d \geq 2$
SMAXd	$O(n \log^{d-1} n)$	$d \geq 2$
SFMAXd	$O(n \log^{d-2} n)$	$d \geq 3$

In the experiments presented, input points were randomly drawn from a uniform distribution over the d-dimensional unit cube.[6] Other experiments showed, however, that the parallel algorithms are quite insensitive in this regard. This is due to their "oblivious" nature; the same number of routing steps is performed (for fixed n, that is), irrespective of the actual point distribution. The sequential algorithms are somewhat more vulnerable, mainly because quicksort is employed. Still, the underlying distribution is not crucial for the overall picture conveyed by our experiments. (This was also confirmed by other experiments.) It should be added that, for each particular input size, the execution times finally reported were averaged over the execution times actually recorded for five different input sets.

Finally, for the parallel algorithms some predictions concerning execution times were made. These predictions were based on the communication costs analysis in Subsection 3.2, and turned out to be quite accurate (even though a relatively small portion of the total execution time is actually spent on communication per se), as we shall see. Using PDOMd and the case $d = 2$ as a norm, we have compiled the results of this analysis into Table 3 (lower-order terms were omitted). These results are also relevant for the parallel MAXd algorithms, as explained in Subsection 3.3.

TABLE 3. Normalized communication costs for parallel algorithms.

	$d = 2$	$d = 3$	$d = 4$	$d = 5$	$d = 6$	$d = 7$
PDOMd	1.00	5.00	21.3	85.6	335	1,290
PFDOMd	0.56	3.14	13.7	55.2	216	832

In the first set of experiments, performance was studied for the case $n \leq N$. Execution times were recorded for seven distinct input sizes $n : 256 \leq n \leq 16,384$ (see Figure 6). For $d = 2$, the parallel algorithms are about ten times faster than the corresponding sequential algorithms when $n = 16,384$. As indicated by the case $d = 3$, this modest "speedup" tends to grow somewhat by increasing dimension d. (The cases $d=4$ and 5 were also investigated; the speedup is about 20 when $d=5$.) A detailed analysis of the sequential algorithms could partially explain this behaviour. (For results in this direction, see [**3**] and further references given therein.)

Let us also relate to theoretical results (cf. dotted curves). As compared to PDOMd, the actual improvement obtained by PFDOMd is close to the expected improvement. A similar remark applies to the parallel MAXd algorithms, though the analysis was less precise for these algorithms.

---

[6]As suggested by Tables 1 and 2, we have consistently used multidimensional algorithms also for the planar problems (cf. Subsection 3.1).

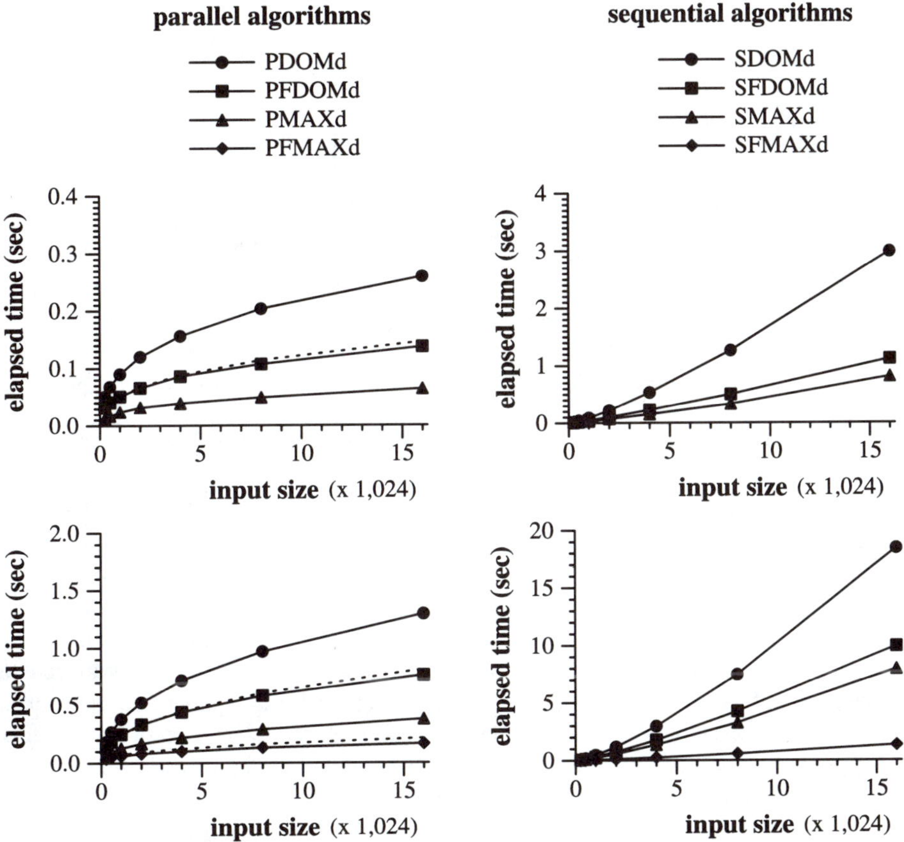

FIGURE 6. Performance of parallel and sequential algorithms for $d = 2$ and 3.

Figure 7 summarizes the performance of our algorithms in the multidimensional case. Execution times for PFMAXd are indeed comparable to execution times for PFDOMd in one dimension less, but the corresponding approximation for PMAXd and PDOMd appears to be somewhat less accurate. Based on the case $d = 2$, execution times for PDOMd were predicted for dimensions $d \geq 3$ (cf. dotted curve). The deviation in higher dimensions could partially be explained by simplifications used in calculations for Table 3 (for this relatively small value of n).

Figure 7 demonstrates the validity of the $O(d\,(2+\sqrt{2}\,)^d\,\sqrt{n}\,)$ time upper bound for our algorithms (cf. dotted curve). However, Figure 7 also reveals that these algorithms become less attractive in higher dimension. For the sake of comparison, we have implemented a parallel *brute-force* method that runs in time $O(dn)$ and requires $4d\,(n - \sqrt{n}\,)$ routing steps. When $n = 16,384$, such a method should be competitive already for $d = 4$ or 5, depending on problem (cf. dashed curve).

In the second set of experiments, performance was studied for the case $n \geq N$. Execution times for virtualized PFDOMd were recorded for nine distinct input sizes $n : 16,384 \leq n \leq 4,194,304$, that is, for values $m = n/N : 1 \leq m \leq 256$ (see Figure 8). (Due to limitations of the workstation, the "speedup" was recorded only for $n \leq 524,288$, that is, for $m \leq 32$.) Needless to say, experimental results should be interpreted carefully for these relatively small values of m.

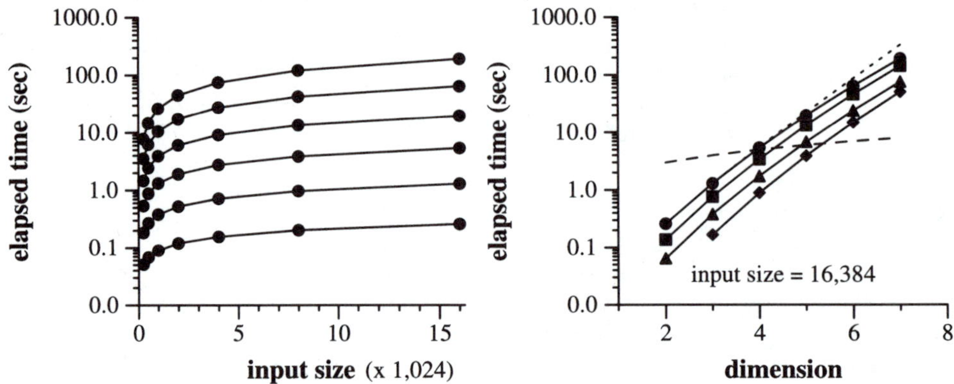

FIGURE 7. Performance of parallel algorithms for $d = 2, 3, \ldots, 7$.

For $d = 2$, overheads for virtualization are about 40 % (cf. Figure 6). However, the execution time is close to linear in m, and the speedup therefore tends to grow logarithmically in m. (Let us recall that SFDOMd has $O(n \log^{d-1} n)$ performance.) As indicated by the case $d = 3$, overheads for virtualization are somewhat larger for $d \geq 3$, about 70 %. More importantly, however, execution times remain almost linear in m, and the speedup therefore tends to grow somewhat faster by increasing dimension d. (The cases $d = 4$ and 5 were also investigated; the speedup is about 24 when $d = 5$ and $m = 16$.) It should finally be noticed that the parallel brute-force method becomes less competitive in this context (at least when local computations are also carried out in a brute-force manner).

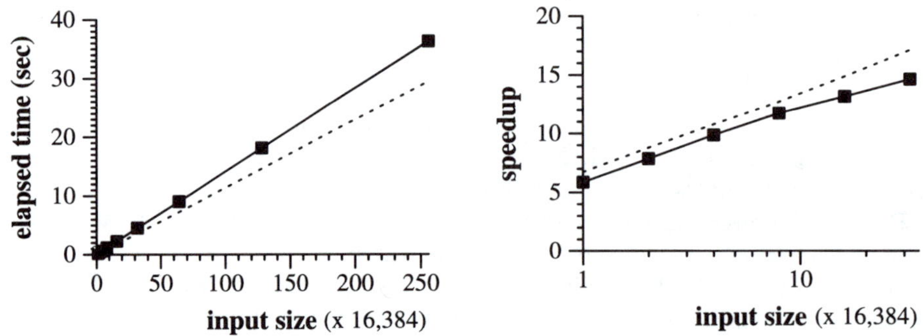

FIGURE 8. Performance of virtualized PFDOMd for $d = 2$ and 3. For $d = 3$ (dotted curve), execution times should be taken times 10.

6. Final remarks

We have presented efficient mesh-connected computer (MCC) algorithms for the d-dimensional Dominance Counting (DOMd) and Maxima (MAXd) problems. Our algorithms are based on the multidimensional divide-and-conquer technique of [3], and run in time $O(d\,(2 + \sqrt{2}\,)^d \sqrt{n}\,)$ on a mesh of size $\sqrt{n} \times \sqrt{n}$, which is optimal for any fixed dimension $d \geq 2$. To determine constant factors hidden by the asymptotic analysis, communication costs have been closely examined. To obtain constant-time improvements, a technique analogous to presorting has been used. Virtualization has been discussed. In the planar case, specifically, our algorithms run in time $O(m \log m + m\sqrt{N}\,)$ on a mesh of size $\sqrt{N} \times \sqrt{N}$, where $m = N/n \geq 1$. It remains, however, to analyze performance in higher dimensions.

As mentioned in the introduction, MCC algorithms for DOMd and MAXd have also been studied by [10, 12, 21]. The first paper, i.e. [10], deals mainly with the planar problems. The algorithms presented can be extended to higher dimensions, but are not optimal for $d \geq 4$. The last two papers address the general problems. The algorithms proposed are also based on multidimensional divide-and-conquer, and run in time $O((\sqrt{2}+1)^d\sqrt{n}\,)$ [21], or even $O(\sqrt{n}\,)$ [12], according to the authors. It is, however, not clear whether these results are due to more novel applications of multidimensional divide-and-conquer, or simply reflect less scrupulous analyses.[7] Anyway, in our case the $d\,(2 + \sqrt{2}\,)^d$ coefficient could be reduced by successively dropping the last coordinate in the recursive calls through dimensions. This would, on the other hand, call for further data movements (and auxiliary information) when such calls are completed, thereby increasing constant factors in the running time expression. It would hence be worthwhile only in higher dimensions. But then, again, a parallel $O(dn)$ brute-force method would become increasingly competitive, at least for realistic input sizes. Still, this matter should be further investigated.

We have also presented experimental results for the MasPar MP–2, a massively parallel computer with $N = 16,384$ simple processing elements. These results have by far confirmed theoretical results presented in this paper. To better assess the performance in practice, comparisons with the corresponding sequential algorithms were included in the experiments. For limited input sizes $(n \leq N)$, running times on the MP–2 would be just about comparable to running times that could be obtained on powerful workstations. For larger input sizes $(n \geq N)$, however, our algorithms would become increasingly competitive, due to a simple yet efficient technique used for virtualization. The "speedup" would, of course, also be improved if the mesh size were larger or the constituent elements faster (relative to conventional systems). For parallel computers like the MP–2, however, significant such developments are not likely within the near future. Hence, virtualization remains an important issue, and should certainly be addressed more carefully than has been done in this paper.

One might finally question how the algorithms of [3], hence our algorithms, compare empirically to the other sequential algorithms listed in the introduction. To our knowledge, no experimental results have been published for the worst-case efficient algorithms of [13, 25], but these asymptotically faster algorithms would probably not perform any better in practice since they are fairly complicated.[8] The linear expected-time algorithms of [4, 5, 7] would, on the other hand, outperform the MAXd algorithms of [3] in most cases (for experimental evidence, see e.g. [4]). Let us therefore recall that the MAXd algorithms of [3] can be adapted to run in expected time $O(n \log n)$, for a wide class of point distributions. This can simply be obtained by removing input points found to be non-maximal in the recursive step from further consideration. Even though we can "only" hope for a constant-time improvement, the same idea should indeed be studied in a parallel setting.

---

[7]The analysis in [12] is obviously somewhat simplified.

[8]We are actually not aware of any other experimental results for the algorithms of [3] either. In [4] it is indicated that no such results have previously been published.

ACKNOWLEDGEMENTS. The algorithms presented were developed on the Mas-Par MP–1 at the National Supercomputer Center (NSC), Linköping University, Sweden. Experimental results were recorded on the MasPar MP–2 at the Parallel Processing Laboratory (Parallab), University of Bergen, Norway. The author would also like to thank an anonymous referee for helpful comments and suggestions.

References

1. M.J. Atallah, R. Cole, and M.T. Goodrich, *Cascading divide-and-conquer: A technique for designing parallel algorithms*, SIAM Journal on Computing **18** (1989), 499–532.
2. M.J. Atallah and M.T. Goodrich, *Efficient plane sweeping in parallel*, Proc. 2nd Annual ACM Symposium on Computational Geometry, 1986, pp. 216–225.
3. J.L. Bentley, *Multidimensional divide-and-conquer*, Communications of the ACM **23** (1980), 214–229.
4. J.L. Bentley, K.L. Clarkson, and D.B. Levine, *Fast linear expected-time algorithms for computing maxima and convex hulls*, Algorithmica **9** (1993), 168–183.
5. J.L. Bentley, H.T. Kung, M. Schkolnick, and C.D. Thompson, *On the average number of maxima in a set of vectors and applications*, Journal of the ACM **25** (1978), 536–543.
6. J.L. Bentley and M.I. Shamos, *A problem in multivariate statistics: Algorithm, data structure, and applications*, Proc. 15th Annual Allerton Conference on Communication, Control, and Computing, 1977, pp. 193–201.
7. ______, *Divide and conquer for linear expected time*, Information Processing Letters **7** (1978), 87–91.
8. P. Berthomé and A.G. Ferreira, *Efficiently solving geometric problems with large hypercube multiprocessors*, Proc. IMACS/IFAC International Symposium on Parallel and Distributed Computing in Engineering Systems, 1992, pp. 123–128.
9. I.W. Chan, *Parallel algorithms for the ECDF problem*, Proc. of a JSPS Seminar. Parallel Programming Systems, 1993, pp. 192–200.
10. F. Dehne, $O(n^{1/2})$ *algorithms for the maximal elements and ECDF searching problem on a mesh-connected parallel computer*, Information Processing Letters **22** (1986), 303–306.
11. F. Dehne and J.-R. Sack, *A survey of parallel computational geometry algorithms*, Proc. 4th International Workshop on Parallel Processing by Cellular Automata and Arrays, 1988, pp. 73–88.
12. F. Dehne and I. Stojmenović, *An optimal parallel solution to the ECDF searching problem for higher dimensions on a mesh-of-processors*, Proc. 25th Annual Allerton Conference on Communication, Control, and Computing, 1987, pp. 660–661.
13. H.N. Gabow, J.L. Bentley, and R.E. Tarjan, *Scaling and related techniques for geometry problems*, Proc. 16th Annual ACM Symposium on Theory of Computing, 1984, pp. 135–143.
14. C.S. Jeong and D.T. Lee, *Parallel geometric algorithms on a mesh-connected computer*, Algorithmica **5** (1990), 155–177.
15. S.K. Kim, *Parallel algorithms for planar dominance counting*, Parallel Computing **15** (1990), 241–246.
16. H.T. Kung, F. Luccio, and F.P. Preparata, *On finding the maxima of a set of vectors*, Journal of the ACM **22** (1975), 469–476.
17. P.D. MacKenzie and Q.F. Stout, *Asymptotically efficient hypercube algorithms for computational geometry*, Proc. 3rd Symposium on the Frontiers of Massively Parallel Computation, 1990, pp. 8–11.
18. ______, *Practical hypercube algorithms for computational geometry*, Proc. 3rd Symposium on the Frontiers of Massively Parallel Computation, 1990, pp. 75–78.
19. R. Miller and Q.F. Stout, *Mesh computer algorithms for computational geometry*, IEEE Transactions on Computers **C-38** (1989), 321–340.
20. D. Nassimi and S. Sahni, *Bitonic sort on a mesh-connected parallel computer*, IEEE Transactions on Computers **C-28** (1979), 2–7.
21. S.-J. Oh and M. Suk, *Parallel algorithms for geometric searching problems*, Proc. Supercomputing '89, 1989, pp. 344–350.
22. J.F. Prins and J.A. Smith, *Parallel sorting of large arrays on the MasPar MP–1*, Proc. 3rd Symposium on the Frontiers of Massively Parallel Computation, 1990, pp. 59–64.

23. I. Stojmenović, *Computational geometry on a hypercube*, Proc. 1988 International Conference on Parallel Processing, 1988, pp. 3:100–103.
24. C.D. Thompson and H.T. Kung, *Sorting on a mesh-connected parallel computer*, Communications of the ACM **20** (1977), 263–271.
25. D.E Willard, *Applications of the fusion tree method to computational geometry and searching*, Proc. 3rd Annual ACM-SIAM Symposium on Discrete Algorithms, 1992, pp. 286–295.

DEPARTMENT OF COMPUTER AND INFORMATION SCIENCE, LINKÖPING UNIVERSITY, S–581 83 LINKÖPING, SWEDEN
E-mail address: jpe@ida.liu.se

DIMACS Series in Discrete Mathematics
and Theoretical Computer Science
Volume **30**, 1997

The ⋆Socrates Massively Parallel Chess Program

Christopher F. Joerg and Bradley C. Kuszmaul

ABSTRACT. Computer chess provides a good testbed for understanding dynamic MIMD-style computations. To investigate the programming issues, we engineered a parallel chess program called ⋆Socrates (pronounced "star-Socrates"), which running on the Sandia National Laboratories 1824-node Paragon, placed second in the 1995 World Computer Chess Championship. ⋆Socrates uses the Jamboree algorithm to search game trees in parallel and uses the Cilk 1.0 language and runtime system to express and to schedule the computation. In order to obtain good performance for chess, we use several mechanisms not directly provided by Cilk, such as aborting computations and directly accessing the active message layer to implement a global transposition table distributed across the processors. We found that we can use the critical path C and the total work W to predict the performance of our chess programs. Empirically ⋆Socrates runs in time $T \approx 0.95C + 1.09W/P$ on P processors. For best-ordered uniform trees of height h and degree d the average available parallelism in Jamboree search is $\Theta((d/2)^{h/2})$. ⋆Socrates searching real chess trees under tournament time controls yields average available parallelism of over 1000.

1. Introduction

Computer chess provides a good testbed for understanding dynamic MIMD-style computations. The parallelism in computer chess is derived from a dynamic expansion of a highly irregular game-tree, which makes computer chess difficult to express, for example, as a data-parallel program. To investigate how to program this sort of dynamic MIMD-style application, we engineered a parallel chess program called ⋆Socrates (pronounced "Star-Socrates".) The program, based on Heuristic Software's serial Socrates program, has an informally estimated rating of over 2400 USCF. ⋆Socrates, running on the 512-node CM-5 at the National Center for Supercomputing Applications (NCSA) at the University of Illinois, tied for third place in the 1994 ACM International Computer Chess Championship held at the end of June 1994 in Cape May, New Jersey; and running on the 1824-node Intel Paragon ⋆Socrates beat Grandmaster Gennady Sagalchik at the 1995 Maryland Theory Day; and again on the Paragon, placed second at the May 1995 World Computer Chess Championship held in Hong Kong.

⋆Socrates is a step forward from StarTech [**Kus94**], our previous chess program. Star-Tech was based on H. Berliner's serial Hitech program [**BE89**], and running on NCSA's 512-node CM-5, tied for third in the 1993 ACM International Computer Chess Championship. ⋆Socrates borrowed many of the techniques we developed for StarTech, including

---

1991 *Mathematics Subject Classification.* Primary 68M20, 68Q22; Secondary 68N99, 90-08.

This research was supported in part by the Advanced Research Projects Agency (DoD) under Grants N00014-94-1-0985, N00014-92-J-1310, and N00014-91-J-1698.

the basic search algorithm and the transposition table. $\star$Socrates uses a new programming language and runtime system called Cilk 1.0 [**BJK$^+$96**] to separate the chess program from the problems of scheduling and load balancing on a parallel computer.

To help manage the complexity of our chess systems, we divided the programming problem into two parts: an application and a scheduler. The application can be thought of as a dynamically unfolding directed acyclic graph, where the graph vertices correspond to instructions, and the graph edges correspond to control-flow dependencies between various instructions. An instruction may not execute until all its predecessors have executed. The scheduler, on the other hand, takes such a DAG and decides on which processor each instruction should run, and when it should run. The application's job is to expose parallelism. The scheduler's job is to run the program as fast as possible, given the available parallelism in the application, without running out of memory. Thus, in $\star$Socrates, we use Cilk 1.0 to address the scheduling problem, and the chess program itself can focus on only those issues which are unique to a chess program.

We had learned from our previous parallel chess program, StarTech, how to predict the performance of a parallel chess program. It was not clear from the outset how to predict the performance of a parallel chess program. Chess programs search a dynamically generated tree, and obtain their parallelism from that tree. Different branches of the tree have vastly different amounts of total work and available parallelism. Chess programs use large global data structures and are nondeterministic. We wanted predictable performance. For example, if one develops a program on a small, readily available, machine, one would like to be able to instrument the program and predict how fast it will run on a big, tournament sized, machine. How can predictable performance be salvaged from a program with these characteristics? We had found from StarTech that there are two performance complexity measures that actually can predict the performance of chess programs: the total work W and the critical path length C.

The total work and critical path length give us a chance to understand how the performance of a parallel program will scale as the number of processors increase, and also gives us a chance to understand the effectiveness of our scheduler. For example, the effectiveness with which the available work is scheduled into the machine can be measured by comparing it to the bound from Brent's theorem [**Bre74**, Lemma 2], which states that the runtime on P processors with a perfect scheduler and no communications overhead can always be brought down to no more than $C + W/P$.

For many applications, the values of W and C depend on the parallel algorithm, rather than on the scheduler. In our game-tree search algorithm, however, the values of W and C are partially dependent on scheduling decisions made by the scheduler, but we believe that W and C are mostly independent of those decisions. A good algorithm reduces W and C. We can compare W to the runtime of a corresponding serial chess program, and we can compare C to W. The ratio of the work done by the serial program to W is the *efficiency* of the program, and indicates how much overhead is inherent in the parallel algorithm. The ratio W/C is the average available parallelism of the program. We can hope, because of Brent's theorem, to use as many as W/C processors with an efficiency of at least 50%.

The rest of this paper explains how we obtain predictable high-performance from the $\star$Socrates program. Section 2 describes the Jamboree game-tree search algorithm and some analytical performance results for the algorithm. Section 3 describes the Cilk 1.0 language and runtime system. The modifications made to Cilk in order to run the chess program are described in Section 4. Section 5 outlines several other mechanisms used in the chess program. Section 6 presents a description of how the Jamboree algorithm relates to the algorithms used by other chess programs. We make some concluding remarks in Section 7.

2. Parallel Game Tree Search

The *Socrates chess program uses an efficient parallel game-tree search algorithm called "Jamboree" search. In this section we explain Jamboree search, starting with the basics of negamax search and serial α-β search, and present some analytical performance results for the algorithm.

The basic idea behind Jamboree search is to do the following operations on a position in the game tree that has k children:

- The value of the first child of the position is determined (by a recursive call to the search algorithm.)
- Then, in parallel, all of the remaining $k - 1$ children are tested to verify that they are not better alternatives than the first child.
- Each child that turns out to be better than the first child is searched in turn to determine which is the best.

If the move ordering is best-first, i.e., the first move considered is always better than the other moves, then all of the tests succeed, and the position is evaluated quickly and efficiently. We expect that the tests will usually succeed, because the move ordering is often best-first due the the application of several chess-specific move-ordering heuristics.

Negamax Search Without Pruning

Before delving into the details of the Jamboree algorithm, let us review the basic search algorithms that are applicable to computer chess. (Readers who are familiar with the serial game tree search algorithms may wish to skip directly ahead to the description of the Jamboree algorithm.) Most chess programs use some variant of negamax tree search to evaluate a chess position. The goal of the negamax tree search is to compute the value of position p in a tree T_p rooted at position p. The value of p is defined according to the negamax formula:

$$v_p = \begin{cases} \texttt{static\_eval}(p) & \text{if } p \text{ is a leaf in } T_p, \text{ and} \\ \max\{-v_c : c \text{ a child of } p \text{ in } T_p\} & \text{if } p \text{ is not a leaf.} \end{cases}$$

The negamax formula states that the best move for player A is the move that gives player B, who plays the best move from B's point of view, the worst option. If there are no moves, then we use a static evaluation function. Of course, no chess program searches the entire game tree. Instead some limited game tree is searched using an imperfect static evaluation function. Thus, we define the *chess knowledge* of a program as the combination of T_p, which tells us what tree to search, and $\texttt{static\_eval}$, which tells us how to evaluate a leaf position.

The naive Algorithm $\texttt{negamax}$ shown in Figure 1 computes the negamax value v_p of position p by searching the entire tree rooted at p. It is easy to make Algorithm $\texttt{negamax}$ into a parallel algorithm, because there are no dependencies between iterations of the *for* loop of Line (N5). One simply changes the *for* loop into a parallel loop. But negamax is not a efficient serial search algorithm, and thus, it makes little sense to parallelize it.

(N1) Define $\texttt{negamax}(p)$ as
(N2)   If n is a leaf then return $\texttt{static\_eval}(n)$.
(N3)   Let $\vec{c} \leftarrow$ the children of n, and
(N4) $b \leftarrow -\infty$.
(N5)   For i from 0 below $|\vec{c}|$ do:
(N6)   Let $s \leftarrow -\texttt{negamax}(\vec{c}_i)$.   *;; Recursive Search*
(N7)   if $s > b$ then set $b \leftarrow s$.   *;; New best score*
(N8)   enddo
(N9)   return b.

FIGURE 1. Algorithm $\texttt{negamax}$.

FIGURE 2. White to move and win. In this position, White need not consider all of Black's alternatives to 40. ♔f1, since almost any move Black makes will keep the queen, a worse outcome than just taking the queen with 40. ♔×h2.

Alpha-Beta Pruning

The most efficient serial algorithms for game-tree search all avoid searching the entire tree by proving that certain subtrees need not be examined. In this section we review the α-β serial search algorithm in preparation for the explanation of how the Jamboree parallel search algorithm works.

An example of how pruning can reduce the size of a game tree search can be seen in the chess position of Figure 2. Suppose White has determined that it can win Black's queen with 40. ♔×h2. White's other legal move 40. ♔f1 fails to capture the queen. White does not need to consider every possible way for Black's queen to escape. Any one of a number of possibilities suffices. Thus, White can stop thinking about the move without having exhaustively searched all of Black's options.

The idea of pruning subtrees that do not need to be searched is systematically embodied in the serial α-β search algorithm [**KM75**], which computes the negamax score for a node without actually looking at the entire search tree. The algorithm is expressed as a recursive subroutine with two new parameters α and β. If the value of any child, when negated, is as great as β, then the value of the parent is no less than β, and we say that the parent *fails high*. If the values of all of the children, when negated, are less than or equal to α, then the value of the parent is no greater than α, and we say that the parent *fails low*.

(A1) Define $\texttt{absearch}(n, \alpha, \beta)$ as
(A2)   If n is a leaf then return $\texttt{static\_eval}(n)$.
(A3)   Let $\vec{c} \leftarrow$ the children of n, and
(A4) $b \leftarrow -\infty$.
(A5)   For i from 0 below $|\vec{c}|$ do:
(A6)   Let $s \leftarrow -\texttt{absearch}(\vec{c}_i, -\beta, -\alpha)$.
(A7)   If $s \geq \beta$ then return s.   *;; Fail High*
(A8)   If $s > \alpha$ then set $\alpha \leftarrow s$.   *;; Raise α*
(A9)   If $s > b$ then set $b \leftarrow s$.
(A10)   enddo
(A11)   return b.

FIGURE 3. Algorithm $\texttt{absearch}$.

Procedure $\texttt{absearch}$[1] is shown in Figure 3. When Procedure $\texttt{absearch}$ is called, the parameters α and β are chosen so that if the value of a node is not greater than α and less than β, then we know that the value of the node can not affect the negamax value of the root of the entire search tree. After the score is returned from the subsearch on Line (A6), the algorithm, on Line (A7), checks to see if the negated score is as great as β. If so, we know that the value of the node is at least as great as β and we can skip searching the remaining children; the node has failed high. Just because one of the children has a negated score less than α, however, does not mean that some other child might not be within the α-β window. The algorithm can only fail low after considering all of the children.

The α-β algorithm can substantially reduce the size of the tree searched. The α-β algorithm works best if the best moves are considered first, because if any move can make the position fail high, then certainly the best move can make the position fail high. Knuth and Moore [**KM75**] show that for searches of a uniform best-ordered tree of height H and degree D, the α-β algorithm searches only $O(\sqrt{D^H})$ leaves instead of D^H leaves.

For any $k \geq 0$, before searching the $(k + 1)$st child, the α-β algorithm obtains the value of the kth child and possibly uses that value to adjust α or return immediately. This dependency between finishing the kth child and starting the $(k + 1)$st child completely serializes the α-β search algorithm.[2]

Scout Search

For a parallel chess program, we need an algorithm that both effectively prunes the tree and can be parallelized. We started with a variant on serial α-β search, called *Scout* search, and modified it to be a parallel algorithm. This section explains the Scout search algorithm.

Figure 4 shows the serial Scout search algorithm, which is due to J. Pearl [**Pea80**]. Procedure $\texttt{scout}$ is similar to Procedure $\texttt{absearch}$, except that when considering any child that is not the first child, a *test* is first performed to determine if the child is no better a move than the best move seen so far. If the child is no better, the test is said to *succeed*.

---

[1] This variant on the standard α-β algorithm is apparently due to Fishburn [**Fis83**], who called it *fail-soft α-β search*. Fail-soft α-β search can return a value that is less than α, in which case the value returned is an upper bound to the true value of the node, or the search can return a value that is greater than β, in which case the value returned is a lower bound to the true value.

[2] R. Finkel and J. Fishburn showed that if the serialization implied by α-β pruning is ignored by a parallel program, then it will achieve only $\sqrt{P}$ speedup on P processors [**FF82**].

```
(S1)   Define scout(n, α, β) as
(S2)       If n is a leaf then return static_eval(n).
(S3)       Let  c⃗ ← the children of n, and
(S4)             b ← −scout(c₀, −β, −α).
(S5)             ;; The first child's valuation may cause this node to fail high.
(S6)       If b ≥ β then return b.
(S7)       If b > α then set α ← b.
(S8)       For i from 1 below |c⃗| do:                    ;; the rest of the children
(S9)             Let s ← −scout(c⃗ᵢ, −α − 1, −α).          ;; Test
(S10)               If s > b then set b ← s.
(S11)               If s ≥ β then return s.                ;; Fail High
(S12)               If s > α then                          ;; Test failed
(S13)                     Set s ← −scout(c⃗ᵢ, −β, −α).      ;; Research for value
(S14)                     If s ≥ β then return s.           ;; Fail High
(S15)                     If s > α then set α ← s.
(S16)                     If s > b then set b ← s.
(S17)             enddo
(S18)       return b.
```

FIGURE 4. Algorithm scout.

If the child is determined to be better than the best move so far, the test is said to *fail,* and the child is searched again *(valued)* to determine its true value.

The Scout algorithm performs tests on positions to see if they are greater than or less than a given value. A test is performed by using an empty-window search on a position. For integer scores one uses the values $(-\alpha - 1)$ and $(-\alpha)$ as the parameters of the recursive search, as shown on Line (S9). A child is tested to see if it is worse than the best move so far, and if the test fails on Line (S12) (i.e., the move looks like it might be better than the best move seen so far), then the child is valued, on Line (S13), using a nonempty window to determine its true value.

If it happens to be the case that $\alpha + 1 = \beta$, then Line (S13) never executes because $s > \alpha$ implies $s \geq \beta$, which causes the *return* on Line (S11) to execute. Consequently, the same code for Algorithm scout can be used for the testing and for the valuing of a position.

Line S10, which raises the best score seen so far according to the value returned by a test, is necessary to insure that if the test fails low (i.e., if the test succeeds), then the value returned is an upper bound to the score. If a test were to return to its parent a score that is not a proper bound, then the parent might return immediately with the wrong answer when the parent performs the check of the returned score against β on Line S11.

A test is typically cheaper to execute than a valuation because the α-β window is smaller, which means that more of the tree is likely to be pruned. If the test succeeds, then algorithm scout has saved some work, because testing a node is cheaper than finding its exact value. If the test fails, then scout searches the node twice and has squandered some work. Algorithm scout bets that the tests will succeed often enough to outweigh the extra cost of any nodes that must be searched twice, and empirical evidence [**Pea80**] justifies its dominance as the search algorithm of choice in modern serial chess-playing programs.

(J1) Define jamboree(n, α, β) as
(J2)   If n is a leaf then return static_eval(n).
(J3)   Let $\vec{c} \leftarrow$ the children of n, and
(J4) $b \leftarrow -$jamboree$(c_0, -\beta, -\alpha)$.
(J5)   If $b \geq \beta$ then return b.
(J6)   If $b > \alpha$ then set $\alpha \leftarrow b$.
(J7)   In Parallel: For i from 1 below $|\vec{c}|$ do:
(J8)   Let $s \leftarrow -$jamboree$(\vec{c}_i, -\alpha - 1, -\alpha)$.
(J9)   If $s > b$ then set $b \leftarrow s$.
(J10)   If $s \geq \beta$ then abort-and-return s.
(J11)   If $s > \alpha$ then
(J12)   Wait for the completion of all previous iterations
(J13)   of the parallel loop.
(J14)   Set $s \leftarrow -$jamboree$(\vec{c}_i, -\beta, -\alpha)$. *;; Research for value*
(J15)   If $s \geq \beta$ then abort-and-return s.
(J16)   If $s > \alpha$ then set $\alpha \leftarrow s$.
(J17)   If $s > b$ then set $b \leftarrow s$.
(J18)   Note the completion of the ith iteration of the parallel loop.
(J19)   enddo
(J20)   return b.

FIGURE 5. Algorithm jamboree.

Jamboree Search

The Jamboree algorithm, shown in Figure 5, is a parallelized version of the Scout search algorithm. The idea is that all of the testing of the children is done in parallel, and any tests that fail are sequentially valued. A parallel loop construct, in which all of the iterations of a loop run concurrently, appears on Line (J7). Some synchronization between various iterations of the loop appears on Lines J12 and J18. We sequentialize the full-window searches for values, because, while we are willing to take a chance that an empty window search will be squandered work, we are not willing to take the chance that a full-window search (which does not prune very much) will be squandered work. Such a squandered full-window search could lead us to search the entire tree, which is much larger than the pruned tree we want to search.

The *abort-and-return* statements that appear on Lines J10 and J15 return a value from Procedure jamboree and abort any of the children that are still running. Such an abort is needed when the procedure has found a value that can be returned, in which case there is no advantage to allowing the procedure and its children to continue to run, using up processor and memory resources. The abort causes any children that are running in parallel to abort their children recursively, which has the effect of deallocating the entire subtree.

The actual search algorithm used in ⋆Socrates also includes some *forward pruning* heuristics that prune a deep search based on a shallow preliminary search. The idea is that if the shallow search looks really bad, then most of the time a deep search will not change the outcome. Forward pruning techniques have lately been shown to be extremely powerful, allowing programs running on single processors to beat some of the best humans at chess. The serial Socrates program uses such a scheme, and so does ⋆Socrates. In the ⋆Socrates version of Jamboree search, we first perform the preliminary search, then we search the first child, then we test the remaining children in parallel, and research the failed tests serially.

Parallel search of game-trees is difficult because the most efficient algorithms for game-tree search are inherently serial. We obtain parallelism by performing the tests in parallel, but those tests may not all be necessary in a serial execution order. In order to get any parallelism, we must take the risk of performing extra work that a good serial program would avoid.

Analysis of Jamboree Search

The Jamboree search algorithm can be analyzed for a few special cases of trees of uniform height and degree. Here we summarize our results. The complete statement of the theorems and proofs can be found in [**Kus94**]. It turns out that we have two analytical results, one for best ordered trees and one for worst ordered trees.

Theorem 1 states how Jamboree search behaves on best-ordered trees. A best-ordered tree is one in which it turns out that the first move considered is always the best move, and thus the tests in the jamboree search algorithm always succeed.

THEOREM 1. *For uniform best-ordered trees of degree d and height h the following hold:*

- *The total work performed is $\Theta(d^{h/2})$, which is the same as serial α-β search would perform. That is, the work efficiency is 1.*
- *The critical path length is $\Theta(2^{h/2})$, and thus the average available parallelism is $\Theta((d/2)^{h/2})$.*

Chess trees typically have degree of between 30 and 40 in the middle-game, and since we hope to search at least to depth 11 or 12, a best-ordered chess tree would have several hundred-thousand fold parallelism.

If the tree is not best-ordered, then the performance of the parallel algorithm can be much worse, however. Theorem 2 addresses worst-ordered trees. A worst-ordered tree is one in which the worst move is considered first, and the second worst move is considered second, and so-on, with the best move considered last.

THEOREM 2. *For uniform worst-ordered trees of degree d and height h the following hold:*

- *The total work performed is $\Theta(d^h)$.*
- *The critical path is $\Theta(d^h)$.*

For large d and h, the constants work out so that the total work performed is approximately three times as much as the serial α-β search would perform (thus the efficiency is 1/3), and the critical path length is equal to the work performed by serial α-β (with the speedup approaching 1 from below.)

Surprisingly, for worst-ordered uniform game trees, the speedup of Jamboree search over serial α-β search turns out to be under 1. That is, Jamboree search is worse than serial α-β search for such trees, even on a machine with no overhead for communications or scheduling. For comparison, parallelized negamax search achieves linear speedup on worst-ordered trees, and Fishburn's MWF algorithm achieves not-quite linear speedup on worst-ordered trees [**Fis84**].

Real Chess Trees

For real chess trees, we found that the better the move ordering, the lower the critical path and the less total work is performed. Thus, the move ordering heuristics of a chess program, which are important for serial programs because it reduces the work, are doubly important for our parallel algorithm because it also decreases the critical path length.

It is difficult to analyze Jamboree search for arbitrary game trees, because it is difficult to characterize the tree itself, and the tree that is actually searched can depend on how the work is scheduled. Unlike many other applications, the shape of the tree traversed by Jamboree search can be affected by the order of the execution of the work, sometimes increasing the work and sometimes decreasing work. Thus, measurements of "critical path length" and "work" on a particular run may be different than the measurements taken on another run, because the trees themselves are different. It is not clear what "critical path" and "work" mean for Jamboree search on arbitrary trees. Nonetheless, we have found that we can use the measured critical path length and total work to tune the program.

Our strategy is to measure the critical path and the work on a particular run, and to try to predict the performance from those measurements. (The details of how we measure critical path length are discussed in Section 3.) We measured the program on a set of eight problems,[3] shown in Figure 6. For each problem the program was run to various depths up to those that allowed the program to solve the problem by getting the "correct" answer, as identified by Kaufman. We also measured the program running on a variety of different sized machines. All of the performance numbers presented here are for the Connection Machine CM-5. We then performed a curve-fit of the data to a performance model of the form

$$T_{\text{predicted}} = c_1 \cdot C + c_2 \cdot \frac{W}{P} + c_3.$$

We found that the performance can be accurately modeled as

$$(1) \qquad T \approx (0.95 \pm 0.04)C + (1.091 \pm 0.001)\frac{W}{P} + 0$$

with a sample correlation coefficient[4] of 0.999947, a mean error of 14.2% and a mean relative error of 4.85%. To us, these small coefficients are quite amazing, because chess is a very demanding application. For our previous program StarTech, we found that according to measurements of the ideal parallelism profile (which shows the amount of parallelism as a function of time, running the program on an ideal infinite processor machine), for half the runtime on an infinite-processor machine there is less than 10-fold parallelism. The low coefficients on Equation 1 indicate that the program quickly finishes the available work during the times of low parallelism, and when there is much parallelism the program efficiently load balances the work. [5]

We also found that the work increases by about a factor of two to three as the number of processors increases from 1 to 128 processors, and that the critical path length is fairly

---

[3]Our eight problems were provided by $\star$Socrates team member L. Kaufman, who is an International Master. Kaufman has published several larger sets of benchmarks [**Kau92, Kau93**] which were used to understand StarTech [**Kus94**].

[4]For a definition of sample correlation coefficients and other statistical terms see, for example, [**HL93**, page 51].

[5]The results presented here are for $\star$Socrates. A more complete analysis of the statistical properties of the measurements for our older program StarTech can be found in Kuszmaul's dissertation [**Kus94**].

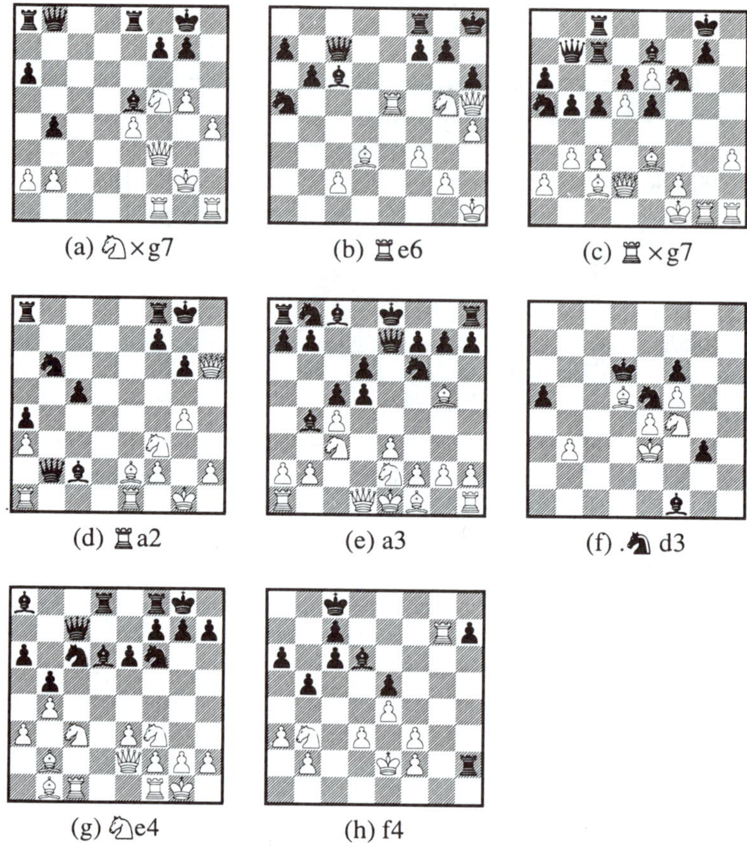

FIGURE 6. The 8 chess positions used in this paper. Below each position
is shown Kaufman's "correct" move for that position. All positions are
"White to move", except for Position (f).

stable as the number of processors increases. Most of the difficulty of predicting the performance of the chess program comes from the fact that the amount of work is increasing. The processors end up expanding subtrees that are pruned in the serial code.

We found that the critical path does not limit the speedup for our test problems, or for the program running under tournament conditions. By using critical path to understand the parallelism of our algorithm, we are able to make good tradeoffs in our algorithm design. Without such a methodology it can be very difficult to do algorithm design. For example, Feldmann, Monien, and Mysliwietz find themselves changing their Zugzwang chess program to increase the parallelism without really having a good way to measure their changes [**FMM93**]. They express concern that by serially searching the first child before starting the other children they have reduced the available parallelism. Our technique allows us to state that there is sufficient parallelism to keep thousands of processors busy without changing the algorithm. We can conclude that we should try to reduce the total amount of work done by the program, even if it reduces the available parallelism slightly.

We experimented with some techniques to improve the work efficiency, and found several techniques to improve the work efficiency at the expense of increasing the critical path length. For example, on StarTech we considered a algorithm change that would value the first two children before starting the parallel tests of all the remaining children. The idea is that by valuing more children, it becomes more likely that the best of the children that have been valued will be able to prune some of the remaining children. When we measured the runtime on a small machine, the program ran faster but on a big machine the runtime actually got worse. To understand why, we looked at the work and critical path length. We found that this variant of Jamboree search actually does decrease the total work, but it increases the critical path length, so that there is not enough available parallelism to keep a big machine busy. By looking at both the critical path length and the total work we were able to extrapolate the performance on the big machine from the performance on the little machine, however, and so we avoided introducing modifications that would hurt us in tournament conditions.

3. The Cilk Work-Stealing Scheduler

Now that we have explained the search algorithm used in ⋆Socrates, we need to explain how the computation is distributed across the machine. We use a runtime system called Cilk 1.0 [**BJK**$^+$**96**] (pronounced "Silk") to distribute work among the processors. This section explains how a program is expressed in Cilk and how the computation is distributed across the machine.

To distribute work among the processors of a parallel machine, Cilk uses a randomized work-stealing approach, in which idle processors request work. Processors run code that is nearly serial. When a processor discovers some work that could be done in parallel, it *posts* the work into a local data structure. When a processor runs out of work locally, it sends a message to another processor, selected at random, and removes work from that processor's collection of posted work.

The Cilk system was originally based on the Parallel Continuation Machine (PCM) runtime system of Halbherr, Zhou and Joerg [**HZJ94**]. In PCM, the scheduler uses a double ended queue (a *deque*) on every processor. When a processor posts work, it pushes it on the bottom of the deque. When a processor needs more work to do locally, it pops it off the bottom of the deque. When a processor steals work, the work is stolen from the top of the deque on the remote processor. It turns out that we modified this basic scheduler, as we shall describe in Section 4.

Cilk requires that the programmer explicitly break the algorithm into threads. To give an idea of how programs are expressed, consider the doubly recursive Fibonacci program shown in Figure 7. First we convert the program to a dataflow graph, and then for each node of the graph, we write a thread, which looks like a C function. Thus, in the final Cilk code, there are two threads, the `sum` thread and the `fib` thread. The `sum` thread accepts two values, adds them, and sends the result to an explicitly provided continuation. The `fib` thread creates a thread to sum two results, and passes continuations (denoted `x` and `y`) for that thread to two subsidiary `fib` threads. For a more complete description of the Cilk syntax, including a tutorial, see [**BHJ**$^+$**94**].

Similarly for the Jamboree algorithm, we transform the search code shown in Figure 5 into a dataflow graph, as shown in Figure 8. Then we express the program in Cilk analogously to the Fibonacci example.

Cilk automatically computes the critical path length and total work of a computation. The computation of the critical path is done by a system of time-stamping, as shown in Figure 9.

The Cilk 1.0 system runs on the CM-5, the Intel Paragon, and a network of workstations. Soon we expect to provide Cilk versions that run on shared memory multiprocessors

```
P1      int fib (int n)
P2      {
P3              if(n¡2) return n;
P4              else return fib(n-1)+fib(n-2);
P6      }
```

(a) The program written in serial C.

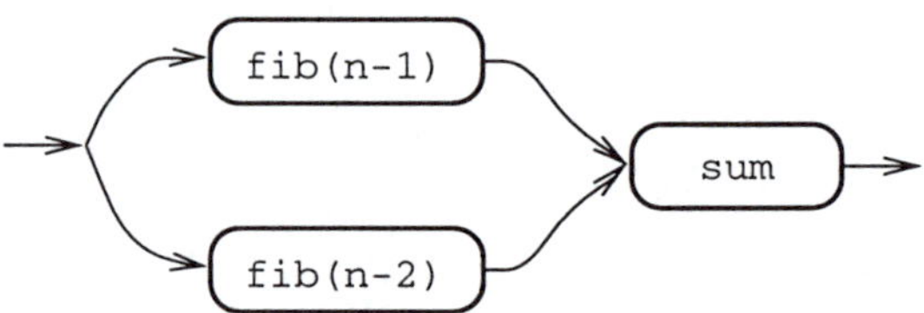

(b) The dataflow graph for the program.

```
F1      thread sum (cont k, int x, int y)
F2      {
F3              SendWordArgument (k, x+y);
F4      }
F5
F6      thread fib (cont k, int n)
F7      {
F8              if (n¡2) SendWordArgument (k, n);
F9              else
F10             {    cont x, y;
F11                  spawn_next sum (k, ?x, ?y);
F12                  spawn fib (x, n-1);
F13                  spawn fib (y, n-2);
F14             }
F15     }
```

(c) The corresponding Cilk code.

FIGURE 7. Expressing the doubly recursive Fibonacci program in Cilk 1.0.

and a variety of other parallel computing platforms. Later versions of Cilk are now available which improve the runtime system to provide better support for global data structures and to help automatically break up a program into threads.

4. Using Cilk for Chess Search

In the following two sections we describe the implementation of ⋆Socrates using Cilk. These sections are an interesting case study in implementing a large, multithreaded, speculative application. As mentioned in the introduction, ⋆Socrates is a parallelization of a

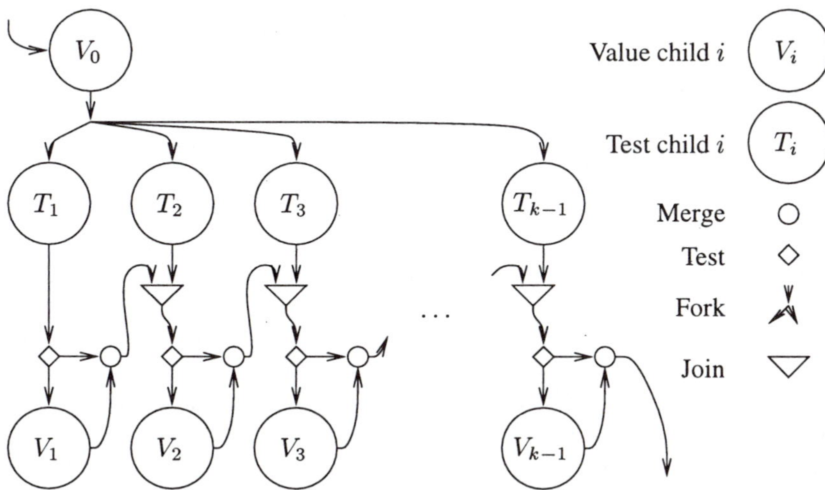

FIGURE 8. The dataflow graph for Jamboree search. First Child 0 is searched to determine its value, then the rest of the children are tested in parallel to try to prove that they are worse choices than Child 0, and then each of the children that fail their respective tests are serially researched. This dataflow graph can be used to measure the critical path length of the computation by using time-stamping. Compare this description of the Jamboree algorithm to the textual description in Figure 5.

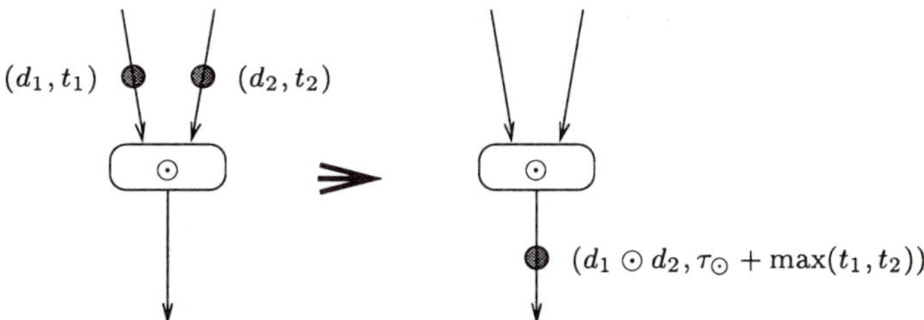

FIGURE 9. The time at which an instruction in a dataflow graph is executed in a perfect infinite-processor schedule can be computed by time-stamping the tokens. In addition to the normal data-value of a token (d_1, d_2, and $d_1 \odot d_2$ respectively in the figure), the token includes a time-stamp (t_1, t_2, and $\tau_\odot + \max(t_1, t_2)$ respectively.) The time-stamp on the outgoing token is computed as a function of the time-stamps of the incoming tokens and the time to execute the instruction.

serial chess program. Much of the code, including the static evaluator, is identical in the parallel and the serial versions and is not be discussed here. Instead, we focus on the portions of the code which were written specifically for the parallel version.

This section focuses on those parts of the Cilk scheduler that we had to change in order to make Cilk behave more like the scheduler used in StarTech. The changes we made include implementing migration handlers, aborting computations that are in progress, changing the order in which threads are stolen, and adding level waiting.

Migration Threads

We use a large, variable sized data structure (nearly 200 bytes) to describe the state of a chess board. In the serial code we pass around pointers to this structure and copy it only when necessary. In the parallel code we cannot just blindly pass pointers between threads, because if the thread is migrated the pointer will no longer be valid. A naive solution is to copy the state structure into every thread, but this adds a significant overhead to the parallel code. This overhead is especially distasteful when you realize that well under 1% of threads are actually migrated, so most of the copying would be wasted effort.

To solve this problem we use *migration threads*. Any thread can have a migration thread associated with it. When the scheduler tries to migrate a thread that has an associated migration thread, the scheduler will first call the migration thread. This migration thread will return a new closure which is migrated instead of the original closure.

Using this mechanism we are able to pass threads a pointer to a state structures. Any thread that is passed a state pointer is also given a migration thread which will copy the state, by value, into the closure if the thread is stolen. Once the closure arrives at the stealing processor, the stolen thread can then be called with a pointer to the copied state structure. This allows the overhead of copying the state to be paid only when it is actually necessary.

Abort

In order to implement the jamboree search algorithm we must be able to abort a computation. This is needed when a position fails high, that is, when we discover that at least one child has a score greater than beta, so there is no need to search the rest of the children. The Cilk system has no built-in mechanism for aborting a computation, so aborting had to be added as "application" code. Our goal in designing the abort mechanism was to keep it as self contained as possible and to minimize changes to the rest of the code. Eventually we would like to add support for aborting to Cilk itself.

In order to abort a computation we must be first able to find all of the threads that are working on this computation. To implement this we use *abort tables* to link together all the threads working on a computation. When a computation, say A, needs to create several children it first creates an abort table containing an entry for each child of the computation. If a child of A, say B, itself spawns off children, then the entry for B is updated to contain a pointer to the abort table that B creates. Once B and all its children have completed, B's table is deallocated and the entry for B is updated. With this mechanism in place the abort code is able to find all the descendants of any computation. When performing an abort, the abort code does not actually destroy any threads, instead it merely makes a mark in the affected abort tables. When a user's thread runs its first action should be to check to see if it has been aborted, and if so skip the rest of its computation. This check allows the user's code to do any cleaning up that may be necessary. (For example, the code may need to free some data structures.)

The abort mechanism provides functions to create, update, and deallocate the abort structures; to check if a thread is aborted; and to start an abort. By using these functions and passing around a few pointers to abort tables, the search code was modified to include aborting without too many changes.

One difficulty encountered in implementing the abort tables was in keeping the tables correct when a computation migrates. When a computation is stolen an abort table is allocated on the stealer's side and the existing abort table is modified to point to it. The difficulty arises because at the time a computation is stolen there is not yet an abort table on the stealer's side to point to. This abort table is not be allocated until after the thread begins to run (unless we change the run time system, which we wanted to avoid). So instead we create a unique identifier (UID) for each stolen computation, and store that into the abort table. Then on the stealer's side we have a hash table to map the UID into a pointer to the abort table. The protocol for accessing the hash table is quite tricky since there are many cases which require special handling. For example, the network of the CM-5 can reorder messages, therefore we have to handle the case where a message to abort a computation arrives before the thread that will allocate the hash table entry and abort table for that computation. Unfortunately, we did not consider all such possibilities before beginning the design, so getting this mechanism working correctly took longer than anticipated.

Steal Ordering

In the original Cilk runtime system the thread queue consisted of a single double ended queue. Newly enabled threads were placed at the front of the queue and the local processor took work out of this side as well (i.e. LIFO). When stealing occurs, threads were stolen from the other side of the queue (i.e. FIFO). For a tree shaped computation, the LIFO scheduling allowed the computation to proceed locally in a depth first ordering, thus giving us the same execution order a sequential program would have. However when stealing occurs the FIFO steal ordering caused a thread near the top of the tree to be stolen, so a large piece of work will be migrated, thus minimizing stealing. Since jamboree search is a tree shaped computation this mechanism worked reasonably well.

With this scheduling mechanism, the order in which children are executed depends on whether or not a child is stolen. For most computations this execution order does not matter; but for jamboree search it does. Execution order has an effect because if one child fails high, the rest of the children do not need to be searched. Our program orders the children such that when no children are stolen (the common case) the children most likely to fail high are executed first; this order minimizes the total work W. The problem is that when stealing occurs we steal the child least likely to fail high.

Ideally we would like to steal from the top of the tree, but still steal the child that is most likely to fail high. To do this modified the scheduler to keep track of the level, in the tree-search, of each thread. Each thread in the queue is assigned a level and threads at the same level are be executed in a fixed order, regardless of whether they are stolen or executed locally. Between levels, however, scheduling is done as before. We execute locally at the shallowest (newest) level and steal from the deepest (oldest) level. The search code then marks all the children of a computation as being at a level one shallower than the level at which the computation is currently executing. This gives us exactly the ordering of threads that we want. Adding this to ⋆Socrates reduced the amount of work performed for searching a position and seemed to give a speedup of 20-25%. This idea seemed important enough that we included a cleaner version of this mechanism in the released version, Cilk 1.0.

Level Waiting

The final change we made to the scheduler was a further attempt to reduce the extra work being performed by the parallel version. When a processor is searching a board position, A, it spawns off a bunch of children to test. If a processor ran out of children to work on while some children were still being worked on elsewhere, that processor would steal another closure and begin working on that.

Consider the case where one (or more) of the children is stolen and the processor finishes the rest of the tests before the test of the stolen child completes. The processor may then be out of work to do. This processor will then steal some closure from another processor and begin searching its board position, call it B. Eventually the test of the stolen child will complete. When this result comes back it will restart the computation on position A and preempt B. Since position A may still have additional value searches to perform, this is potentially a long computation. We are now in a position where B, no matter how little work it has, will not complete until the potentially long computation for A completes. The computation which spawned B will continue without it. It may eventually block (and thereby artificially lengthen the critical path C) or it may be able to continue, but will use looser bounds than if B had completed (and will thereby increase the total work W).

To avoid this stalled work we further modified the scheduler. We added "level waiting", a feature which makes uses of the same levels that were used in the previous section for optimizing the steal ordering. When a computation spawns children all the sub-computations are placed at the same level. The level waiting mechanism simply requires that all of these sub-computations have completed before we may begin any work at a shallower level. This prevents us from starting, and then preempting, an unrelated search. Implementing this change seemed to give us a 15-20% speedup.

5. Other Chess Mechanisms

The previous section described issues that arose in getting the search routines to run in our parallel environment. This section describes other aspects of the serial code that had to be modified to run in a parallel system. These aspects include the transposition table, detecting repeated moves, and debugging support.

Transposition Table

Most serial chess programs include a Transposition Table, which is basically a hash table of previously evaluated nodes. After a node is searched we create (or update) the hash entry for this node. The information stored in this entry includes a score, a move, a depth and a check key. The score tells us the value of the node; the move tells us what move achieves this score; and the depth tells us how deep a search was done. The check key is used to distinguish between the many positions which may hash to the same entry.

Before searching a node we first check to see if it is present with a deep enough depth, in which case we need not search this node again, we just use the stored value. The value may already be present because the same position can be reached by many different sequences of moves (i.e. a transposition). Much of the time when we get a hit the depth is not sufficient for the current search. But even in this case the table is still useful because it gives us the best move found by an earlier search, and often the best move at a shallower depth is the best move at a deeper depth. By using the returned move as our predicted best move, we increase our chances of accurately predicting the best move, which, as we saw in Section 2, reduces the work and critical path of the computation.

For ⋆Socrates we implemented a distributed transposition table. We had a choice between implementing a blocking or a non-blocking interface to the table. When a thread begins a search of a node the first thing it typically does is to do a transposition table lookup on that node. In a blocking implementation, this thread would send off a lookup request to the appropriate node and busy-wait until the response arrives, and then continue. The obvious disadvantage of blocking is that we waste time busy-waiting.

In a non-blocking implementation we would break this thread into several threads. When the time came to do a lookup, a thread would be posted on the node that would hold the entry. This thread would do the lookup and send the result back to the original node, enabling the continuation of the search. This implementation has the advantage that we do not spend any time busy-waiting while we do a table lookup. But it has one big disadvantage in that it may lead to many searches taking place on the same node concurrently. Intermixing two or more searches on the same node can cause both the work and the critical path to increase. To avoid these increases the scheduler would have to be modified to keep the two computations separate. To avoid the complexity involved in such a modification we chose to implement a blocking transposition table.

Since there is no way to implement this blocking mechanism using Cilk primitives, we dropped to a lower level and used the Strata active message library [**BB94**]. We designed the transposition table such that all accesses are atomic. For example when a value is to be put into the table, the information about the position is sent to the node where the entry resides, and that node updates the entry as required. Alternatively, we could have implemented a non-atomic update by performing a remote read of the entry, modifying the entry, and then doing a remote write. Non-atomic updates would have required more messages and would have had to either lock the entry while the update was in progress, or risk losing some information if two update operations overlapped.

To determine how much the busy-waiting hurts us, we instrumented our code to measure the time spent busy-waiting.[6] Our experiments show that the mean time between sending the request and receiving the reply is around 1600 cycles on the CM-5 with 33 megahertz SPARC processors. This works out to about 7% of the execution time.

We tried to keep the hash entries small so that we could have many entries.[7] The score and the move each require 16 bits. The bits describing the depth and type of search required another 9. The only other piece of an entry is the check bits. In our implementation each position had a 64-bit key. Of these bits 9 were used to select a processor and 21 were used to select a hash line on a given processor, so there is no need to store these bits in the entry itself. Of the remaining bits 34 bits we stored only 23 of them as the check bits since this allowed us to fit an entry in one 64-bit double word. When executing on a 512 node CM-5 we have 10^9 entries in our hash table!

The last aspect of the transposition table we will examine is subsumptions. The issue is what, if anything, do we do if two independent searches are concurrently searching the same position (i.e. one search "subsumes" the other). For example, Processor P1 may begin a search of Position B and before it completes and writes its result into the hash table Processor P2 begins another search of Position B. This leads to part of the search being duplicated. In the serial code these searches would be performed sequentially so this problem would not occur.

We considered trying to avoid this overhead in the following manner. When a search begins if the transposition table lookup fails an entry is created for that position and it is marked as "search in progress." Then if another lookup occurs on this position we know that a search is already being done. We would then have the option of waiting for the earlier search to complete.

---

[6] Not all this time is wasted since while busy-waiting we poll the network so we may spent part of this time responding to arriving messages. Our measurements provide an upper bound to the cost of busy-waiting.

[7] Hsu claims that increasing the size of the hash table by a factor of 256 can easily give a factor of 2 to 5 speedup [**hH90**]. Kuszmaul found similar results for StarTech [**Kus94**].

We chose not to implement this mechanism. Implementing it would have been somewhat complicated, and there were a number of issues that this would raise that we did not have a clear understanding of. For example, when we were about to abort a search would it be necessary to first check to see if anyone else is waiting for the results of this search. Another example is deciding when to wait: If a position is already being searched to depth d, and we want to search it to depth $d - 1$, do we wait for the deeper search? If we don't wait we are doing extra work, if we do wait we may wait much longer than if we had just done it ourself. We instrumented our program to estimate how much duplicate work was being done. Each time we completed a search and were about to write the hash table entry we first did a hash table lookup to see if we would get a hit if we began the search now. (If so, then someone else must have completed a search of this node during the time since we began the search.) We found that this occured less than 1% of the time. Furthermore, we had actually implemented a similar mechanism for StarTech, and it sometimes speeds the program up, and sometimes slows it down.

Repeated Moves

To fully describe a position in a chess game we need more than just a description of where each piece is on the board; some history is needed as well. A simple example is we need to know if the king has moved. If it has then we cannot castle, even if the king has moved back to its original position. This sort of information can easily be stored in a few bits in the state so this causes no difficulty.

Other required history can not be stored so easily. In chess if the same position is repeated 3 times then the game is a draw. Similarly if 50 moves are made by each player without an irreversible move being made, the game is a draw.[8] To handle these cases we need to keep track of all moves since the last irreversible move. (Once an irreversible move is made earlier positions cannot be repeated.) We do this by adding an array of positions to our state structure. This array contains all the positions (represented by their 64 bit hash key) since the last irreversible move.

This array greatly increases the size of the state structure (from about 160 bytes to nearly 1000 bytes). For a serial program the size of the state may not be significant since the code could just modify and unmodify the same state structure. For parallel code, however, it is often necessary to make copies of the state so a large state can slow down the program. To prevent this from occuring when we copy a state we only copy the part of the repeated position array that is meaningful. Since the average length of this list is quite small (under 2) copying this list adds very little overhead.

Debugging

In order to make it easier to debug our code, we make liberal use of 'assert' statements. Not only did this cause bugs to be detected sooner, it was also helpful in pinpointing the cause of the bug. One of our biggest problems initially was making sure that the parallel version was working correctly. This was difficult because if the parallel version was close to the serial, but not exactly the same, it would usually produce the exact same answers. We were often modifying both the parallel and the serial search algorithms and keeping them consistent was quite error prone. One method we occasionally used to test whether

---

[8] An irreversible move is one which cannot be undone; that is, one which captures a piece or moves a pawn. When we say that the game is drawn, technically the rule is that either side may unilaterally claim a draw. Players who both think they can still win could conceivably continue to play indefinitely. Our program always claims the draw.

both versions were identical was to run the parallel code on one processor and run the serial code and make sure they both searched exactly the same number of nodes. Unfortunately we did not do this check often enough and at one point so many minor variations had crept in that we wound up spending almost a week trying to make both versions consistent again.

One of the most useful assertions we added was to check at every node of the tree that the results of the parallel code were the same as the serial code. In the debugging version of the code, after the search of a position was complete we would call the serial code on the same position and assert that the results were the same. (We do this with the hash table turned off, otherwise the serial code simply finds the result in the hash table.) This was extremely slow, but it is an easy way to detect any differences between the serial and parallel searches, and to pinpoint exactly where the differences lie. After we started using this check, keeping both versions identical became much easier. We think this is an approach that is applicable to many parallel programs, not just chess.

Even with this grandiose verification not all our bugs were detected. At one point the debugging mode worked fine when run on any number of processors, as did the non-debugging program when run on one processor. But when we ran on more than one processor the speedup was quite small. It turned out that debugging mode was not being completely turned off as the flag which says whether or not to use the hash table was being set correctly only on processor 0. Therefore all other processors would never use the hash table. As is often the case, bugs which affect only performance can be harder to detect than bugs that affect correctness.

6. Related Search Algorithms

Our chess program uses *Jamboree* search [**Kus94**], a parallelization of the Scout search algorithm [**Pea80**]. In Jamboree search, at every node of the search tree, the program searches the first child to determine its value, and then tries to prove, in parallel, that all of the other children of the node are worse alternatives than the first child. This approach to parallelizing game tree search is quite natural, and it has been used by several other parallel chess programs, including Cray Blitz [**HSN89**] and Zugzwang [**FMM91**]. Still others have proposed or analyzed variations of this style of game tree search [**ABD82, MC82, Fis84, hH90**]. We do not claim that the search algorithm is entirely novel, although the details of Jamboree search are quite different from the details of the other algorithms. Instead, we view the algorithm as a testbed for evaluating mechanisms needed for the design of scalable, predictable, asynchronous parallel programs.

Jamboree search was used in our previous program, StarTech [**Kus94**]. ⋆Socrates is a step forward compared to StarTech because we introduced a linguistic layer and runtime system called Cilk 1.0 [**BJK⁺96**] to make it easier to program the application without worrying about the scheduling issues. Many of the techniques originally used in StarTech were borrowed for ⋆Socrates. Inspired by some problems we had with early versions of our StarTech program, Leiserson and Blumofe designed a provably good scheduler that has good space and time bounds, as well as low communications requirements [**BL94**].

Other parallel algorithms based on Scout search include minimal tree search, mandatory work first, and principal variation splitting. S. Akl, D. Barnard and R. Doran [**ABD82**] proposed the *minimal tree search*, which performs the weak α-β search by searching the minimal tree (i.e., the Knuth-Moore critical tree [**KM75**]). Each position is kept in an expanded form, potentially for a long time, resulting in unrealistic storage requirements. The Deep-Thought parallel algorithm as described in Hsu's thesis [**hH90**] is a variant of the high-storage-requirement minimal tree search.

J. Fishburn [**Fis84**] proposed the *mandatory work first* (MWF) algorithm. Algorithm MWF is based on the weak version of α-β search. It explicitly computes the number of *critical children* of the position being searched. A child of a position is *critical* if the child is in the Knuth-Moore critical tree, which means that the child would definitely be searched by the α-β algorithm. If the position being searched has more than one critical child, then MWF searches the first child and then searches the other children in parallel. If the first child turns out to be worse than some other child, MWF then researches the children that might be the best, all in parallel. In contrast, Jamboree researches sequentially. For nodes with exactly one critical child, MWF searches just the first child. Fishburn analyzed MWF for best-ordered and worst-ordered trees, but not for realistic game trees. One can construct game trees that are mostly best-ordered, in which the MWF algorithm does almost as badly as the naive parallel α-β search's $O(\sqrt{P})$ speedup.

Fishburn's MWF algorithm can be viewed as being separate from the scheduler, but his analysis depends on the scheduler. For example, Fishburn proves that worst-ordered game-trees achieve speedup using mandatory-work-first on a tree-of-processors scheduler, in which the depth of the game-tree is much greater than the depth of the processor tree. Our Theorem 2, in contrast, states that for an infinite processor perfect scheduler the average available parallelism is less than 3 and the speedup is less than one. Even though the MWF algorithm is tangled up with the tree-of-processors scheduler, one can interpret Fishburn's results somewhat independently of the scheduler. Fishburn's results indicate, for example, that if one has a tree of processors that is half as deep as the game tree and the degree of the processor tree is greater than the degree of the game tree, then the critical path is short and the work efficiency is good. Such a tree is as good as "infinite processors" for an algorithm in which the shallowest $h/2$ plies of the game tree are searched in parallel and the deepest $h/2$ plies of the game tree are searched serially. It turns out that the half-the-depth-serially strategy, when applied to Jamboree search, reduces the average available parallelism even further, down to about 2 for worst-ordered trees. Fishburn did not analyze what happens if the tree of processors is as deep as the game tree. The reason that MWF achieves speedup on worst-ordered trees is that MWF researches the children who failed their tests in parallel, while the Jamboree algorithm serially researches all the failed children. Hence, for worst ordered trees, Jamboree search finds little parallelism, while MWF finds much parallelism. Any chess program that is searching worst-ordered trees is not competitive, however.

Several programs use principal variant splitting (PV-splitting) [**MC82**], which is a another variation on MWF, but the ideas behind PV-splitting are, like MWF, somewhat obscured by the fact that a tree-of-processors scheduler is entangled into the search algorithm. Later work has separated the scheduler from the algorithm. For example, Cray Blitz [**HSN89**] apparently uses PV-splitting with something like a work-stealing scheduler. No critical path analysis or measurement has been performed for Cray Blitz, however.

The Zugzwang program, developed by R. Feldmann, P. Mysliwietz, and B. Monien [**FMM91**], uses a parallel search algorithm that is very similar to Jamboree search. Zugzwang achieves high work-efficiency, searching to within a few percent the same number of nodes in a parallel search as in a sequential search. The efficiency of our programs appears to be somewhat lower, probably because the Zugzwang team has gone to substantial effort to try to ensure that they search the tree in a mostly best-first order.

The parallel aspiration search algorithm [**Bau78**] divides the α-β window into segments, and gives each processor a different segment of the window to search. Aspiration search achieves only small parallel speedups. Surprisingly, the serial version of aspiration search often runs faster than a infinite window search. Today most state-of-the-art chess programs, including StarTech, use a serial aspiration search in which the game tree is searched with a small α-β window, and if the score is outside of the window, the tree is researched.

R. Karp and Y. Zhang [**KZ89**] show how to search an AND/OR tree in parallel by carefully allocating the right number of processors to each subtree. C. Stein [**Ste92**] employs Karp and Zhang's algorithm as a subroutine to do a parallel α-β search. Stein performs a binary search for the value of the game tree, at each stage converting the game tree to an AND/OR tree with the question "Is the value of the root greater than s?".

There are several other approaches to game tree search that are not based on α-β search. H. Berliner's B* search algorithm [**Ber79**] tries to prove that one of the moves is better with respect to a pessimistic evaluation than any of the other moves with respect to an optimistic evaluation. D. McAllester's Conspiracy search [**McA88**] expands the tree in such a way that to change the value of the root will require changing the values of many of the leaves of the tree. The SSS* algorithm [**Sto79**] applies branch and bound techniques to game tree search. These algorithms all require space which is nearly proportional to the run time of the algorithm, but the the constant of proportionality may be small enough to be feasible. While these algorithms all appear to be parallelizable, they have not yet been successfully demonstrated as practical serial algorithms. We wanted to be able to compare our work to the best serial algorithms.

7. Conclusions

The history of ⋆Socrates illustrates some the problems encountered when developing a high-performance parallel program. The ⋆Socrates chess team, which initially included R. Blumofe, M. Halbherr, C. Joerg, B. Kuszmaul, C. Leiserson, and Y. Zhou of MIT as well as D. Dailey and L. Kaufman of Heuristic Software, decided to start with a new chess program rather than to try to parallelize the original Socrates program. The difficulty with the original Socrates program is that it uses many global variables which are modified throughout the search. We felt that it would be easier to start with a program that was designed to modify its state in a non-destructive fashion by always making a new copy of the variables that represent the state of a chess board in the tree search. It turned out that the decision to start with a new program resulted in the program being substantially weaker than we had hoped, because we did not have sufficient time to get all of the chess knowledge transfered from Socrates to ⋆Socrates.

The program was developed on a very tight schedule. Dailey implemented a barebones chess program that copies chess boards and provided it to the MIT contingent in May 1994. During June, Dailey visited MIT to help tune the program, but we spent most of June simply getting the parallel version of the program to work correctly. The program started playing predictably only a few days before the tournament. The tournament was to start on Saturday morning, and on Thursday night the program crashed 2 out 3 times that we played it. Friday morning we packed up two X-terminals and two modems into the trunk of our cars and drove the eight hours to Cape May, New Jersey, wondering whether we were going to be embarrassed by a program that would crash during tournament play. Friday night we logged in and made changes to the program until 3am. Then the tournament began. Saturday morning we played and won our first game. We noticed some problems with the program, and modified it for the Saturday evening match, which we also won. Saturday night we made some more modifications to the program, and on Sunday morning we won our third game. We left the program alone for the Sunday evening game, which we lost to Deep Thought. ⋆Socrates's insufficient appreciation of the value of castling rights resulted in a poor move that Deep Thought punished brilliantly in what the on-site commentators called "one of the all-time greatest games of computer chess". Our fifth game resulted in a disappointing loss to Zarkov, in which ⋆Socrates made two mistakes due to insufficient chess knowledge. The first mistake was similar to the mistake in the game against Deep Thought, but ⋆Socrates managed to salvage the game to a drawn rook and pawn endgame. Unfortunately, ⋆Socrates managed to find a losing move in a position that the commentators thought was nearly a forced draw. Throughout the tournament the program ran without crashing, and searched quite deeply. If only we had given Dailey more time to tune the chess knowledge...

In 1995 R. Riesen of Sandia National Laboratories, and M. Frigo and K. Randall of MIT, joined the team to help port the program to the 1824-node Intel Paragon at Sandia. On that platform, ⋆Socrates played, and won, against Grandmaster Gennady Sagalchik in the "Man vs. Machine Chess Match" at the 12th Maryland Theory Day in March 1995. *Socrates won second place at the 1995 ICCA 8th World Computer Chess Championship, held in Hong Kong on May 25–30 1995.

One of the important organizational differences between StarTech and ⋆Socrates is that ⋆Socrates separates the application from the scheduler, whereas in StarTech the scheduler and the application were wound up together. More importantly, ⋆Socrates employs a linguistic layer to help the programmer express the program independently of the scheduler. Separating the system greatly simplified the implementation of ⋆Socrates, and allowed us to implement several other parallel applications including a protein folding program [**PJGT94**] which was the first program to find the number of Hamiltonian paths in a $4 \times 4 \times 3$ grid, and some smaller programs such as the doubly recursive Fibonacci routine, a backtracking search to solve the problem of determining how many ways there are to place n queens on an n by n chess board, a ray-tracing image rendering program, and a radiosity image rendering program.

We are now developing additional mechanisms for Cilk to provide high performance on a wider variety of applications. We are trying to improve the linguistic layer, to develop abstractions for manipulating shared data structures, and to simplify the interface to input/output and the operating system.

Acknowledgments

Robert D. Blumofe, Matteo Frigo, Michael Halbherr, Charles E. Leiserson, Keith Randall, and Yuli Zhou, all of MIT, contributed to making the chess program work and to developing the underlying parallel technology used in ⋆Socrates. Don Dailey and Larry Kaufman of Heuristic Software provided the serial program, Socrates, on which our parallel program is based, and Don worked many hours to help us get our parallel program working. Rolf Riesen, of Sandia National Laboratories, ported Cilk to the Intel Paragon and helped get ⋆Socrates running on the Paragon. Hans Berliner and Chris McConnell of CMU provided the serial version of Hitech that we first used as a testbed to develop our ideas for parallel game tree search. The National Center for Supercomputing Applications at the University of Illinois at Urbana-Champagne (NCSA) provided a 512-processor CM-5 for both the 1993 and the 1994 ACM Computer Chess Championships under NCSA Grant TRA930289N. Sandia National Laboratories provided access to the 1824-node Intel Paragon for the 1995 matches.

References

[ABD82]   Selim G. Akl, David T. Barnard, and Ralph J. Doran. Design, analysis, and implementation of a parallel tree search algorithm. *IEEE Transactions on Pattern Analysis and Machine Intelligence*, PAMI-4(2):192–203, March 1982.

[Bau78]   G. M. Baudet. The design and analysis of algorithms for asynchronous multiprocessors. Technical Report CMU-CS-78-116, Carnegie Mellon University, Pittsburgh, PA, April 1978. Ph.D. thesis.

[BB94]   Eric A. Brewer and Robert D. Blumofe. Strata: A multi-layer communications library. Technical report, MIT Laboratory for Computer Science, January 1994. To appear. (Available as `ftp://ftp.lcs.mit.edu/pub/supertech/strata`).

[BE89]   Hans Berliner and Carl Ebeling. Pattern knowledge and search: The SUPREM architecture. *Artificial Intelligence*, 38(2):161–198, March 1989.

[Ber79]   Hans Berliner. The B* tree search algorithm: A best-first proof procedure. *Artificial Intelligence*, 12:23–40, 1979.

[BHJ+94]   Robert D. Blumofe, Michael Halberr, Christopher F. Joerg, Bradley C. Kuszmaul, Charles E. Leiserson, Phil Lisiecki, Keith H. Randall, Andy Shaw, and Yuli Zhou. *Cilk 1.1 Reference Manual*. MIT Laboratory for Computer Science, 545 Technology Square, Cambridge, MA 02139, September 1994. (Available as `ftp://theory.lcs.mit.edu/pub/cilk/manual1.0.ps.Z`).

[BJK+96]   Robert D. Blumofe, Christopher F. Joerg, Bradley C. Kuszmaul, Charles E. Leiserson, Keith H. Randall, and Yuli Zhou. Cilk: An efficient multithreaded runtime system. *Journal of Parallel and Distributed Computing*, 37(1):55–69, August 25 1996. (An early version appeared in the *Proceedings of the Fifth ACM SIGPLAN Symposium on Principles and Practice of Parallel Programming (PPoPP '95)*, pp. 207–216, Santa Barbara, California, July 1995.) (Available as `ftp://theory.lcs.mit.edu/pub/cilk/cilkjpdc96.ps.gz`).

[BL94]   Robert D. Blumofe and Charles E. Leiserson. Scheduling multithreaded computations by work stealing. In *Proceedings of the 35th Annual Symposium on Foundations of Computer Science (FOCS '94)*, November 1994. To appear.

[Bre74]   Richard P. Brent. The parallel evaluation of general arithmetic expressions. *Journal of the ACM*, 21(2):201–206, April 1974.

[FF82]   Raphael A. Finkel and John P. Fishburn. Parallelism in alpha-beta search. *Artificial Intellgence*, 19(1):89–106, September 1982.

[Fis83]   John P. Fishburn. Another optimization of alpha-beta search. *SIGART Newsletter*, (84):37–38, April 1983.

[Fis84]   J. P. Fishburn. *Analysis of Speedup in Distributed Algorithms*. Number 14 in Computer Science: Distributed Data Base Systems. UMI Research Press, Ann Arbor, MI, 1984.

[FMM91]   R. Feldmann, P. Mysliwietz, and B. Monien. A fully distributed chess program. In D. F. Beal, editor, *Advances in Computer Chess 6*, pages 1–27, Chichester, West Sussex, England, 1991. Ellis Horwood. Conference held in August 1990 in London.

[FMM93]   R. Feldmann, P. Mysliwietz, and B. Monien. Game tree search on a massively parallel system. In H. J. van den Herik, I. S. Herschberg, and J. W. H. M. Uiterwijk, editors, *Advances in Computer Chess 7*, pages 203–219, 1993.

[hH90]   Feng hsiung Hsu. Large scale parallelization of alpha-beta search: An algorithmic and architectural study with computer chess. Technical report CMU-CS-90-108, Computer Science Department, Carnegie-Mellon University, Pittsburgh, PA 15213, February 1990. Ph.D. thesis.

[HL93]   Robert V. Hogg and Johanenes Ledolter. *Applied Statistics for Engineers and Physical Scientists*. Macmillan Publishing Company, New York, second edition edition, 1993.

[HSN89]   Robert M. Hyatt, Bruce W. Suter, and Harry L. Nelson. A parallel alpha/beta tree searching algorithm. *Parallel Computing*, 10(3):299–308, May 1989.

[HZJ94]   Michael Halbherr, Yuli Zhou, and Chris F. Joerg. MIMD-style parallel programming based on continuation-passing threads. Computation Structures Group Memo 355, MIT Laboratory for Computer Science, 545 Technology Square, Cambridge, MA 02139, April 1994. A shorter version appeared in Proc. of 2nd Int. Workshop on Massive Parallelism: Hardware, Software and Applications. Capri, Italy, Oct. 1994.

[Kau92]   Larry Kaufman. Rate your own computer. *Computer Chess Reports*, 3(1):17–19, 1992. Published by ICD, 21 Walt Whitman Rd., Huntington Station, NY 11746, 1-800-645-4710.

[Kau93]   Larry Kaufman. Rate your own computer — part II. *Computer Chess Reports*, 3(2):13–15, 1992-93.

[KM75]   Donald E. Knuth and Ronald W. Moore. An analysis of alpha-beta pruning. *Artificial Intelligence*, 6(4):293–326, Winter 1975.

[Kus94] Bradley C. Kuszmaul. *Synchronized MIMD Computing*. PhD thesis, Massachusetts Institute of Technology, Department of Electrical Engineering and Computer Science, May 1994. (Available as Technical Report MIT/LCS/TR-645 and as `ftp://theory.lcs.mit.edu/pub/bradley/phd.ps.Z`).

[KZ89] Richard M. Karp and Yanjun Zhang. On parallel evaluation of game trees. In *Proceedings of the 1989 ACM Symposium on Parallel Algorithms and Architectures (SPAA '89)*, pages 409–420, Santa Fe, New Mexico, June 1989.

[MC82] T. A. Marsland and M. S. Campbell. Parallel search of strongly ordered game trees. *ACM Computing Surveys*, 14(4):533–552, December 1982.

[McA88] David Allen McAllester. Conspiracy numbers for min-max search. *Artificial Intelligence*, 35:287–310, 1988.

[Pea80] Judea Pearl. Asymptotic properties of minimax trees and game-searching procedures. *Artificial Intelligence*, 14(2):113–138, September 1980.

[PJGT94] Vijay S. Pande, Chris Joerg, Alexander Yu Grosberg, and Toyoichi Tanaka. Enumeration of the Hamiltonian walks on a cubic sublattice. *Journal of Physics A.*, 1994. To appear.

[Ste92] Clifford Stein. Evaluating game trees in parallel. In Charles E. Leiserson, editor, *Proceedings of the 1992 MIT Student Workshop on VLSI and Parallel Systems*, pages (47–1)–(47–2), MIT Endicott House, July 1992. Available from Leiserson at 545 Technology Square, Cambridge, Massachusetts 02139.

[Sto79] G. C. Stockman. A minimax algorithm better than alpha-beta? *Artificial Intelligence*, 12(2):179–196, August 1979.

MIT LABORATORY FOR COMPUTER SCIENCE, 545 TECHNOLOGY SQUARE, CAMBRIDGE, MA 02139

Current address: Dr. Christopher F. Joerg; Digital Equipment Corporation; Cambridge Research Laboratory; One Kendall Square, Building 700, 2nd Floor; Cambridge, MA 02139.
  E-mail address: `cfj@jj.lcs.mit.edu`
  World wide web home page: `http://csg-www.lcs.mit.edu:8001/Users/cfj/`

Current address: Prof. Bradley C. Kuszmaul; Yale University; Department of Computer Science; 51 Prospect Street; New Haven, CT 06520.
  E-mail address: `kuszmaul-bradley@cs.yale.edu`
  World wide web home page: `http://arch.cs.yale.edu/~bradley`

DIMACS Series in Discrete Mathematics
and Theoretical Computer Science
Volume **30**, 1997

Concurrent Data Structures and Load Balancing Strategies for Parallel Branch-and-Bound/A* Algorithms

V.-D. Cung, S. Dowaji, B. Le Cun, T. Mautor and C. Roucairol

ABSTRACT. In this article, we propose new concurrent data structures and load balancing strategies for Branch-and-Bound (B&B)/A* algorithms in two models of parallel programming: shared and distributed memory.

For the shared memory model (SMM), we present a general methodology which allows concurrent manipulations for most tree data structures, and show its usefulness for implementation on multiprocessors with global shared memory.

Some priority queues which are suited to basic operations performed by B&B algorithms are described: the *Skew-heaps*, the *Funnels* and the *Splay-trees*. We also detail a specific data structure, called *treap* and designed for the A* algorithm. These data structures are implemented on a parallel machine with shared memory: KSR1.

For the distributed memory model (DMM), we show that the use of partial cost in the B&B algorithms is not enough to balance nodes between the local queues. Thus, we introduce another notion of priority, called *potentiality*, between nodes that takes into account not only their partial costs but also their capacities to generate other nodes. We have developed three load balancing strategies using this potentiality.

The B&B implementation was carried out in a network of heterogeneous Unix workstations used as a single parallel computer through the Parallel Virtual Machine (PVM) software system.

In order to test the efficiencies of concurrent data structures and load balancing strategies for B&B and A* algorithms, we implemented them to solve Combinatorial Optimization Problems (COPs) such as the Quadratic Assignment Problem (QAP), the Vertex Cover Problem (VCP) and puzzle games.

1. The challenge

Processing larger problems in a shorter time has always been one of the main challenges in computer science.

This point is particularly important for the solution of Combinatorial Optimization Problems (COPs) which require high processing speed and a lot of memory space. Numerous scientific, military and industrial applications are expressed as

---

1991 *Mathematics Subject Classification.* Primary 90C10; Secondary 90C27.
This work was partially supported by the projet Stratagème of the French CNRS.

COPs (e.g. VLSI circuit design, production control, resource allocation, command system, robots, etc).

Massively parallel processing, which has been developed to satisfy these needs, is therefore a natural choice. The challenge is how to take advantage of the huge processing capacity provided by a large number of processors in terms of performance (speed-up and/or scale-up). Parallel algorithm development (design, analysis and implementation) is thus the price to pay to obtain the expected results.

1.1. COPs and Branch-and-Bound/A* formulations. Formally, a COP in its minimization release can be defined as follows: Given a finite discrete set X, a function $F : X \to \mathbb{R}$, and a set S where $S \subseteq X$, find an *optimal* solution $x^* \in S$, such that $F(x^*) = \min\{F(x)|\forall x \in S\}$. The set S is called the domain of constraints and all the elements $x \in S$ are *feasible* solutions. We assume that S is finite or empty.

For example, in Operational Research (OR), the Quadratic Assignment Problem (QAP) and the Vertex Cover Problem (VCP) fit the above definition. In Artificial Intelligence (AI), solving a puzzle game is generally stated as finding the shortest path from an initial configuration to the final configuration. All these COPs are *NP-complete* or *NP-hard*.

To find an exact solution to a COP, the best way consists in using a Branch-and-Bound (B&B) paradigm including B&B algorithms in OR and A* algorithm in AI [**34**]. The B&B paradigm explores - cleverly - the set X. The knowledge acquired along the search path is used to discard the exploration of the useless parts of X. Synthetically, the B&B paradigm may be summed up as follows:

Building the search tree:
- a *branching scheme* splits X into smaller and smaller subsets,
- a *search strategy* selects one node among all pending nodes to be developed.

Pruning branches:
- a bounding function $f : 2^S \to \mathbb{R}$ gives a *lower bound* for the value of the best solution in each set S_i of S created by branching,
- the *exploration interval* is revised periodically, as the upper bound is updated every time a feasible solution is found;
- in certain applications, *dominance relationships* may be established between subsets S_i, and will thus also lead to discard non-dominant nodes[1].

From an algorithmic point of view, a B&B algorithm carries out a sequence of basic operations on a set of elements with their priority value:

- *DeleteMin* selects and deletes the highest priority node,
- *Insert* adds a new node with computed priority,
- *DeleteGreater* deletes nodes with lower priorities than a given value which is usually the upper bound.

In practice, *priority queues* are usually chosen as suitable data structures for implementing these operations.

---

[1]The A* algorithm uses this kind of relationships for graph search.

1.2. Data structures and programming models. Unlike Numerical Computation which generally manipulates regular and static data structures (e.g. arrays), B&B/A* algorithms use *irregular* and *dynamic* data structures (e.g. priority queues, hash tables and linked lists) for the storage of the search tree, as its size is not known at the outset. It grows exponentially with the size of the problems and often remains too large to be solved successfully as the program stops for lack of time or memory space. Parallelism is then used to speed up the construction of search trees and to provide more memory space. The management of the irregular and dynamic data structures in parallel processing is therefore the key to high performance of computation.

Research during the last decade in the parallelization of B&B/A* algorithms showed that MIMD architecture is suitable. However, from experimental machines with exotic architectures to commercial distributed multiprocessors and networks of workstations, there still are two main high-level programming models: the shared memory model (SMM) and the distributed memory model (DMM). Vendors are beginning to offer parallel machines (KSR1, CRAY T3D) with programming environments supporting both models.

In the SMM, data is stored in a global shared memory which can be accessed by all the processors. This model could be implemented on distributed memory machines via the *Virtual Shared Memory* mechanism (e.g. ALLCACHE system on KSR1). On the other hand, in the DMM, each processor can only access its local memory: data is exchanged by a message-passing mechanism (e.g. PVM, MPI). Problems involved in these programming models are completely different.

As data is shared in the SMM (section 2), the main issue is the contention access to the data. The higher the *concurrent access* to the data is, the higher the performance. Data consistency is provided by a mutual exclusion mechanism, and load balancing is easy to achieve since data can be accessed by any processor.

On the other hand, *load balancing* is the key point to tackle in the DMM (section 3). As each processor can only access its own memory, if all the data have been processed in a local memory, the corresponding processor becomes idle while the other processors are still running.

In this paper, we propose new concurrent data structures and load balancing strategies for the SMM and the DMM respectively. In order to test their efficiency on the COP, we implemented them for B&B and A* algorithms to solve QAP, VCP and a 15 puzzle game.

2. Concurrent access to data structures

In the SMM, the data structure is stored in the shared memory. Each asynchronous processor must be able to access it. The simplest method to allow concurrent access to a data structure is each asynchronous process to lock the entire data structure whenever it makes an access or an operation. This exclusive use of the entire data structure to perform a basic operation serializes the access to the data structure and thus limits the speed-up obtained with the parallel algorithm.

The next section presents a better technique which is termed **Partial Locking**.

2.1. Partial locking protocol. An operation is composed of successive elementary operations. At a given moment, a processor only needs few nodes of the tree. Severity of contention can be reduced if each processor locks only the part of the data structure that it actually modifies. Hence, the time delay, during which the access to the structure is blocked, is decreased.

We reiterate the definition of *user view serialization* of the structure introduced by Lehman and Yao, 1981 [**28**], Calhoun and Ford, 1984, [**5**] in the context of data base management. In this approach, the processors that access the data structure with a well-ordering scheme, inspect a part of the structure that the previous processors would never change further, and leave all parts of the data structure (modified or not) in a consistent state.

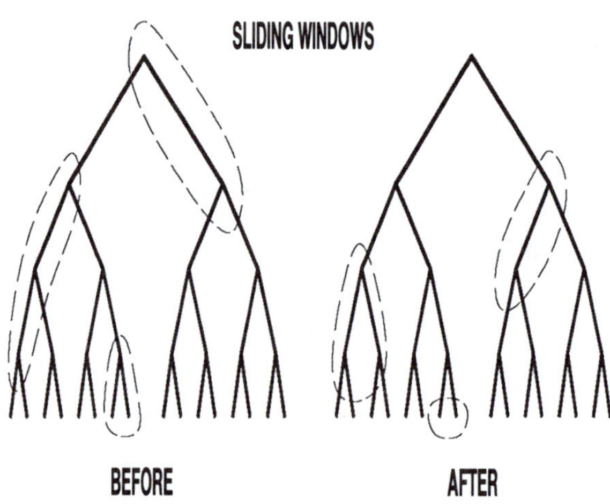

FIGURE 1. Example of applying the partial locking protocol to a tree data structure.

Figure 1 shows an example of this method applied to a tree data structure. A sliding window of a processor executing a basic operation on a tree data structure, is defined as the set of nodes of this data structure to which the processor has an exclusive access.

To forbid the creation of a cycle of processors waiting for resources (deadlocks), we have to force each processor to follow a specific locking scheme.

A simple scheme of this top-down method can be described as follows. Each operating window will be moved down the path, from the root to a leaf.

Notations: an ancestor of x is defined as a node which belongs to the (only) path between x and the root.

DEFINITION 1. *Let S be a tree data structure in which all basic operations are executed downwards. The scheme is defined by the following rules:*

Lock: *: a processor can request a lock on a node x only in the following cases*
  1: *: if the processor has a lock on the parent of x,*
  2: *: if the processor has a lock on an ancestor of x and a lock on a descendant of x,*
  3: *: a processor can lock the root r of S iff the processor has no more locks in S.*
Unlock: *: no specific rule.*

The full description of the variant schemes and the proofs can be found in [**6**].

2.2. Partial locking boolean protocol. If the scheme described above allows concurrent accesses, it implies an overhead due to the number of locks used: these have an expensive execution time.

In respect to the locking scheme defined in 1, if a processor P_i has a lock on a node A of the data structure S, P_i is the only processor that can request a lock on a node B, child of A (figure 2).

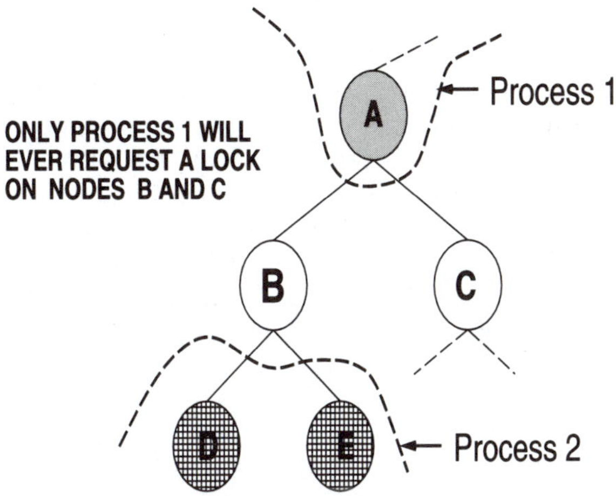

FIGURE 2. Only one process can ever request a lock on a node.

Hence, expensive mutual exclusion primitives are not needed. Locks could be replaced by a boolean-like protocol. This is just a flag, which indicates if the node is in use or free. Since the root node has no parent, several processors can try to access it. A lock will be necessary only for this specific node.

To illustrate this optimization, we test a Skew-heap using the partial locking paradigm [21] in the context of a simulation of B&B (table 1) on the KSR1 machine with one processor. The execution time shows that the lock protocol overhead is really bigger than the boolean protocol overhead. Further, boolean protocol time is not very different from the serial time.

Serial	Locks	Boolean
22 s	57 s	28 s

TABLE 1. Times of Skew-heap to perform 200000 operations.

2.3. Related studies. We can find in the literature two main kinds of techniques which allow "parallel" operations on data structures for shared memory machines. They are usually called *Parallel data structures* and *Concurrent data structures*.

Parallel Data structures offer several synchronous operations performed by several processors. Processors cooperate to perform their operations [10, 11, 9]. Deo and Prasad in [11] have proposed an optimal parallel heap. P processors can simultaneously perform P operations. But these P operations are synchronous. Thus, a processor that wants to access the data structure, has to wait for the other processors to terminate their current operations. These kinds of parallel data structures is not very well suited to our applications, since the time between two accesses to the data structure is never the same on two processors. Some solutions use specialized processors to handle the data structure. We prefer to employ each processor to execute the tree search algorithms

Concurrent data structure algorithms allow concurrent accesses to a data structure by asynchronous processors. Each processor performs a serial operation which is modified in order to keep the others processors unblocked. Processors make their operations themselves and do not need some other processors to access the data structure. They do not cooperate to perform their operations. These methods are very useful if the delay between two accesses is unknown. Therefore, mutual exclusion primitives are generally used to make atomic update operations with respect to the other processors. Partial locking protocols are such techniques. Initially the idea of partial locking can be found in articles dealing with data base management. Several solutions have been proposed to allow concurrent access on Search Tree such as AVL-Tree, B-Tree and B+Tree [12, 13, 26]. Afterwards, this technique was used for different priority queues such as D-heap [3, 39], Skew-heap [21], Fibonacci Queue and priority pool [19]. Sometimes, these concurrent algorithms need specialized processors to rebuild the data structure. Our contribution is an optimized version of a partial locking method. We have reduced the overhead due to the mutual exclusion primitives. For example, Jones' Skew-heap in [21] has $\log n$ mutual exclusion primitives calls for one operation. Our solution uses only one mutual exclusion primitive and $\log n$ boolean-like protocol calls. Table 1 shows the importance of this optimization.

In the next two sections, we show the efficiency of our partial locking boolean protocol by applying it to data structures used in a parallel best-first B&B and in a parallel A* algorithm.

2.4. Priority queues for best-first B&B. Best-first strategy in B&B algorithms seems to be the most efficient, because the number of evaluated nodes is optimal. The data structure used in the best-first B&B is a priority queue (PQ). The basic operations are given in section 1.1.

In serial, PQ are usually represented by heaps. There exist several algorithms which manage a heap : D-heap [22], Leftist-heap [22], Skew-heap [47], Binomial queue [4], Pairing heap [15, 45]. The most popular one is the D-heap[2] as used in the heapsort [49]. This is the oldest PQ implementation with $O(\log n)$ performance. In a heap, the priority structure is represented as a binary tree that obeys the heap invariant, which states that each item always has a higher priority than its children. In a D-heap, the tree is embedded in an array, using the rule that location 1 is the root of the tree, and that locations 2i and 2i+1 are the children of location i. In a B&B, each item contains an external pointer to store the subproblem information. Bistwas and Browne [3], Rao and Kumar [39] have proposed a concurrent version of the D-heap. Both have used a partial locking protocol. Our partial locking boolean protocol cannot be used with the D-heap, because the operations of the algorithm require direct accesses to the tree.

Serial experimental results [20, 6] show that the D-heap is not an efficient PQ implementation. Tarjan and Sleator proposed in [47] a better heap algorithm, the Skew-heap. Their algorithm is the self-adjusting version of the Leftist-heap. The

---

[2]Jones in [20] called it Implicit-heap.

basic operation which is used to implement *DeleteMin* and *Insert* operation is called the merge operation. Its *amortized complexity* is $O(\log n)$. It seems that the Skew-heap is one of the most efficient serial algorithms for heap implementation [**20, 6**]. Jones [**21**] has proposed a concurrent Skew-heap using a partial locking protocol with only mutual exclusion primitives. Applying our locking boolean protocol to the Skew-heap offers better performances (table 1).

The complexity of the heap *DeleteGreater* operation is $O(n)$, because the tree must be entirely explored. Another problem is that heaps are not stable. In [**31**], Mans and Roucairol demonstrated that the PQ must be stable. The order of the nodes with the same priority must be fixed (LIFO or FIFO). This property avoids some anomalies of speed-up. Then, several PQ which are not a heap structure have been proposed. We can mention the Funnels [**30, 6**] (table and tree) and the different Splay-trees [**47, 20**]

The Funnel data structures were developed by Mans and Roucairol in 1990 [**30**] for a best-first B&B implementation. However, they can be used in many other applications. The B&B algorithms only need a small bounded interval of priority. The size of the interval is denoted by S. Initially S is equal to $ub - lb$ (ub is the cost of the best known solution and lb is the evaluation of the problem). During the execution of the algorithm, lb increases and ub decreases, then S decreases until it reaches 0. Then, there is a very simple way to achieve an efficient representation for the PQ. The idea is to use an array of FIFOs of size S, where each FIFO j of the array is associated to a possible priority[3]. The serial experimental results show that the Funnel table is the most efficient priority queue. Our partial locking boolean protocol cannot be used to make concurrent the access to the Funnel table, because it is not a tree data structure. Details of the Funnel table can be found in [**30, 6**]. The Funnel tree uses a complementary binary tree with S external nodes, where S is the smallest power of 2 which is greater than $ub - lb$. Each internal node of the tree has a counter which represents the number of subproblems contained in the FIFOs below it. This tree is used to drive the *DeleteMin* operation to the FIFO containing the best nodes. The operation complexity is $O(\log S)$. The Funnel tree operations are made concurrent using our partial locking boolean protocol.

Splay-trees are initially self-adjusting binary search trees. Jones in [**20**] shows that Splay-trees could be used as efficient priority queues. There exist several versions of serial Splay-tree data structures depending on the Splay operation : Splay, Semi-Splay, Simple-Semi-Splay. Each of them has a Top-Down and a Bottom-Up version. These different versions of Splay-trees support search operations on any priority. We create new versions of Splay-trees (called Single) where each tree node is associated with a fixed priority value. We apply our partial locking boolean protocol to the Top-Down versions of the Semi-Splay, the Simple-Semi-Splay, Single-Semi-Splay and the Single-Simple-Semi-Splay.

The Funnels and Splay-trees support efficient *DeleteGreater* operations and have the stability property.

Table 2 shows the complexities and the properties of each priority queues.

2.4.1. *Experimental results.* We have tested these data structures on a best-first B&B algorithm solving the Quadratic Assignment Problem. The Quadratic Assignment Problem (QAP) is a combinatorial optimization problem introduced by

---

[3]We make the assumption that priority values are integers.

PQ	Insert	DeleteMin	DeleteGreater	Perf	Stab
Funnel-Table	O(1)	O(1)	O(1)	1	Y
Splay	O(log n)	O(log n)	O(log n)	2	Y
Single-Splay	O(log S)	O(log S)	O(log S)	2	Y
Funnel-Tree	O(log S)	O(log S)	O(log S)	3	N
Skew-heap	O(log n)	O(log n)	O(n)	3	N
D-heap	O(log n)	O(log n)	O(n)	4	N

TABLE 2. Summary of all priority queues.

Koopmans and Beckman, in 1957, [**23**]. It has numerous and various applications, such as location problems, VLSI design [**36**], architecture design [**14**], etc.

The goal of QAP is to assign n units to n sites in order to minimize the quadratic cost of this assignment, which depends both on the distances between the sites and on the flows between the units. We modified the algorithm developed by Mautor and Roucairol [**32**] which uses the depth-first strategy, to use the best-first strategy.

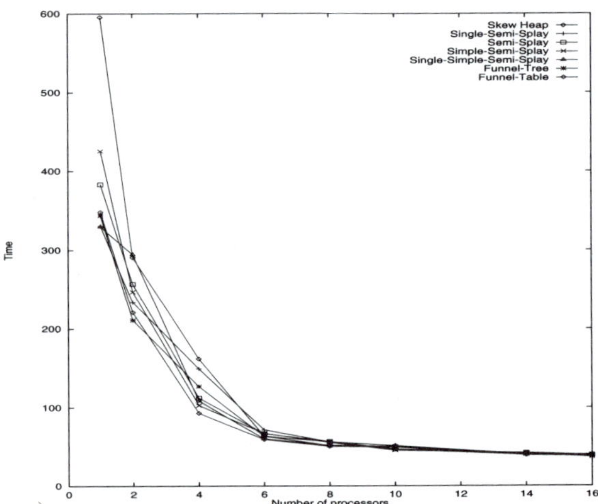

FIGURE 3. Time results on KSR1 machine solving the nugent15 problem.

Figure 3 shows the results obtained on a KSR1 machine with virtual shared memory. The programs solve the nugent15 problem which can be found in the QAP Library. We can see that the Splay-trees and the Funnel PQs are more efficient than the Skew-heap up to 6 processors. That confirms the theoretical complexities, and that the heap is not a good PQ representation for the best-first B&B. The single Splay-trees seem to be more efficient than the non single ones. The speed-ups obtained are also very good up to 6 processors. With more than 6 processors, the times of the different PQs no longer decrease and they are quite the same. This phenomenon is due to the problem size (96000 nodes are evaluated with the nugent15). If the size of the problem is small, the number of nodes in the data structure is small, and so the depth of the priority queue is small. The number of simultaneous accesses depends on the depth of PQ. Thus, the speed-up is limited by the size of the problem. We began to test our program with a bigger problem (nugent 16) to verify this conclusion. However, the time obtained with 6 processors is very good according to the machine and the problem.

2.5. Concurrent Treap for parallel A*. In this section, we present an application of the partial locking protocol (section 2.1) on a *double criteria* data structure called a *treap*. This data structure is particularly suitable for the implementation of our parallel A* algorithm because there is no cross-referencing between two data structures as we will see later. Therefore, in the data structure management we save memory space and avoid deadlock problems.

2.5.1. *The A* algorithm.* The space of potential solutions of a problem is generally defined in Artificial Intelligence in terms of state space. A state space is defined by:

1. an initial description of the problem called *initial state*,
2. a set of operators that transform one state into another,
3. a termination criterion which is defined by the properties that the solutions or the *set of goal states* must satisfy.

Generally, the state space is represented by a graph $G = (E, V)$, where E is a set of edges labelled by the operators and the costs of transformation, and V a set of nodes/states. To find an *optimal* solution to a problem is equivalent to exhibiting a least cost path from the initial state to a goal state in the associated graph. The A* algorithm [35, 37] is generally used to find out such an optimal path.

At the theoretical level, the A* algorithm is a special case of the B&B paradigm. Like the B&B algorithm with the best-first strategy [34], an evaluation function $f = g + h$ is defined to give a priority between nodes. Thus, useless parts of the graph can be discarded and the *combinatorial explosion* reduced. The g function gives the cost of the path from the initial state to the current state and the h heuristic function estimates the cost of the path from the current state to a goal state.

When the A* algorithm is used to make a tree search on the state graph, it is similar to a best-first B&B algorithm. However, the A* algorithm is more difficult to deal with when it makes a graph search. In a graph search, a state could be reached by several paths with different costs. Therefore, a comparison mechanism must be added to find out whether a state has already been explored or not and thus avoid redundant work. Afterwards, we study a suitable data structure for the A* algorithm in graph search.

From an algorithmic point of view, the A* algorithm manages two lists, named OPEN and CLOSED. The OPEN list contains the states to be explored in the increasing order of their priorities (f-values), while the CLOSED list keeps the states already explored without priority order. The basic operations to access the OPEN list O are:

- $Search(O, state)$ finds the node x in O such that $x.state = state$;
- $Insert(O, x)$ adds the node x in O but $x.state$ must be unique in O;
  let y be a node already in O such that $y.state = x.state$,
    - if $y.priority < x.priority$, x is inserted, y is removed,
    - if $x.priority \leq y.priority$, x is not inserted;
- $DeleteMin(O)$ selects and removes the node x in O with the highest priority;
- $Delete(O, state)$ removes the node x from O such that $x.state = state$.

For the CLOSED list C, only three operations are necessary:

- $Search(C, state)$ finds the node x in C such that $x.state = state$;
- $Insert(C, x)$ adds the node x in C;

- *Delete*(C, *state*) removes the node x from C such that $x.state = state$.

2.5.2. *Towards a double criteria data structure.* The simplest way to parallelize the A* algorithm, in the shared memory model, is to let all available processors work on one of the current best states in the OPEN list, following an asynchronous concurrent scheme. Each processor gets work from the global OPEN list. This scheme has the advantage providing small search overheads, because global information is available for all processors [25] via the OPEN list. This scheme is also named centralized scheme. The main difficulty in this scheme is the management of the OPEN list in a concurrent environment.

Several parallelizations of the A* algorithm have been proposed for tree search, just like the best-first B&B algorithm (see [18] for a large survey). But to the best of our knowledge, there are only a few specific parallel implementations of the A* algorithm [25, 8]. The reason is that the A* algorithm seems to be difficult to parallelize [38]. The only work to do in parallel in A* is the management of OPEN and CLOSED global lists. Furthermore, no suitable concurrent data structures for the OPEN and CLOSED lists have been proposed for parallel formulations in the literature.

Priority queues [1, 44] have generally been used up to now and may be suitable for the *DeleteMin* operation according to the priority criterion (section 2.4). But, they are completely inefficient for the *Search* operation with the state criterion. Other data structures such as hash tables, AVL-trees [1], Splay-trees [13, 47], etc, are efficient for the *Search* operation but not for *DeleteMin*. There have been no data structures with *both operations* working on each criterion. This is why the data structure used for OPEN is usually a combination of a priority queue (heap) and a hash table, and the one for CLOSED is a hash table. The hash table is relatively easy to implement and the access can be concurrent without any problem. In contrast, concurrent access to a priority queue is not simple to achieve as we have seen in section 2.1.

Furthermore, parallelism increases some specific problems as synchronization overheads, because operations have to be done in an exclusive manner. The combination of two data structures for the OPEN list also implies cross-references and thus deadlock problems and memory space overhead.

Thus, we propose a new data structure called a *concurrent treap* which combines the two criteria (the priority for *DeleteMin* and the state for *Search*) into one structure. This suppresses cross-references and limits synchronization overheads.

In the following sections we discuss this data structure in more detail and how concurrent access may be implemented.

2.5.3. *Treap data structure.* Serial treap was introduced by Aragon and Seidel [2]. The authors use it to implement a new form of binary search trees : Randomized Search Trees. McCreight [33] also uses it to implement a multi-dimensional searching. He calls it *Priority Search Trees*[4].

---

[4]Vuillemin introduced the same data structure in 1980 and called it *Cartesian Tree*. The term *treap* was first used for a different data structure by McCreight, who later abandoned it in favor of the more commonly used *priority search tree* [33].

Let O be a set of n nodes, a *key* and a *priority* are associated to each node. The keys are drawn from some totally ordered universe, and so are the priorities. The two ordered universes need not be the same.

A *treap* for O is a rooted binary tree with a node set O that is arranged in In-order with respect to the keys and in Heap-order with respect to the priorities.

In-order means that for any node x in the tree $y.key \leq x.key$ for all y in the left subtree of x and $x.key \leq y.key$ for all y in the right subtree of x. *Heap-order* means that for any node x with parent z the relation $x.priority \leq z.priority$ holds.

It is easy to see that for any set X such a treap exists. The node with the largest priority is in the root node.

The A* algorithm uses an OPEN list where a *key* (a state of the problem) and a priority (f-value of this state) are associated to each node. Thus, we can use a treap to implement the OPEN list of the A* algorithm.

Let T be the treap storing the node set O. The operations presented in the literature that could be applied on T are *Search*, *Insert* and *Delete*. We add one more operation *DeleteMin* and modify the *Insert* operation to conform to the basic operations of A* (section 2.5.1).

Given the key of x, a node $x \in O$ can be easily accessed in T by using the usual search tree algorithm.

As with several binary search trees [**43, 47, 13, 26, 6**], the update operations use a basic operation called *rotation*.

In the literature, the *Insert* operation works as follows. First, using the key of x, it attaches x to T in the appropriate leaf position. At this point, the keys of all the nodes of the modified tree are in In-order. To establish again the Heap-order, it simply rotates x as long as its parent has a smaller priority.

To keep the properties of the *Insert* operation as defined above, the *Insert* algorithm cannot be used in this form. We design a new algorithm which inserts a node x in T.

Using the key of x, we search the position, with respect to the In-order and to the Heap-order. That is, we use the *Search* algorithm but it stops when:

- a node y is found such that $y.priority < x.priority$ (cases (1) and (2) of figure 4),
- a node z is found such that $z.key = x.key$ (case (3) of figure 4).

If a node z is found, the algorithm ends because it is guaranteed that $x.prority < z.priority$. Thus x must not be inserted in T. On the other hand, if such a node y is found, the node x is inserted at this position (between y and the parent of y).

Let SBT_x be the subtree of T rooted in x. At this point, the priorities of all the nodes of the modified tree (SBT_x) are in Heap-order. To establish again the In-order we use the splay operation [**43, 47**]. SBT_x is split into a left subtree and a right subtree. The left subtree (resp: right) contains all the nodes of SBT_x with the key smaller (resp: larger) than the key associated with x. Finally, the left subtree and the right subtree are attached to x. Then, SBT_x and T are in In-order and in Heap-order.

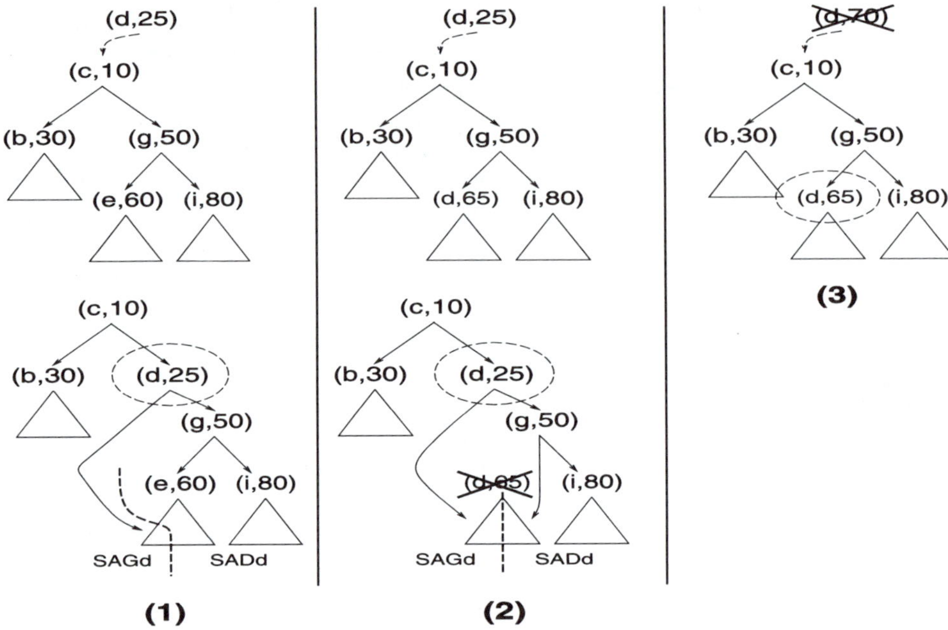

FIGURE 4. Insertion algorithm.

If we find a node y such that $y.key = x.key$, during the splay operation, the node y, is deleted (the y priority will be smaller then the x priority).

The *DeleteMin* and *Delete* operations are not very different. The *DeleteMin* operation removes the root of T, and the *Delete* operation removes the root x of a subtree of T such that $x.key = key$. Thus, first we search for such a node x and then we apply a *DeleteMin* on the subtree rooted in x.

The *DeleteMin* operation is achieved as follows. Let x be the root of the treap T. We rotate x down until it becomes a leaf (where the decision to rotate left or right is dictated by the relative order of the priorities of the children of x), and finally clip away the leaf.

Each node contains a key and a priority. Thus, the set occupies $O(n)$ words of storage. The time complexity of each operation is proportional to the depth of the treap T. If the key and the priority associated with a node are in the same order, the structure is a linear list. However, if the priorities are independent and identically distributed continuous random variables, the depth of the treap is $O(\log n)$ (the treap is a balanced binary tree). Thus, the expected time to perform one of these operations, is still $O(\log n)$ (n number of nodes in T) [**33**].

To get a balanced binary treap in an implementation for the A* algorithm, the problem is *reversed*. The priority order cannot be modified. However, we can find an arbitrary bijective function to encode the ordered set of keys into a new set of randomized ordered keys. The priority order and the key order are then different.

To allow concurrent access to the treap, we use the partial locking boolean protocol described in section 2.2.

2.5.4. *Experimental results.* The implementation of this algorithm has been done on the shared memory architecture KSR1 [**7**].

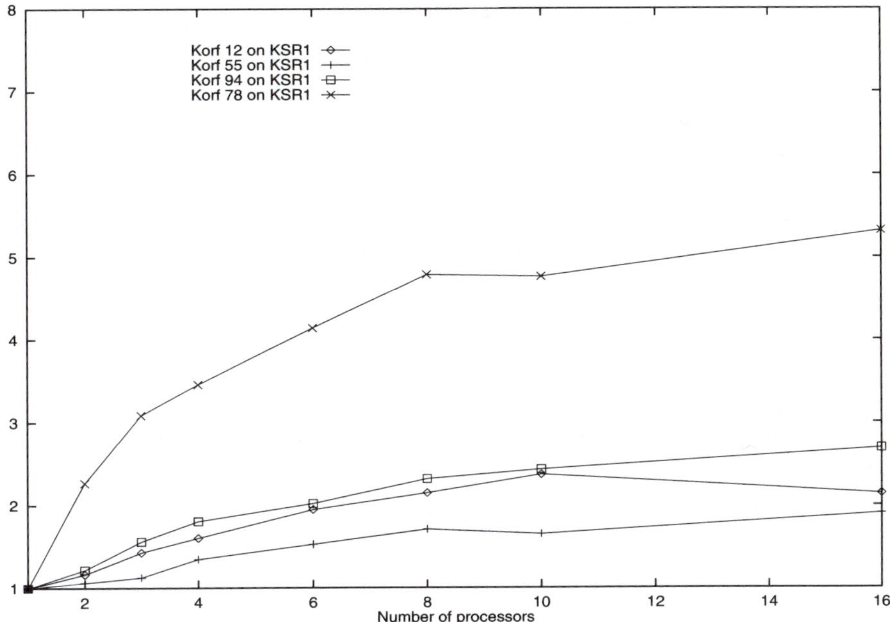

FIGURE 5. Results on KSR1 with some 15 puzzle games.

Applied on some relatively small instances of the 15 puzzle problem proposed by Korf [24], we have compared these results (figure 5) with those obtained under the same experimental conditions, but with a combination of two data structures (a Skew-heap with a Splay-tree) for the OPEN list. The release with the combination of two data structures gives no speed-up. We have also compared them with the results obtained by Rao, Kumar and Ramesh [38]. On the 15 puzzle game, their speedup reached a limit with less processors. Moreover, their implementation was done on a Sequent Balance 21000 which had a physical shared memory, the communication speed over computation speed ratio is greater on their machine than on the KSR1. Our data structures would then be more efficient on the Sequent than on the KSR1. Therefore, we could already claim that the *concurrent treap* surpasses all the other data structures proposed for the centralized parallelization of A*.

Another on-going study is to apply this algorithm on other discrete optimization problems such as allocating processes on processors in order to reduce communication cost.

3. Load balancing strategies

Load balancing is an important factor in parallel processing to reduce processor idleness and optimize performance, especially in the DMM. With B&B algorithms, nodes are classified in function of their priorities into several queues, and solutions may be reached more efficiently if priorities given to nodes by queues are taken into consideration during the parallel execution of the algorithm.

Existing load balancing schemes use partial cost to balance nodes generated by best-first B&B distributed algorithms.

In this section, we show that using partial cost might lead to a big accumulation of high priority tasks on a few processors, while the other processors continue to work with low priority nodes. In such a situation, another notion of priority is needed. It must take into account not only the partial cost of nodes but also their capacity to generate other nodes. Our aim is to develop an efficient load strategy that uses priority of tasks.

We have developed three load balancing strategies with this new notion of priority: a *one-by-one* and two versions of *partial distribution* strategies.

Our new notion of priority is applicable to various applications including those using best-first B&B algorithms and those from the area of Operations Research. We have chosen to evaluate the strategy with a B&B solution to the Vertex Cover Problem (VCP).

The implementation of the B&B algorithm was carried out in a network of heterogeneous Unix workstations used as a single parallel computer through the Parallel Virtual Machine (PVM) software system. All experiments in this section have been done with 3 SUN workstations (1 SPARCstation ELC and 2 SPARCstations IPC).

3.1. The PVM environment. PVM [**16**] is a software system that permits a network of heterogeneous Unix computers (workstations in our case) to be used as a single large parallel computer (named the *virtual machine*). Thus, larger computational problems may be solved by using the aggregate power of many computers.

PVM supplies functions to automatically start up tasks on the virtual machine and allows tasks to communicate and synchronize with each other. PVM may start up more than one process on any processor in the PVM virtual machine. This assignment is done by calling the routine *pvm_spawn()*. A task is for us a Unix process.

Applications, such as B&B algorithms, can be parallelized by using message-passing constructs common to the most distributed-memory computers. By sending and receiving messages, multiple tasks of an application can cooperate to solve a problem in parallel.

Like that, PVM provides the flexibility to develop parallel applications using its communication facilities. The interested user can refer to [**16, 46**] for more details about PVM.

3.2. Distributed best-first B&B. We use our distributed version of best-first B&B to solve the VCP.

3.2.1. *B&B for VCP.* For an undirected graph $G = (V, E)$ a subset $U \subseteq V$ of nodes is called a vertex cover if every edge is covered by a node from U, i.e. $\{u, v\} \in E$ implies $u \in U$ or $v \in U$. This problem aims to find the vertex cover with minimal cardinality.

All nodes are coded as tuples (SC, pc) where SC is a sub-cover (a set of nodes that cover some edges of the graph G) and pc is the number of nodes in SC; from now on, we refer to the **partial cost** of the treated node (lower bound on the sub-cover cardinality).

Our B&B algorithm generates two new nodes (SC_1, pc_1), (SC_2, pc_2) from a given node (SC, pc). The generation of SC_1 and SC_2 by the branch procedure is done by searching for a node v with maximum degree in the rest-graph (part of the original graph that has not yet been covered). $SC_1 = SC \cup \{v\}$, $SC_2 = SC \cup \{w \in E\}$ (for more details, see [**29**]).

3.2.2. *Implementation.* We have implemented the distributed B&B scheme of [29] with different strategies of load balancing as we will see later. Our aim is to develop an efficient load balancing strategy that uses priority of nodes. Therefore, the chosen algorithm is sufficient for our purpose (for more information about B&B algorithms and their parallelizations, refer to [**40, 27, 17, 48, 50**]).

The chosen B&B algorithm uses a distributed queue organization to temporarily stock the generated nodes. We chose to execute only one process per processor in the PVM machine. Each processor has a local queue in its local memory and executes the sequential B&B algorithm using this queue.

In the best-first search strategy, nodes are classified in many queues in decreasing order of their priority. The evaluation of a node is given by its partial cost.

With the distributed B&B scheme, communication plays an essential role in determining the performance especially when we use multi-user machines (like workstations). To improve performance, we must try to reduce the number of messages exchanged during the execution, as we will show in subsequent sections.

3.3. Motivations and justifications of our approach. We have developed three load balancing strategies, a one-by-one and two versions of partial distribution, to understand load distribution between the different slaves. We started by testing all of these strategies with the generated nodes of each processor classified into a local queue according to their associated **partial cost**.

In the one-by-one load balancing strategy, each slave needing work receives only one node from the beginning of the queue of another loaded processor (figure 6 shows an execution for a graph of 75 vertices with average degree of 50%).

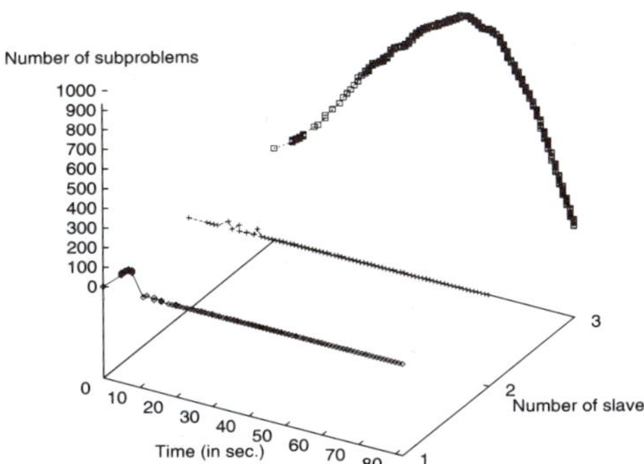

FIGURE 6. The load distribution by "one_by_one" load balancing strategy.

In the partial distribution strategies, the number of tasks received by a processor requiring work is variable. The number of nodes sent from the maximum loaded slave to the one requiring work is equal to the minimum of the average load and the local load minus the average load.

The first version of partial distribution load balancing strategy performs load balancing by sending nodes from the beginning of the local queue whereas the second one sends nodes from the end of the queue.

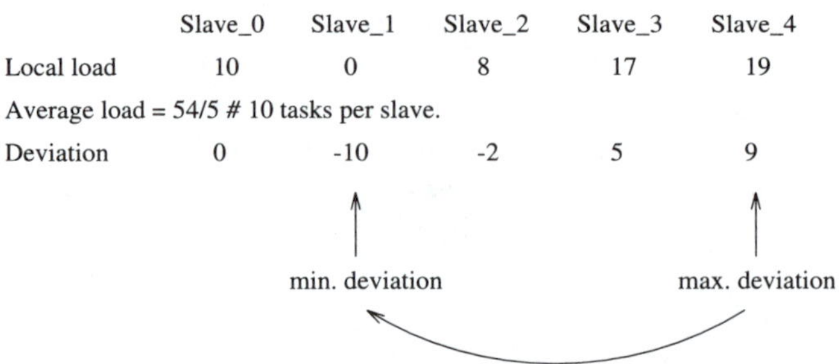

FIGURE 7. An example application of partial distribution load balancing strategy, where slave_1 asks the other slaves for work.

3.4. Results with classical priority notion. We have noticed that we get a very bad load distribution in the case of the one-by-one strategy. At the beginning all slaves have the same quantity of work, but after that, one of them (the second slave) becomes strongly loaded although this slave is not the one to which the root node in the B&B tree has been assigned.

We can explain this situation by the fact that some nodes potentially generate more work than the others in the search space.

We have also noticed that with version 2 of the partial distribution load balancing strategy, the loads of different slaves are globally more equally distributed compared to version 1, and that with version 2 load balancing operations occur less frequently than with version 1. This proves that the **partial cost** used as a criterion to classify nodes within the queues is not the only parameter to apply to get a good load balancing strategy.

The above results indicate that it is important to take into consideration the potential work that nodes can generate.

Any efficient load balancing strategy should ensure, as much as possible, that the processing of nodes occurs in the global order of their partial cost and should take into consideration their associated potential work. Consequently, we need to define a priority notion between different nodes which takes these two parameters into account.

3.5. A new notion of priority : potentiality. A node generated during the execution of a B&B algorithm has two associated values : its cost and an indicator representing the potential work it can generate successively to reach an optimal solution (figure 8). These two values depend on the treated problem. In the VCP for example, the first one is equal to the partial cost, and the other value will be taken as equal to the number of edges in the rest-graph.

Each generated node is characterized by its position in the indicated region in figure 8. The execution of a B&B algorithm starts from **Start** point (where we have the root of the B&B tree) and terminates at **End** point (the searched optimal solution).

The potentiality of a node sp is defined as follows :

DEFINITION 2.

$$Potentiality(sp) = (dist(sp, End), potential\_work, ancestors\_nb).$$

Where

sp :: *is the considered node,*
dist(sp, End) :: *the distance between the position of sp and the* **End** *point,*
potential_work :: *the value of the associated potential work of sp,*
ancestors_nb :: *the number of the ancestors of sp.*

In this definition of priority, we introduced a third parameter, the number of ancestors, to select between nodes that have the same distance from the **End** point and the same quantity of potential work. We chose to give priority to those having the less number of ancestors.

In practice, the value of the optimal solution is not known before the end of the execution, but usually we start execution with an upper bound that maximizes this value.

In the VCP, for example, we can use the number of nodes of a given graph as an **End** point and we compute distances relative to it.

Generated nodes are classified into the different queues during the execution of a B&B distributed algorithm as a function of their priorities. A node sp_1 has greater priority than another node sp_2, if it verifies one of the following rules:

(1)
$$dist(sp_1, End) < dist(sp_2, End)$$

(2)
$$(dist(sp_1, End) == dist(sp_2, End))\&\&$$
$$(sp_1.potential\_work > sp_2.potential\_work)$$

(3)
$$(dist(sp_1, End) == dist(sp_2, End))\&\&$$
$$(sp_1.potential\_work == sp_2.potential\_work)\&\&$$
$$(sp_1.ancestors\_nb < sp_2.ancestors\_nb)$$

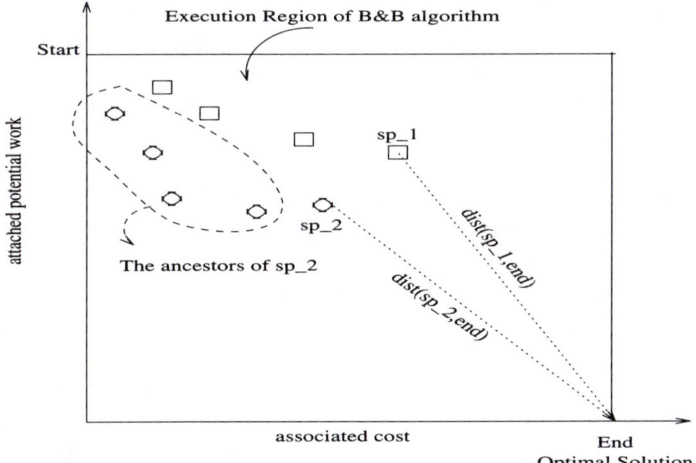

FIGURE 8. Definition of priority of two nodes sp_1 and sp_2.

3.6. Load balancing strategies with potentiality. This notion has led to improvements such as a better load distribution among the different processors in the PVM machine, and a reduction in the number of messages exchanged during the execution.

3.6.1. *Influence on load distribution.* For the one-by-one load balancing strategy, we remark that at the beginning of the execution, the assigned nodes have greater priority than the others so that the number of load balancing operations is lower than it would be without using our priority notion. At the end, we have a lot of load balancing operations when the priority of nodes begins to decrease (figure 9 with the same graph as figure 6).

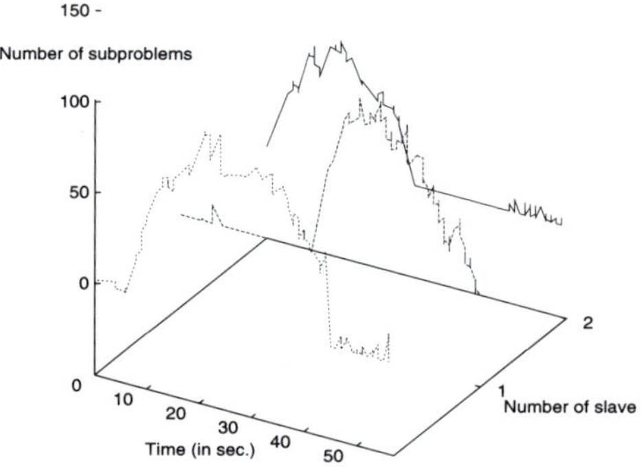

FIGURE 9. The load distribution by "one_by_one" strategy using the notion of potentiality.

The load is equally distributed with partial distribution load balancing strategies (versions 1 and 2).

We can also see that the load of the most loaded slave does not exceed the 110 nodes while it was around 450 nodes (with version 1) and 600 nodes (with version 2), without using our priority notion.

3.6.2. *Influence on communication costs.* To show the importance of the communication factor, we have chosen to study the messages exchanged between the master and all of its slaves.

For the one-by-one strategy, we have remarked that there is a clear difference in the number of messages sent and received with and without using the potentiality notion. This number is less in the first case (figure 10).

For the two versions of partial distribution load balancing strategy, we have remarked that the number of messages sent and received takes an asymptotic value. In version 1, the number of messages exchanged remains approximately the same, while in version 2 the utilization of our priority notion slightly increases the number of messages exchanged. In fact, with this version, when an unloaded slave takes nodes from the end of the queue of a loaded slave, this unloaded slave executes the work and rapidly becomes unloaded. This slight increase in the number of load balancing operations shows that nodes are really classified in queues as a function of their priority of execution.

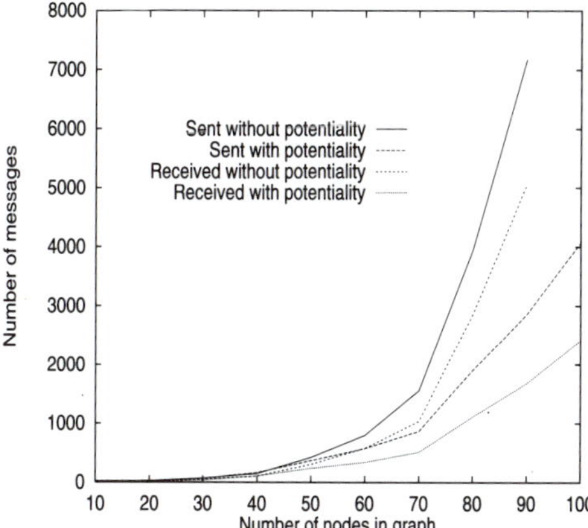

FIGURE 10. The messages sent and received using the "one_by_one" strategy with and without the notion of potentiality.

4. Concluding remarks & perspectives

For the SMM, we have proposed a set of concurrent data structures suitable for Tree/Graph search algorithms such as best-first B&B and A* algorithms. Parallel best-first B&B need efficient concurrent PQ. Theoretically, the Funnel and the Splay-tree priority queues are more efficient than the classical Heap or Skew-heap. The experimental results, obtained on the KSR1 machine with a parallel B&B solving the Quadratic Assignment Problem, seem to confirm this fact. The problem of the partial locking method is that the number of simultaneous accesses is limited by the depth of the tree. But as far as we know, if we want to keep the strict best first strategy and to allow asynchronous access, it seems that the partial locking method is the only solution.

Our contribution is an optimized version of the partial locking protocol in the case of tree structures called the *partial locking boolean protocol*. We have reduced the number of mutual exclusion primitive calls. Thus, the overhead is reduced. We plan to test our concurrent priority queues to solve bigger instances of the QAP and other problems such as TSP, Graph coloring.

In this model, we have also presented a double criteria data structure: the *concurrent treap*, with the operations *DeleteMin* and *Search*. This data structure allows to store a set of items containing a pair of key and priority. We can apply on the same data structure the basic operations of binary search trees and those of priority queues. We have implemented concurrent access for these operations with the technique of partial locking.

The coexistence basic operations of binary search trees and priority queues applied to the same data structure is essential in order to implement the A* algorithm efficiently. This data structure could also be used in other applications in which the management of two criteria is needed.

Results obtained on the KSR1 and applied to some 15 puzzle games show that the concurrent treap is efficient for a group of ten processors. The speedups presented are better than those in [**38**] with the same parallel scheme.

For the DMM, we analyzed the behavior of three load balancing strategies and proved the necessity of a new priority order between the different executed nodes in a B&B application.

We introduced the notion of potentiality based upon an estimation of the capacity of a node to generate work, and on an evaluation of the distance between the node and the optimal solution. We believe that this kind of potentiality can be applied to any B&B application where nodes are characterized by the previous parameters.

Furthermore, we studied the impact of this notion on the behavior of load balancing strategies for distributed best-first B&B applications. These strategies show that after taking into consideration the potentiality of nodes, their selection to participate in an operation of load balancing is not the same at the beginning and at the end of the execution.

All these load balancing strategies are developed in a centralized manner (with one master processor that controls the others in the PVM machine). Future work will consist in investigating the effect of using our potentiality notion when several masters instead of only one (like the strategies in [**42, 41**]) are used.

References

1. A.V. Aho, J. Hopcroft, and J. Ullman, *The design and analysis of computer algorithms*, Addison-Wesley, 1974.
2. C.R. Aragon and .G. Seidel R, *Randomized search trees*, FOCS 30 (1989), 540–545.
3. J. Bitwas and J.C. Browne, *Simultaneous update of priority structures*, IEEE international conference on parallele computing (1987), 124–131.
4. M.R. Brown, *Implementation and analysis of binomial queue algorithmms*, SIAM Comput. **7** (1978), 298–319.
5. J. Calhoun and R. Ford, *Concurrency control mechanisms and the serializability of concurrent tree algorithms*, of the 3rd ACM SIGACT-SIGMOD Symposium on Principles of Database Systems (Waterloo Ontario), April 1984, Debut de la theorie sur la serializability.
6. B. Le Cun, B. Mans, and C. Roucairol, *Opérations concurrentes et files de priorité*, RR 1548, INRIA-Rocquencourt, 1991.
7. Van-Dat Cung and Bertrand Le Cun, *A suitable data structure for parallel a**, RR 2165, Institut National de Recherche en Informatique et Automatique (INRIA), January 1994.
8. Van-Dat Cung and Catherine Roucairol, *Parcours parallèle de graphes d'états par des algorithmes de la famille a* en intelligence artificielle*, RR 1900, INRIA, April 1993, In French.
9. S.K. Das and W.-B. Horng, *Managing a parallel heap efficiently*, Proc. PARLE'91-Parallel Architectures and Languages Europe, 1991, pp. 270–288.
10. N. Deo, *Data structures for parallel computation on shared-memory machine*, SuperComputing, 1989, pp. 341–345.
11. N. Deo and S. Prasad, *Parallel heap: An optimal parallel priority queue*, Journal of Supercomputing **6** (1992), no. 1, 87–98.
12. C.S. Ellis, *Concurrent search and insertion in 2-3 trees*, Acta Informatica **14** (1980), 63–86.
13. ______ , *Concurrent search and insertion in avl trees*, IEEE Trans. on Cumputers **C-29** (1981), no. 9, 811–817.
14. A. Elshafei, *Hospital layout as a quadratic assignment problem*, Operational Research Quarterly **28** (1977), 167–179.
15. M.L. Fredman, R. Sedgewick, D.D. Sleator, and R.E. Tarjan, *The pairing heap: A new form of self-adjusting heap*, Algorithmica **1** (1986), 111–129.
16. Al Geist, Adam Beguelin, Weicheng Jiang, Robert Manchek, and Vaidy Sunderam, *Pvm 3 user's guide and reference manual*, Oak Ridge, Tennessee 37831, May 1993.
17. B. Gendron and T. G. Crainic, *Parallel branch-and-bound algorithms: Survey and synthesis*, Tech. Report 913, Centre de recherche sur les transports, Montréal (Canada), May 1993.
18. Ananth Y. Grama and Vipin Kumar, *A survey of parallel search algorithms for discrete optimization problems*, Personnal communication, 1993.

19. Qin Huang, *An evaluation of concurrent priority queue algorithms*, Third IEEE Symposium on Parallel and Distributed Processing, December 1991, pp. 518–525.

20. D.W. Jones, *An empirical comparaison of priority queue and event set implementation*, Comm. ACM **29** (1986), no. 320, 191–194.

21. ______, *Concurrent operations on priority queues*, ACM **32** (1989), no. 1, 132–137.

22. D.E. Knuth, *The art of programming: Sorting and searching*, vol. 3, Addison-Wesley, 1973.

23. T.C. Koopmans and M.J. Beckman, *Assignment problems and the location of economic activities*, Econometrica **25** (1957), 53–76.

24. Richard E. Korf, *Depth-first iterative-deepening : An optimal admissible tree search*, Artificial Intelligence (1985), no. 27, 97–109.

25. Vipin Kumar, K. Ramesh, and V. Nageshwara Rao, *Parallel best-first search of state-space graphs : A summary of results*, The AAAI Conference (1987), 122–127.

26. H. Kung and P. Lehman, *Concurrent manipulation of binary search trees*, ACM trans. on Database Systems **5** (1980), no. 3, 354–382.

27. E. L. Lawler and D. E. Wood, *Branch and bound methods: A survey*, Operations Research (1966), no. 14, 670–719.

28. P. Lehman and S. Yao, *Efficient locking for concurrent operation on b-tree*, ACM trans. on Database Systems **6** (1981), no. 4, 650–670.

29. R. Lüling and B. Monien, *Two strategies for solving the vertex cover problem on a transputer network*, proc. of the 3rd Int. Workshop on Distributed Algorithms, number 392 in Lecture Notes of Computer Sciences, 1989, pp. 160–171.

30. B. Mans and C. Roucairol, *Concurrency in priority queues for branch and bound algorithms*, Tech. Report 1311, INRIA, 1990.

31. ______, *Performances des algorithmes branch-and-bound parallèles à stratégie meilleur d'abord*, RR 1716, INRIA-Rocquencourt, Domaine de Voluceau, BP 105, 78153 Le Chesnay Cedex, 1992.

32. T. Mautor and C. Roucairol, *A new exact algorithm for the solution of quadratic assignment problems*, Discrete Applied Mathematics **to appear** (1993), MASI-RR-92-09 - Université de Paris 6, 4 place Jussieu, 75252 Paris Cédex 05.

33. E. M. McCreight, *Priority search trees*, SIAM J Computing **14** (1985), no. 2, 257–276.

34. Dana S. Nau, Vipin Kumar, and Laveen Kanal, *General branch and bound, and its relation to a* and ao**, Artificial Intelligence **23** (1984), 29–58.

35. Nils J. Nilsson, *Principles of artificial intelligence*, Tioga Publishing Co., 1980.

36. C. Nugent, T. Vollmann, and J. Ruml, *An experimental comparison of techniques for the assignment of facilities to locations*, Operations Research **16** (1968), 150–173.

37. Judea Pearl, *Heuristics*, Addison-Wesley, 1984.

38. V. Nageshwara Rao, Vipin Kumar, and K. Ramesh, *Parallel heuristic search on shared memory multiprocessors : Preliminary results*, Tech. Report AI85-45, Artificial Intelligence Laboratory, The University of Texas at Austin, June 1987.

39. V.N. Rao and V. Kumar, *Concurrent insertions and deletions in a priority queue*, IEEE proceedings of International Conference on Parallele Processing (1988), 207–211.

40. C. Roucairol, *Parallel branch & bound algorithms - an overview*, Tech. Report 862, INRIA-Rocquencourt, Domaine de Voluceau - Rocquencourt - B.P. 105 - 78153 LE CHESNAY Cedex (France), 1989.

41. Vikram A. Saletore and Mannan A. Mohammed, *Hierarchical load balancing schemes for branch-and-bound computations on distributed memory machines*, Hawaii International Conference on System Software, January 1993.

42. A. B. Sinha and L. V. Kale, *A load balancing strategy for prioritized execution of tasks*, Workshop on Dynamic Object Placement and Load Balancing in Parallel and Distributed Systems (in co-operation with ECOOP '92), June 1992.

43. D.D. Sleator and R.E Tarjan, *Self-adjusting trees*, 15th ACM Symposium on theory of computing, April 1983, pp. 235–246.

44. ______, *Self-adjusting heaps*, SIAM J. Comput. **15** (1986), no. 1, 52–69.

45. J.T. Stasko and J.S. Vitter, *Pairing heap: Experiments and analysis*, Tech. Report 600, I.N.R.I.A., February 1987.

46. V. S. Sunderam, G. A. Geist, J. Dongarra, and R. Manchek, *The pvm concurrent computing system: Evolution, experiences, and trends*, Parallel Computing **20** (1994), no. 4, 531–546.

47. R.E. Tarjan and D.D. Sleator, *Self-adjusting binary search trees*, Journal of ACM **32** (1985), no. 3, 652–686.
48. Benjamin W. Wah and Chee Fen Yu, *Stochastic modeling of branch-and-bound algorithms with best-first search*, IEEE Transactions on software engineering **SE-11** (1985), no. 9, 922–934.
49. J.W.J. Williams, *Algorithm 232: Heapsort*, CACM **7** (1964), 347–348.
50. Myung K. Yang and Chita R. Das, *Evaluation of a parallel branch-and-bound algorithm on a class of multiprocessors*, IEEE Transactions on parallel and distributed Systems **5** (1994), no. 1, 74–86.

PNN Team, PRiSM Laboratory, University of Versailles-Saint Quentin en Yvelines, 45, avenue des États-Unis, 78035 Versailles Cedex, FRANCE.

E-mail address: `pnn@prism.uvsq.fr`